# THE COMPLETE BOOK
# OF IN-HAND SHOWING

Purebred Arabians must be shown with a full mane and tail.

# THE COMPLETE BOOK
# OF IN-HAND SHOWING

## ALEX FELL

Photographs by the author

**J. A. ALLEN**
London

British Library Cataloguing in Publication Data
A catalogue record for this book is available from the British Library.

ISBN 0.85131.641.7

Published in Great Britain in 1996 by

J. A. Allen & Company Limited
1 Lower Grosvenor Place, London SW1W 0EL

*Photographic acknowledgements*: the photographs on pp. 28 and 62 were taken by Iain Burns, and the photograph on p. 38 by Anthony E. Reynolds. All other photographs by the author.

Designed by Nancy Lawrence

Typeset by Setrite Typesetters Ltd., Hong Kong.
Colour processing by Tenon & Polert Colour Scanning Ltd., Hong Kong.
Printed by Dah Hua Printing Press Co. Ltd., Hong Kong.

# Acknowledgements

This book is dedicated to the horse and to all those who place its welfare above personal achievement.

I would like to thank all the experts consulted for their generosity in sharing their extensive knowledge for the benefit of future standards.

I would also like to thank Nancy Lawrence, Maggie Raynor, Ray Bird and Anthony Reynolds for their kindness and encouragement, and my editor at J. A. Allen for her infinite patience and good humour!

Alex Fell
Devon, 1995

# Contents

# CONTENTS

# CHAPTER ONE

# Introduction

For most people a visit to a County Show means the hunter young-stock and ridden classes, a few pony classes and the show jumping, but in Britain there are a vast number of breeds and types reflecting different aspects of the importance of the horse to the British way of life throughout our history. Since the war we have seen the increasing popularity of imported breeds, some of which now have British-based societies to regulate their breeding and selection. They all demonstrate very varied customs regarding turnout (human and equine), presentation and evaluation, which may sometimes be a combination of European and American customs. The reasons why people choose a particular breed are many and varied. Although much has to do with life style, the unique character of the breed is a big factor which is reflected in the way they are shown.

At first glance showing horses seems a thankless task. It consists of months of preparation and training, expensive travelling and entries, and hours of hard physical work to win a little bit of ribbon worth about a pound, or more usually to be beaten by one of the select band of professional producers of show animals. For most people this is the reality of the experience. Why do they do it?

Win or lose there are many benefits of taking a young horse to a few shows before it is mature enough to be broken in, and this can actually make formal training very much easier. It gets used to loading and travelling, to crowds, to going into strange loose boxes and settling down, and to accepting discipline, and there are also the obvious benefits of learning about leading and standing correctly and trotting in hand.

Once you start to breed horses yourself, even if it is just one foal from your mare, showing acquires new meaning. Finding out how well your stock compares against the best of the breed becomes an intensely interesting and, it is hoped, informative challenge. It is this aspect which brings us to the original and enduring purpose of the show ring, which is to evaluate breeding stock. A glance at any

1

When you show your horse do your best and enjoy yourself.

schedule, whether for a County Show or a breed show, will reveal a hard core of classes for brood mares, foals and youngstock, as well as perhaps classes for stallions. If amateur horse breeding grows into a career the show ring becomes even more important because it is the shop window for your stock, where potential buyers can reassure themselves of your credentials, and so presenting your horse or pony as well as you possibly can is a duty and a matter of pride.

If the show ring is fulfilling its purpose, standards of conformation should (and have) improved over time. So it is inevitable that the production and presentation of horses and ponies have become increasingly significant in the selection of winners. Learning how to produce, train and present your kind of horse or pony can take a lifetime of observation, questioning, eavesdropping and, particularly, practice. The nature of and balance between correct conformation and suitable production in the judging process of the different breeds and types, and its desirability, is food for thought and the subject of this book.

The desirability of the production process is not usually discussed in this context, so its practical examination has been placed in a separate section (Part Two) to distinguish between ethics and pragmatism, although one could argue that ethics should guide pragmatism, not be separate from it.

The practical reality of the judging process is found in Part Three where approved judges of the various breed societies and showing organisations give the benefit of their experience. They are, almost without exception, also commercial breeders, and so are well qualified to comment on the inherent weaknesses of their breed and the best way to show them to advantage, as well as the relative importance of conformation and production. When it was not possible to interview an approved judge, which happened with some foreign breeds that have not yet got a list of British approved judges, and additionally where it was helpful, I interviewed experienced producers and breed society officials to obtain as authoritative a view as possible. After considerable thought their identities have been withheld to allow full weight to be given to their opinions, rather than have their opinions redefined by any personal relationship. All interviews are printed in italics in the text.

The inclusion of a breed in Part Three was based on whether or not it has organised shows or show classes in this country. Although the differences between breeds are very striking there are many aspects of their care and training common to all – they are all horses, after all! Guidance on their general production, training, and presentation in the show ring can therefore be found in Part One.

At horse shows, at all levels of importance the length and breadth of the country, there is now a proliferation of classes both in hand and under saddle for all breeds, colours, ages and sexes of horse. To some extent this has focused attention away from the importance of breeding stock so that showing has become an entertaining activity in its own right, attractive to a wider range of owners and riders and resulting in a change of emphasis. Taking part, dressing up and winning have taken over, in the eyes of many competitors, from breeding the best from the best. In other words, showing for them is mainly about production, and conformation is largely consigned to the original purchase. Parallel to this the breed societies have multiplied and, partly as a result of political changes, now play a decisive role in setting and maintaining standards of conformation, fertility and performance. That these trends are occurring simultaneously may not be coincidental and the result may be that the breed societies examine more effectively, through inspection, grading and premium schemes, the factors the show ring was originally designed to assess.

When you show your horse do your best, enjoy yourself and be proud of yourself if you win, but if you don't remember that you are there to learn the judge's opinion. You have asked for this by attending the show, so even if you disagree – and by other criteria you may still have the best horse in the competition – accept this opinion in the spirit in which it is given.

All roads may lead to Rome but although there is much in common the scenery is different along the various routes. This book can be considered as a map – a help, but no substitute for the journey.

*Opposite* Presence – the elusive 'look at me' factor that can win or lose competitions.

# PART ONE
# Practical Considerations

# CHAPTER TWO

# Planning

Months before the show season starts you have to make an important decision about just how hard you are going to work to prepare your horse. About twenty years ago, if not longer, it was possible to take a horse in good condition out of the field, trim it, bathe it, plait it, take it to a fairly important show and win. This is rarely possible today! Depending on the breed, however, you may still have a certain amount of success at the smaller shows in this way providing your horse is good enough and the professionals aren't there. If it is the fun of taking part that appeals to you, you would be happy just to be placed and you are not trying to establish a reputation as a commercial breeder, there is no reason why you shouldn't go about it in this way. A word of warning, though; you need to have a strong enough character to withstand the annoyed looks or comments from the other competitors who don't share your attitude and object to what they consider to be 'scruffiness' and bad manners. This is even more true of ill-prepared, badly behaved horses that may put the performance or safety of others at risk. It is inescapable, too, that if your horse is good enough to be placed under these conditions it would do better still if produced in a more professional manner, and that can be a tantalising thought.

## LONG-TERM PLANNING

Preparing the horse is only part of the campaign for the season. At the outset you have to identify the factors that require time and planning, including just how far and to how many shows you will be travelling. Whether you decide you are going to attend all the County Shows in England or just concentrate on all shows within a twenty-mile radius, your operation has to be planned with military precision right down to the last detail: advance booking of the farrier for all his visits through the showing season, the order, purchase and breaking in of equipment, paperwork for show secretaries, planning the journeys so that you arrive early enough and so on. It is not a hobby for the faint hearted or the bone idle, and, let's face it, it does help to have a deep purse, although there are ways that you can avoid paying through the nose.

*A good diary* is essential and it needs to be big enough for you to include notes for future reference. Into this should go show secretaries' names and addresses which are published early in the year (March/April) in the equestrian press, dates of events, closing dates for entries and when entries were posted, specific information about routes and show grounds, worming, vaccination and shoeing dates. Do not forget to include important information about your horsebox or trailer, because services, tests and taxes have a habit of getting overlooked and your transport must be safe, roadworthy and reliable.

Many shows require the production of *vaccination certificates* against equine influenza, although this is no guarantee that your horse won't catch it if the virus is on the show ground. For this reason you may decide not to risk an overnight stay in the show stables which can be draughty as well as small, but prefer to travel very early in the morning. A very lively horse can be calmed by travelling so may only need to arrive an hour or two before the class.

The influenza vaccination programme is usually combined with protection against tetanus which is very important for all equines regardless of their showing careers. Foot injuries, and particularly puncture wounds, are very common and can pass unnoticed initially just when treatment against tetanus, a potential killer, is imperative. Up-to-date vaccination can avoid a lot of worry. The complete programme consists of three injections over a six-month period followed by an annual injection. From then on influenza protection is annual and tetanus every two years. The certificate that confirms this contains a section for the physical identification of the horse by the veterinary surgeon. The requirements of individual shows can vary, but racecourses categorically require every equine, for whatever purpose on the premises – horse sales, shows, Pony Club camp – to be vaccinated.

*Height certificates* may be required for classes with height restrictions, in addition to any measurement on the day that the organisers wish to conduct. These are obtained by telephoning the Joint Measurement Board to find the nearest vet to administer the scheme, and then taking your horse or pony to be measured. Feet have to be prepared as for shoeing, but the horse should not be shod. If your pony is a bit close to the limit don't be tempted to over-pare the feet or indulge in any of the tricks that contemporary myth would have us believe can reduce height, because the vets are encouraged to look for them and send people away if guilty. There isn't a great deal of point in any case because some shows measure all competitors before the class and others only at random, but between the two you will invariably get caught, especially if someone lodges a complaint.

Certificates apply more to affiliated shows which are run strictly according to the rules of various showing authorities such as the National Pony Society, the National Light Horse Breeding Society (HIS), the British Show Hack, Cob and Riding Horse Association and the British Show Pony Society, as well as the various breed societies. Unaffiliated shows do not require height certificates. They may check height on the day but as the system is administered by vets and requires a measuring site that is unequivocally level this usually only occurs at the larger shows. As always, *read the rules!*

Certificates are issued annually until the animal is seven years old, when a life certificate is issued, and obtaining one will need to be organised well in advance. If your horse is seven or over when it is first measured it will still be issued with an annual certificate for the first year, so that it is measured twice before being issued with a life certificate. Certificates have to be submitted when the horse or pony is registered with the appropriate showing authority, such as the National Pony Society etc., before entering their classes at specific shows. Youngstock in these categories are usually allowed to grow an inch a year before attaining the maximum height at four years of

Measurement on site, a private activity requiring absolutely level ground and performed by a vet.

age, so they are just as liable to measurement on the day as well.

If your horse has needed medication for any illness or injury you must take care that banned substances are free of the system in good time, because *drug testing* is a feature of modern showing. The International Equestrian Federation (FEI) has strict guidelines on this, as has the Jockey Club, and great efforts are made to ensure uniformity by harmonising the policies of all the societies and associations involved with equine competitions. The object is to avoid false performances from horses that have received stimulants or, more frequently, tranquillisers and painkillers. There is even the threat of artificial growth enhancers. As with height testing, the organisers are within their rights to require all or some competitors to be blood tested on the day, and at the big shows this is to be expected. Don't forget that homoeopathic remedies too can be against the rules. You will need to find out if you are likely to fall into this category and inform your vet so that he can advise you and change treatment if necessary.

The show's own veterinary surgeon will use the facilities available, such as a spare stable, to take a blood sample which will be sent away for analysis and screened for suspected substances. The resulting report will be sent to the show authorities who will decide what action is necessary, which may include informing the relevant regulating authority which has the power to impose sanctions of an enduring nature.

Don't forget that if your horse should require treatment on the show ground for any reason, you have to involve the official veterinary surgeon and will need his/her permission to call your own vet.


# SHORT-TERM PLANNING

Nearer the time of the show you will need to ensure that any membership cards, horse registration documents, vaccination and height certificates, car park and groom/competitor passes, schedules and programmes are put in a special folder which can then be put in the front of the car or horsebox at the last minute along with relevant maps and the diary.

You will also need to sort out and put in the car, trailer or horsebox everything you are likely to need for the length of time you will be away, allowing for any unforeseen delays.

This will include:

*For the horse*
Water in a water carrier and at least one bucket
Haynet with hay (not while travelling if the horse is already plaited
    because of hayseeds in the plaits)
Baler twine for tying up in the show stable
Extra hay from same batch as being currently eaten at home
Bedding for the show stable (to supplement what is provided)
Mucking out equipment
Usual hard food plus extra bran, beet or chaff in case you have to
    substitute a laxative diet (in case of injury etc.)
Feeding bowl

*For the rider/handler*
Showing clothes on hanger in plastic bag
Showing boots in plastic bag
Bag of rest of clothes (e.g. tie, tie pin, hair net, socks etc., as well as
    spare clothes, mucking out clothes and boots)
Camping equipment if necessary (bedding, cooking etc.)
Food and drink (always useful regardless of plans)
Torch
Rainwear

For *travelling*, leg protection and knee caps are essential and,
depending on the weather and the horse's susceptibility, a rug held
securely in place with a surcingle and a fillet string may also be
required. As part of your preparation you will have to make sure
that your equipment is suitable and fits. The tail needs to be protected
from rubbing and soiling. For breeds with pulled or tidy tails a tail
bandage applied the length of a damped dock is a good idea. The
rest of the tail can be loosely plaited and secured with an elastic
band, folded back on itself, covered with a stocking (half a pair of
tights) or a pillow case and bandaged again. If the horse has a
tendency to lean against the back of the box or if you don't use a tail
bandage, a tailguard should go over the top and be secured to the
surcingle in the normal way. If your horse sweats while travelling
give some thought to the type of headcollar you use, because you
don't want saddle soap stains all over its head.

On the subject of leg protection there are a number of products
on the market that wrap round the leg and are secured by velcro.

*Left* Four-fold double thickness cotton jersey, machined and blanket stitched. *Right* Standard travelling bandage with ¾ of an inch of the padding showing above and below.

These are quick and easy but they don't go right down around the coronary band and into the heel, which is where most injuries occur from treads etc. Cotton stable bandages (for ease of washing) with cotton jersey pads underneath (instead of disposable and expensive gamgee tissue) take a lot of beating but they need to be applied evenly and properly so that they stay on without restricting the circulation. This needs practice. If you can't find the cotton jersey pads they can be made relatively easily and cheaply from rolls of one-foot wide cotton jersey sold for car maintenance, which is then cut up into six-foot lengths and folded to make a pad roughly one foot by eighteen inches, four layers thick and machined round the edges. You will need to experiment to get the size right for your horse as it should cover from below the knee right down to the heel, with ½ to ¾ of an inch sticking out above and below the bandage, and it should go around the leg with a couple of inches of overlap (towards the outside of the leg, like brushing boots). These pads are

11

relatively cheap, washable and very effective and they will last indefinitely with the odd bit of darning if the edge of the pad slips (which it will if you use artificial shine on the legs) and gets trodden on. One advantage of protecting the coronary band and the heels in this way is that it keeps the legs clean too. Whereas rugs and hock boots may not always be necessary I consider leg and knee protection essential especially if you are going to a number of shows.

You will also need *an equipment box* that you keep in your horsebox with all your showing requirements. If you compile a checklist of everything you might need the box can be prepared well in advance and just topped up from time to time. The sort of things that go into the box are:

Claw hammer and equipment for dealing with rogue nails etc. in the
    show stable
Grooming kit
Plaiting kit
Spare (dark) tape and scissors for the competitor's number
Hoof kit
Horse washing and white hair/stain kit
Quarter mark equipment (if used)
Tack cleaning kit including metal polish equipment
First aid kit for horse
Ditto for people
Travelling clothing when not in use
Spare rugs/sweat rugs and bandages (for dealing with sweating or
    cold stables)
Show tack plus emergency spares (e.g. plain browband, halter, lead
    rein)
Working-in tack (lungeing equipment/saddle and bridle)
Spare hair nets and gloves
Boot cleaning kit
Clothes brush
Showing cane (and lungeing whip if necessary)

# CHAPTER THREE

# Assess Your Horse

Long before you start planning your outfit or sending for schedules you have to be quite sure what level you are aiming at. It is the dispassionate assessment of your horse at the very beginning that is the single most important factor in successful showing. This point was stressed by everyone I interviewed for this book. So more than money you need access to someone who really has an eye for a horse, and particularly your kind of horse or pony. Their experience as at least an observer at a good level of competition is extremely useful in evaluating your horse's chances. Cynical though it may seem, a large part of winning in the show ring is about successfully creating the optical illusion that your horse corresponds perfectly to the breed or type profile that the judge has got fixed in his mind's eye. With the help of your expert, you need to find out what the ideal is (and preferably what your judge has got in his mind's eye), just how far short of the ideal your horse is, and what to do about it. It cannot be stressed too strongly that no detail is too small when it comes to creating the optical illusion, and even if you can't be bothered there are lots of others who can!

Written breed profiles are available from breed societies and many are reproduced in Part Three. Type profiles are concerned with suitability for the task and long-term soundness in use, and are largely a question of the preferences of the judge. Most judges will agree about the causes of unsoundness stemming from bad conformation which apply to nearly all breeds and types, such as badly formed hooves, crooked legs, upright pasterns, hooky/sickle hocks, or back at the knee, and the resulting curbs, windgalls, thoroughpins, spavins and ossification of joints, many of which will not have had time to develop in the young horses that go to horse shows. Standards of conformation in general have never been so high as a result of the efforts of various organisations in the sphere of stallion and mare inspections. These days it is in the question of suitability for the task where the judges have the greatest opportunity to exercise their opinions. The variety of opinion can be seen most clearly in the type competitions that are so common at County Shows, such as hunter, hack, cob and riding pony classes. Suitability for the task also has a bearing on the definition of breed type because the primary purpose of many breeds has evolved with the changing role of horses generally, from aid to survival to recreation and competition.

In this country the names of the judges are made public before the day of the competition and successful producers are strongly influenced by this information when it comes to deciding which shows to attend. Many realise that certain judges favour certain types, and bringing the wrong kind before them is probably a waste of time which may even spoil an unbroken winning record. Not very sporting, you may say, but a realistic reflection of the professional approach nevertheless. It is also one of the reasons why professional producers appear to be regularly successful irrespective of the horse they are leading. In addition to knowing their horse and its short-comings intimately and accurately and producing it accordingly, they don't waste their time leaving things to chance. This profession-alism is often open to misunderstanding and claims of favouritism. This same professionalism provides a daunting prospect for the inexperienced judge.

It follows that by far the most important help you will receive from your tame expert is unsentimental analysis of your horse's strengths and weaknesses. It will pinpoint the areas that need working on in the run up to the showing season and, equally importantly, provide the blueprint for how you present your horse in the ring.

There are two aspects to consider: the overall outline and general conformation of your horse, and your horse's gaits and how they can be used to enhance the overall impression.

# OVERALL OUTLINE

This includes general condition and fitness. Your assessment must identify any specific conformation faults, such as cow hocks or curbs or a short neck, as well as vaguer defects like weak second thighs or quarters. The next thought is to work out how to eliminate, improve or disguise your horse's specific weaknesses within a programme that develops general condition and fitness.

There are some conformation faults that are very difficult to disguise and more importantly may be passed on to the next generation. You must remember that the show ring is largely about identifying the best breeding stock and if your horse has too many faults it won't stand much of a chance, so when planning your showing season you may decide at this stage that it may not be worth your while to travel very far. It can be discouraging to be continually placed way down the line. On the other hand the perfect horse does not exist and success is about being better than the others on the day *in that judge's opinion*!

If your horse has a weak top line or other muscular areas you will need to embark on a tailor-made programme of work and feeding to develop it. For the older horse lungeing and riding are possibilities, so also are driving and loose schooling, but for brood mares and the youngster you may only be able to lead in hand. Another possibility is long reining, which is not as strenuous for hocks and young limbs as lungeing in circles, is suitable for all ages, and can effectively build up the back muscles if you insist on the horse tracking up well and walking actively, which in turn will also help with developing the correct head carriage. For tightening the line under the belly faster work is more effective but not suitable for young horses.

In addition to the normal grooming schedule that is designed to present the horse in the peak of condition, there is also the possibility of strategic grooming, which means strapping to build up weak muscles and sweating to reduce fatty areas, over the withers, for example.

Fat hides a multitude of sins, so they say, which is probably why it has been so prevalent in the show ring and why so many people are now concerned about the harmful effects of over-conditioning young horses and ponies. As one international judge told me:

*Most judges prefer to see a young horse muscled and fit than a great fat slob. It is the youngstock which are shown overfat and soft that rarely go on to succeed under saddle. They should still carry some flesh and be well covered but when they are reasonably fit they can then move and develop.*

The temptation is that carrying a bit more condition than is strictly necessary for health (see Part Two on the evils of fat) has the effect of appearing to shorten a long back (and vice versa). A fat horse looks deeper in the body, which is a goal in itself for some breeds, but it also flatters horses with a tendency to be herring gutted as well as those with weak necks or quarters. Horses that are light of bone can appear to have more substance when fat, although a glance below the knee can quickly identify this (see pp. 44–6 regarding substance versus quality).

However, some types and breeds, particularly cobs and ponies, may have short thick necks and are prone to fat over the withers which then appear to be non-existent, which is a serious fault in a riding animal. If you want condition on the rest of the animal you can reduce the fat selectively by covering the area and sweating it off during work or for some time during the day in the stable. Just how you do this is dealt with in Chapter 4 under grooming.

An active, forward-moving trot with knee action, moving from the shoulder. Note the single plait behind the poll, worn by the Welsh breeds (see p. 181).

A forward-moving long, low daisy-cutting action.

## GAITS

Although some horses have naturally good gaits that correspond to
the requirements of their breed or type, e.g. an active, forward-
moving trot with knee action moving from the shoulder for the
Welsh breeds, and equally forward-moving long, low daisy-cutting
action for show ponies, the action of others can be improved with
the right sort of work and shoeing. Going forward is very much an
attitude of mind not only of the horse but also of the handler, who
must never settle for second best at any time. The show ring is only
a reflection of this attitude.

Importantly, however, there are a number of speeds within the gaits and your expert needs to see them in action to decide which one suits your horse and enhances the overall impression. A fraction of a difference in speed can make all the difference to the head carriage and consequently to the overall outline. As nearly all the judges interviewed commented on the importance of first impressions, a simple thing like the speed of the walk when you enter the ring can have a huge influence on the first line up and hence the outcome of the competition. Do not confuse speed and forward movement: it is possible to go slowly and actively. If your horse has a tendency to move wide behind at the trot you may not even be aware of it unless someone stands behind and tells you. As this is something that gets worse the faster you go, you need to know that your horse should be trotted slowly during certain parts of the judging process. Conversely dishing is accentuated if you trot slowly, especially downhill. All of these things need to be practised quietly at home until they are automatic.

# FEET

In addition to a tame expert you may also need a detailed discussion with your farrier. He may well be able to improve your horse's action by remedial trimming or shoeing as part of his long-term plan for presenting your horse in the ring with its feet in the best possible condition.

## The farrier's viewpoint

*If your farrier is doing the job properly in the first place there shouldn't be any preparation for a show because the feet should be correct anyway. Some people like to have aluminium plates on for showing which can make horses move better in certain circumstances — like small ponies, where you are looking for long low action. It is when the foot is not correct that you have to think about special preparation. Cracks can be filled, broken feet can be disguised, and with modern products the most dreadful feet can be made to look good. In my experience over the years I find that judges pay very little attention to the feet, if any at all, which I think is a bit stupid, particularly if you are looking at a breed show because one of the things you want on any horse is decent feet. They don't [notice] very often until you get right up into the top end of the showing world where one or two of the top shows, like Wembley, have a shoeing competition attached to the class. Even then they are only looking at the feet from a shoeing point of view, not from the animal's point of view, and it only generally happens in hunter classes anyway.*

*Feeding plays a big part in the quality of the horse overall and that includes the feet. A good fit horse that has been correctly fed will have much better feet as a rule, but so much comes back to good shoeing.*

*You can make feet look better, straighter or whatever. In principle a good foot should be the same for most breeds but there are variations on a theme. You want a good strong solid foot that is a decent shape, fairly round and weight bearing in front, not too low at the heel, and in line with the limbs. The angles need to be correct. Looking at it from the side the angle of the hoof wall wants to be in line with the angle of the pasterns. You should be able to draw a straight line from the middle of the pastern to the middle of the hoof. The angle of the wall of the hoof should be about 50 degrees but it has got to depend on your horse's legs. The angle of the pastern varies with all of them, a horse with long sloping pasterns will have long sloping feet. The angle is slightly steeper behind.*

*The feet have got to be in proportion to the horse. A nice big Irish Draught horse has got to have nice big feet to take the weight. A little fine show Arab with matchstick legs is going to have little tiny feet otherwise it looks out of proportion. When you start getting into the foreign breeds the foreign Arabs can have small boxy feet, Andalusians also have small boxy feet and are kept that way deliberately because they have to scrabble over rocky ground and it is claimed that it works better like this and it is traditional. The front feet want to have a fairly round open shape that can absorb the concussion and shock. Any native breed rarely has bad feet if pure bred. It tends to be with Thoroughbreds and cross breds that things start to go wrong.*

*If a pony has a tendency to toe in or out it spoils the look of the limbs. In the old days they used to say you should straighten them by cutting the feet unlevel and building them up on one side but this is all wrong because you have got to keep the joints working as they are formed otherwise you are putting excess strain on them. You can change deviations in the fetlock joint up to about four months old and you can change deviations in the knee up to seven or eight months old, after that what you've got is what you've got. After that if you try to straighten them out you will stress another joint somewhere else. Over a period of time you will end up with more problems than you started with. The thinking now is to leave them so that they are bearing the correct weight in the correct place. This is looking at it from the horse's point of view. From the showing point of view people will get up to all sorts of things to try and make them look better. If somebody is insisting on straightening up a twisted joint the easiest thing is to put a light shoe on with no clips because a toe clip on a front shoe draws the eye to the fault.*

*Various varnishes are used nowadays which look very nice but don't do the feet much good because they seal them up. Once you've put it on it is on until such time as it wears off. The foot is a living piece of the horse and it has got to be able to breathe. If you clog it all up the feet dry out and get brittle and again you end up with more problems than you cure after the season is over.*

## Shoes

For showing in hand shoeing is a matter of personal judgement unless directed specifically by the rules of the particular breed society. It is rare for hind shoes to be worn because of the danger of kicking either other horses or incautious members of the general public. Front shoes may be worn if a two or three year old is going to be shown a lot to protect it from getting sore, especially on hard going. Don't forget that horses' feet grow and however perfectly balanced they are at the time of shoeing, they may well be out of balance twenty-eight days later.

# PRESENCE

Presence is something that can win or lose competitions. It can best be described as the innate self-respect of a horse, which is why it is so important, particularly, for potential breeding stallions. Although, generally speaking, horses are born with it, correct handling can develop it. It is accompanied by a general sense of well being and confidence. Good nutrition, lack of worms, overall health and confidence in the handler can all help. Knowing the job and having the discipline that goes with it, as well as being praised for good behaviour, all contribute.

# CHAPTER FOUR

# Conditioning, Feeding and Grooming

## CONDITIONING

By far the most important aspect of the appearance of your horse is its general condition, including the state of its feet, and overall outline. Before you can think about grooming, trimming or plaiting you have to ensure that it is physically healthy and in the peak of condition. This is something that should be uppermost in your mind whether you plan to show or not. No amount of grooming, bathing or strapping can compensate for a poor coat and poor nutrition, or to be more precise faulty nutrition, because a horse does not have to be thin to be unhealthy. Inappropriate food is almost worse than insufficient food. The way to good condition is through the mouth!

Teeth need to be checked periodically for sharp corners, which should be filed by the vet, especially if grains of hard food can be recognised in the dung or if food is seen to drop from the mouth. It is no use feeding expensive hard food if the horse cannot chew it well enough to assimilate it.

Similarly the horse should be wormed regularly because it is the horse you want to feed, not the worms as well. Opinions vary about the best way to do this. Worm counts can be undertaken by the vet who can advise on the brands and frequency of dosing, but it makes sense to worm whenever you change to a fresh paddock if the horse lives out, and modern opinion suggests worming every six weeks in any case to prevent significant internal damage from mature worms. At least once a year, in the autumn, the wormer used should kill migrating bots, however careful you are about removing their yellow eggs from the horse's legs. Ideally droppings should be removed regularly from the field if alternative grazing is difficult to arrange. Alternating horses with sheep helps to keep down worm infestation of pastures, although it has been said that sheep can improve grazing to the point that you have to be even more wary of laminitis in native ponies and in horses that are good converters of food.

On the subject of laminitis, good condition for a native pony means fit not fat, whereas other breeds may need to be fed fattening starchy foods to get them looking rounded and well, even if they need sweating in vulnerable areas.

In the enthusiasm of your preparation don't forget that a period of time out in the field each day offers more benefits than disadvantages for your horse. A controlled amount of fresh grass is dust free and palatable, and a period of relaxation and freedom has benefits for the attitude of mind, which prevents stable vices and makes the horse easier to handle. You need to ensure that there is little or no risk of injury by checking fences regularly, avoiding other horses which might get overexcited or vicious, and protecting your horse from insects by ensuring there is shelter or by bringing it back in before

Good condition takes months of correct feeding and exercise, not just grooming.

the heat of the day. There are some horses, however, such as certain palominos, that have to avoid sunlight on the coat to protect the colour, but they could be turned out at night.

Advice needs to be taken about the use of artificial fertiliser on grazing and the influence of high nitrogen levels on the incidence of laminitis, and their effect generally on horses. New research suggests that more care may be needed than just keeping horses off fertilised land for a few days, but there are no firm conclusions at the time of writing so it would be advisable to check with your vet. One thing is certain: your horse will need fibre as the mainstay of the diet, in the form of good grass or good quality hay that is relatively free of dust and spores, before the addition of any supplementary feed.

The hay bale is the ideal incubator for the minute *Glaucas aspigillus* spores, which with *Glaucas fumigatus* spores can lodge in the minute passageways in the lungs where they expand and cause respiratory problems. If they enter the lung the immune system may develop antibodies which cause hypersensitivity in the horse, which manifests itself as a hay allergy in the form of coughing and wheezing. This can be offset by soaking hay before feeding so that the spores are fully expanded and cannot enter the airways so easily. This kind of inflammatory condition is not to be confused with asthma or farmer's lung in humans, although caused by the same spores. The good news is that with proper management and an environment free of these spores the horse can return to full work. There is no such thing as broken wind. You just have to ensure that affected horses are never exposed to dry hay because you do not want your horse coughing in the show ring, or anywhere else for that matter.

# FEEDING

It would be useful to be able to give you sample menus for the different breeds at different stages, but in practice this is not possible. The basic rules of feeding acknowledge that each equine, let alone every breed, is an individual, has its own way of reacting to certain foods, and has needs which vary constantly according to the work, the age of the horse and the weather. To get the all-important show ring presence one horse will need lots of extra protein while another will need to travel overnight and be worked in on arrival so that it doesn't kill the judge!

Much is written about the use of food supplements to enhance coat condition, including feeding boiled linseed from time to time (once a week, commonly) or adding cod liver oil to the feed. Veterinary opinion generally agrees that if the horse has a balanced diet, commercial mineral supplements are not normally necessary and certainly not on a regular basis when they will simply be excreted. This does not stop experienced producers swearing by them.

Nowadays there are many choices of complete rations available that are scientifically balanced to provide consistently the ideal ratio of proteins and carbohydrates required for the different activities that horses and ponies undertake. They are supplied with information on suggested feeding levels and take a lot of the guesswork out of feeding, however experienced you are. The quality of basic foods can vary considerably depending on their source and the weather from season to season.

The horse's digestive system cannot cope with sudden changes to the diet because the micro-organisms in the gut responsible for digestion need time to adjust or illness will follow, so changes in food have to be introduced slowly. When in doubt take the advice of an expert on the breed and also remember the old adage: 'the eye of the master makes the horse fat'. In other words follow the advice and then watch your horse closely to see if it suits him, including watching for adverse changes in behaviour and temperament and keeping an eye out for humour spots on the back behind the saddle area which suggest over-feeding.

# GROOMING

There is no real substitute for elbow grease in preparing a horse. Regular grooming not only cleans mud, sweat, scurf and grease from the coat but stimulates the circulation and the natural oils in the skin and makes for a much better result than any artificial aids. In the months before the shows grooming serves two purposes: helping to shed the winter coat, and encouraging a shine on a clean, healthy coat, although care should be exercised if your horse is living out that the natural protection is not removed from the coat by body brushing and bathing. If your horse is living in and rugged up, and if you can groom twice a day, the first session in the morning when the rugs are first taken off removes the loose hairs, which come out more easily because the horse is warm and the pores are open. The second session, which should be after training or exercise sessions and after the horse is sponged and dried if necessary, cleans and distributes the natural oil to the ends of the hairs. It is said that a very good conditioner during the weeks of preparation is a mixture of bay rum and liquid paraffin applied externally which produces a wonderful shine.

A large part of the grooming session may well be devoted to the 'body moulding' techniques of strapping and/or sweating to develop certain muscles and reduce fatty areas. Strapping used to be undertaken with a pad made from a rope of twisted hay or straw plaited into a wisp. Nowadays you can buy purpose-made straps that look like body brushes but which have a pad instead of bristles and a strap which passes over the back of the hand that makes it much easier to use effectively. As part of the grooming routine you deliver a number of hefty glancing blows to the muscles that need building up, in a regular rhythm that the horse can anticipate and brace itself against by tensing the muscle in question. In this way the horse develops itself selectively in addition to the general muscular development of regular exercise and work. You have to do both sides equally and to be effective you have to administer anything from 25 to 100 strokes at a time. Once you get the effect you want you must stop. Strapping must not be carried out on sensitive areas where organs are close to the surface, such as the loins, and it is painful and pointless on bony areas. Be prepared for not being able to wear tight sleeves yourself for a while because it does wonders for the physique of the groom as well!

Sweating the fat off specific areas, such as the neck or over the withers, can be tackled in a number of ways. For the neck, some people recommend rubbing glycerine into the area to be reduced and then wrapping the neck with a length of clean, heat-insulating material. Once the area has sweated the glycerine and sweat have to be washed off with warm water. For fat withers a pad is placed over them with plastic on top which again encourages the area to sweat. Wearing a saddle during work also encourages moulding of the tissues over the withers even if the horse cannot be ridden. When sweating the withers, care has to be taken that the area is kept clean and has time to dry and harden in between sessions, because infections can invade soggy skin and, because of the difficulties of drainage, infections in this area can be far more serious than losing in the show ring.

# Rugs

The use of rugs is frequently one of the factors that distinguishes the amateur showman from the professional, and is one of the main reasons why the dedicated stable their horses. Rugs have two purposes: to improve and maintain the condition of the horse by keeping it warm, and to help ensure a clean summer coat as early in the season as possible, without having to rely on the vagaries of the weather to cause the horse to shed its winter coat naturally. Rugs also help to lay the coat and keep it clean and dust-free. Their use would be especially appropriate for any breed or type that is expected to have a particularly fine coat, such as hacks, riding ponies and hunters and, less obviously, some native breeds. However, a word of caution. If you were showing an Exmoor, for example, which is supposed to be one of Nature's greatest survivors, you could even prejudice some judges against your pony and, more likely, against you, if they suspected it had been mollycoddled.

Under normal circumstances we tend to rely on food to keep horses warm unless they are clipped or particularly susceptible to the cold, but in the unnatural environment of show ring production, it is true to say that providing the use and fitting is supervised, practically any animal of any age can be rugged up.

Care has to be taken that rugs are fitted correctly and do not rub the shoulders, which would be counter-productive. There are two ways to do this: by leaving the front fastener of the rug undone during the day, providing the rug is securely fitted and cannot slip causing an accident or the horse to catch cold, or by sewing sheepskin over the areas that might rub. Despite the conservatism of many owners who favour traditional methods and fabrics, there is a school of thought that prefers manmade fabrics that 'breathe' and have a shiny surface next to the horse. The argument is that wool can retain loose hairs which are itchy and provoke the horse into trying to dislodge the rug, whereas shiny fabrics do not and can be shaken free of them easily, keeping the coat cleaner.

*Opposite* The secret of training is practice and discipline. With youngsters control is vital.

# CHAPTER FIVE

# Training

One of the bonuses of showing young horses is that they have to perfect at an early age the sort of training that all horses undergo sooner or later, which helps them to become calm and disciplined. You could say that showing youngstock is the equivalent of nursery education with all its advantages. If shown as foals, they learn to load and lead, because they naturally follow their mothers and if the mare remains calm so will the foal.

Training is simply a question of teaching short lessons, by repetition and reward, until they become automatic. There is no need to hurry or look for short cuts. The secret is practice, discipline and hard work. Start with easy tasks and gradually build on their successful completion so that the horse understands what is expected, knows it can do what you are asking of it, and learns that obedience is compulsory. Short frequent lessons are more effective than occasional long ones because, like children, the young horse has to learn to concentrate.

Success depends very much on the attitude and character of the trainer, who needs to be patient and disciplined. Correction, if necessary, should be appropriate, considered and measured and never administered in anger. There will probably be a clash of wills at some stage but you just have to keep going and work through it calmly, reverting to a previous stage if necessary to restore confidence

Foals naturally follow their mothers. If the mare remains calm, so will the foal.

and to re-establish your authority. The goal at all times is that the horse should be calm, receptive and obedient to your commands.

The easiest way to train young horses is by example. Foals learn much from watching their mothers and if they see them wearing halters and being led as well as having their feet picked out and trimmed they accept it themselves more easily.

# Safety

At all times safety has to be uppermost in the mind. This means that you have to be equipped and ready for the unexpected so that you can deal with it effectively and retain control. Being properly equipped gives you extra confidence to cope, and as well as avoiding injury to you both it gives the horse the confidence to obey your commands in the future. The sort of situations you have to be prepared for can include rearing and striking, shying and pulling backwards, and attempting to take off. To protect the head and the hands a hard hat and gloves should be worn and nylon lead reins avoided like the plague because they are virtually unbreakable. Strong supportive footwear with a non-slip sole is essential. Make sure the horse cannot go too far should it get away from you, so never practise leading without the gate shut, at least in the initial stages. Be prepared for the worst and with luck it won't happen.

The best training methods allow the horse to obey and be rewarded at the first time of asking. The rule is to ask the first time with a clear correct aid, if the horse does not comply ask again with a more pronounced aid, and if necessary ask a third time with a reinforced aid. Methods of reinforcing aids are most commonly the use of the voice, a strategically placed assistant, or the whip used as a signal, not as punishment. If you anticipate confusion, using some of these from the start in a calm manner can be helpful. In all cases the willingness of the horse to obey should be instantly rewarded with the voice and perhaps a pat, even if the task is not entirely correctly performed. Most horses aim to please and disobedience is usually for a reason. Lack of understanding due to insufficient preliminary training is the most common cause but poorly fitting and uncomfortable tack, and fear, are other possible explanations which should be explored before resorting to strong-arm tactics. If pure disobedience is diagnosed a short sharp correction, administered at the right moment followed by a reward for good behaviour can nip bad habits in the bud and prevent a good horse from being ruined and wasted.

When the horse has learnt the lesson and repeated it a couple of times it may well be time to stop because you should always end a lesson on a good note with a sense of satisfaction in a job well done. This is more important than the length of time spent on a training session. You should, in any case, change the activity to keep the interest of your pupil. Rest is a significant reward for concentration and at the right time is more effective than titbits, which can create bad habits if overused.

## Use of the voice

The voice is an essential aid and is the first point of communication between you and your horse. The best trainers talk constantly to their horses in the early stages but make a very clear distinction between soothing 'chat' and commands. It is the contrast between the two that provides the introduction to the trainer/pupil relationship. Horses go by tone of voice and body language, as well as by eye contact, to gauge your mood. The voice should be used so that even when just turning the horse out it becomes accustomed to the commands 'Walk on', 'Whoa' and 'Stand' and, more importantly, to obeying them! At an early stage when there is confusion 'No' should be taught, to mean 'Stop what you are doing and wait for a fresh command'.

# LEARNING TO LEAD

Horses that have been shown as foals have the advantage here and it is hoped that all foals will have been well handled from birth, wearing foal slips from a few days old and learning to be led short distances. Yearlings and two year olds usually live out in the winter but can benefit from the occasions when they move around, for example changing fields, to be led correctly, from both sides, without hanging back. Right from the beginning they should learn as a habit to 'track up', which means walking energetically so that the hind feet step into the tracks of the front feet rather than behind them. In this way they use their backs effectively and develop the muscles which create a nice rounded top line. With normal handling the horse should learn to walk on, stand politely, have its feet picked up, turn and be touched. The only activity which has to be taught specifically for the show ring is trotting on in hand, which should not pose problems once the horse is used to walking at whatever speed you are walking. All you have to do is give a very clear verbal command as you start to run, like 'ter-rot' and then later on 'trot on' when you are asking for some extension.

All horses and ponies have to learn to walk and trot in hand and they all have to learn to behave themselves, but some need more help than others. They should all be taught to lead from both sides so that they do not become one-sided. Some horses swing their heads too much towards the handler, especially if they have been shown a lot in hand, and this has to be corrected otherwise it unbalances the movement. One way to do this is to lead with the rein attached to the offside of the bridle or headcollar, and also for the handler to lead from the offside when practising at home. Another method is carrying a cane in the left hand which is held against the horse's nose to stop the head turning towards the handler. The stick is the last resort and should not be necessary if the horse is taught to walk on well and you can keep up with it. Keeping up with the horse is most important, hence the need for suitable clothing and footwear. If you hang on to the horse's head it will turn towards you and may look as if it is dishing on the side nearest the judge. If the head is straightened the action becomes straighter.

With a particularly difficult horse that plunges and tries to pull away, especially a young horse that you prefer not to use a bit with and risk the mouth becoming one-sided or injured, a lead rein with a short chain attached can be very effective. It is attached to the off-side of the headcollar and goes round, usually behind the jaw but sometimes over the front of the nose, and through the ring on the nearside of the headcollar into the handler's hand. This is similar to the American and Spanish in-hand systems and has to be used with very great care. In the hands of an expert and used properly it can be a marvellous deterrent. It works just like a curb chain and is very similar to the choke chain on powerful dogs. It is very important that it runs freely so that it works immediately you pull it but as soon as the pressure is released it becomes looser and the horse is rewarded for obedience. It should never be jerked.

A softer version which is worth trying first, especially with the ignorant and strong but well-meaning horse, is the old-fashioned rope halter which can be used with the rope running freely through the nearside loop rather than tied in the usual manner. Care has to be exercised that the rope does not get tighter and tighter, however, because it does not run so freely through the loop as a chain does,

although it is less severe.

With an older horse that is used to wearing a bit with couplings on both sides to which the lead rein is attached, a chain can be used independently on a headcollar under the bridle as a 'belt and braces' system for dealing with intermittent disobedience. The handler has two lead reins and only uses the one attached to the chain at difficult moments. As with all aids to enforcing discipline, correction has to be immediate, as do rewards. The horse has to be capable of obeying, and has to understand what is being asked of it and why it is being disciplined, otherwise it does not learn. There is a fine line between correction and training on the one hand and abuse on the other. Once a horse becomes frightened or hurt it may start to pull back, which is very difficult to correct, so this situation is best avoided.

A horse that hangs back when being led can be helped along by carrying a longer whip in the left hand and touching the flank as near to the quarters as can be reached, so that the horse is driven forward and not frightened backwards. An easier system involves a helper walking behind to reinforce the voice and the words of command of the leader.

If a horse has a sloppy lazy handler it can develop a sloppy lazy mentality. This can be counteracted by a certain amount of 'sharpening up' of both of them. If you ask the horse to do something it should learn to do it immediately, not ten minutes later. If you 'click', the horse should learn to react, and can be helped by an assistant walking behind with a lunge whip, used correctly as a visual signal to support the trainer's voice, not to hit the horse. This way the horse learns that a 'click' means 'pay attention'. It must be stressed that this is only effective in the hands of a disciplined trainer, as a temporary phase of a training programme, which ends once the horse recognises the correct signal and the authority of the handler. There is no place for abuse of the horse, which is unmistakable and which is dealt with increasingly severely by officials on show grounds. Abuse is, in any case, counter-productive because the horse loses confidence and presence.

*Top* If the pony's head turns outwards it can produce an unflattering effect on the shoulder and foreleg action. *Base right* The head is held firmly by the handler so that it is facing squarely in the direction it is going, any deviation being inward rather than outward. *Base left* With correct head positioning the body of the pony is able to bend and the shoulder and foreleg action are shown to perfection.

## Tying up

Tying up is best taught gradually by threading a long lead rope through a tie ring and holding the end taut, yielding a little with the movement of the horse so that there is no rigid restraint. Later the horse can be tied to string which will break before injury can occur. This has to be taught and fully accepted before you can progress to teaching the horse to load and travel in a horsebox.

# LEARNING TO LOAD

The best time to teach a horse to load is when it is coming into the yard regularly and thinking about food. Bearing in mind that feeding young horses together out in the field is a hazardous activity, you can kill two birds with one stone and bring them in to be fed with the box parked in the yard.

Ideally the box should be parked beside a wall which can later serve as a wing to the ramp. It should face away from the light so that when the ramp is down the interior is as well lit as possible, because horses are wary of walking into dark places. To start off with just let them get used to the sight of it, progressing to leading them up to it when they are ready so that they can sniff it.

Do not attempt to load a horse formally until you have complete obedience with the in-hand stage of training. Some people load a quiet horse first so that the young horse is encouraged to join its companion. There is a danger here of making a rod for your own back if this is not seen as a temporary phase and the horse learns to expect a companion. If you can, it is better to teach the horse not to fear the box and to be independent.

With a horse that is frightened of a lorry or trailer and in a secure yard you can feed the pupil loose in the yard, placing the food on the ramp at the lowest part so that the horse does not have to stand on it initially. At this stage the ramp must not be unsteady and the food should be in a stable container that will not knock over unexpectedly, as sudden frights are very much to be avoided. The horse does not have to be held for this but should wear a headcollar in case you have to intervene. You should have to hand a leadrope with a clip. Gradually over a period of days you can place the food higher and higher up the ramp. This should be supervised, however, because if the horse stands near the edge of the ramp it may need steadying so it doesn't slip off. Eventually the horse will go right into the box and eat, so that the box becomes completely familiar. When this happens it is helpful to have an assistant to watch the edge of the ramp so that you can go into the box with the horse with a view eventually to tying it up for a brief period.

If you have a trailer take care that the horse does not hit its head on the breast bar. You will need to pick up the bucket and move backwards into the trailer so that the horse has its head up as it moves off the ramp. You can then practise tying up. This should be done with the breeching strap or gate secured behind the horse first and with a reward. Once the horse has settled, reward it again and then untie it before your assistant undoes the breeching/gate and the horse can come out under supervision with its head held by you. You want to avoid the horse straining against the rope while still tied up, or possibly putting a foot off the ramp and then panicking. When the horse is obedient in hand and familiar with the box you can lead it up the ramp to its food, and once it is tied up your assistant can lift and secure the ramp.

Eventually short journeys can be undertaken which should be long enough for the horse to settle. Before returning home the horse should be rewarded but not unloaded and then on returning home the ramp should be undone and the horse allowed to settle before being unloaded. It is a good idea to load the horse again and reward it before unloading it, to leave a good impression.

Once familiarity has replaced fear, any reluctance to move up the ramp can be helped by attaching a lunge line to the side of the box away from the wall and drawing it quietly round behind the quarters above the hocks and supporting the horse with it as an incentive to walk forward. This is more effective and infinitely preferable to the growling, shouting and arm waving which we witness all too often at equine events.

## UNFAMILIAR SIGHTS AND SOUNDS

Playing a radio in the stable can help the young horse get used to the sounds of the show, although it is harder to get it used to small children, pushchairs and balloons without risking the health of family and friends. It is strongly advised that you go to small shows first, even if you do not compete, so that the horse can learn what to expect. There is no substitute for practice and the results will justify the time spent. This is particularly apparent watching mare and foal classes and the behaviour of the older foals.

# CHAPTER SIX

# Turnout

## TACK

Once you and your expert have identified your horse's good and bad points you can then decide about the tack that will show him off to advantage. The type of tack worn for in-hand showing varies with the type and breed of horse and there are very specific rules which are dealt with in Part Three.

For all showing, whether in hand or ridden, the weight of the bridle varies with the weight of the horse so that it is in keeping and enhances the head. A hunter would look coarse and common in a very narrow, fine bridle and a hack would be swamped by a coarse, thick bridle. Ornamentation in the form of coloured or brass brow-bands is not acceptable for hunters, working hunter ponies and cobs, in the same way that it is unacceptable in the hunting field, but is popular with many competitors for hacks, riding horses and riding ponies. Generally speaking big strong horses need big strong bridles, quality heads need fine, light, stitched bridles. The height of the noseband can improve the look of the head and if fitted higher up the nose can cut in half a long head, which is more flattering.

Generally speaking, big strong horses need big strong bridles, quality heads need fine, light, stitched bridles. *Top left* Cob. *Top right* Riding horse. *Base left* Hack. Note the subtle difference in weight between the finer hack bridle and the riding horse bridle, both designed for quality heads. Both have opted for coloured browbands which are popular but not compulsory (see judge's comments, p. 107). Note also that all use lip straps, which are essential to the correct use of a curb chain but, regretfully, increasingly rarely seen these days. The use of a lip strap is one of the factors that distinguish the professional from the amateur. *Base right* Standard in-hand showing bridle with bit. The showing of donkeys is frequently overlooked but shares many features with the showing of ponies and horses regarding conditioning, feeding, training, ringcraft, and, for in-hand showing, tack.

Everyone's worst nightmare.

Do not make the mistake of having too short a lead rein. Young horses, however well trained, have their off days and if a horse rears up and the rein is too short it is much easier for it to get away from you, which is dangerous and disruptive for everybody. For yearlings and two year olds, especially colts, you must have quite a long rein, as then if they should rear up you can let the rein slip a bit and still hang on to them. As a leading judge said to me: 'This tends to happen more in Arab classes than hunter classes. They are a highly strung breed in any case and are fine once they are trained, but are prone to excitability in public whilst learning, particularly if not subject to consistent discipline.' I actually think this can be said of most horses so the tip is useful.

When it comes to leading foals some people use a lunge line so that they never lose contact if the foal should plunge and break away from the restraining right hand of the leader. This is not really advisable unless the leader is experienced with a lunge line because the potential for getting in a tangle is greater the longer the line, and the further away from you the harder the foal is to control.

For all ages of animal most people favour a leather lead rein although webbing can be easier to grip and very smart if whitened, but perhaps not quite so discreet. Brass and leather couplings can be used to attach the lead rein to the bit if one is worn, but they

The further away from you the harder the foal is to control.

need to be fitted with care so that a certain amount of pressure is taken by the noseband to protect young mouths. Where appropriate, riding reins can be used instead of couplings and lead rein, which give more flexibility regarding the side of the bit to take the pressure, in expert hands, to keep the head straight.

## CLOTHING

Frequently people spend an enormous amount of time and effort on the appearance of the horse and forget about themselves and their own clothing and turnout.

In-hand showing allows more leeway with clothes than in ridden classes, and therefore more potential for making a good or a bad impression. There is a world of difference between what you can wear and what you should wear. Don't forget the importance of first impressions, which is when the majority of classes are probably decided. Your aim is to make the judge think you are a knowledge-able person who wouldn't waste time on an inferior horse, that you leave no stone unturned in your determination to qualify for Wembley as usual, and that they will need a very good reason for not putting you first. The interesting thing about the professionals is that they dress to the same standard for the local shows as for the big shows. The moral is always to give the competition of the moment your maximum effort.

The professionals dress to the same standard for local shows as for the big shows. *Above and opposite left* Mountain and Moorland. *Left and below* Welsh. *Opposite right* Hunters.

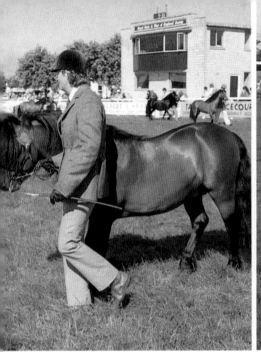

When choosing your clothes the first priority is practicality and the second is suitability. I have heard so many stories of ladies in both in-hand and leading rein classes who couldn't decide whether to put their free hand up to hold their smart, wide-brimmed hat on, or down to control their flimsy skirt and preserve their modesty. Then there are the smart shoes that come off in the mud or get trodden on, and the well-built ladies with non-existent bra elastic who have to decide if they demonstrate their horse's action or their own! The object is for your horse to catch the judge's eye, not you, so smart, discreet, efficient clothing is the order of the day. Quite seriously, being well built can be a problem because clothes that

Wear smart, discreet, efficient clothes that flatter you.

Clean jeans can look good.

don't flatter you cast doubts on your judgement. Some large ladies look better in a skirt than a tight pair of trousers.

There is no excuse for going into the ring without a jacket, unless a different form of dress is specifically required by a breed society. At a very small show on a hot day you do see people showing without jackets, but as this would not be acceptable at a big show it really is not correct anywhere. Similarly you should also always wear a hat that can be relied on to stay on, even if your horse behaves badly. For safety reasons a riding hat is sensible when showing youngstock particularly. Many experts believe that if you are showing young horses you should always wear riding clothes and a hard hat because of the possibility of your horse rearing and striking in the heat of the moment.

You should wear whatever suits you, remembering that you have to run in hand. For this reason long boots and breeches are not quite as practical as trousers and boots or strong shoes. Clean jeans or cords can look good but to be really smart a pair of cavalry twill trousers looks best with a hacking jacket. These should be accompanied by a shirt with a collar and tie, and either a trilby hat or beret or a hard hat for ladies. Men wear bowlers and suits at the very big shows for some breeds and types but otherwise smart trousers, a tweed jacket and a trilby or a flat cap. Hair must be tidy. The American influence on Arab showing accounts for the sight now of smart waistcoats and shirts for ladies, although handlers are expected to wear white clothes for International Arab shows. Even so a big show calls for a jacket and hat.

In-hand clothes are also preferable for the assistant who enters the ring for the stripped phase of ridden classes – tee shirts and jeans just don't look professional enough. Anyone associated with you should aim to look like a travelling head lad, your stud manager or someone gaining valuable experience before going off to take professional exams, not like your dad, sister or mum which is probably more likely to be the case.

It is worth mentioning here the subject of *competitor's numbers.* Reporting to the Secretary to collect them should be your first task when you arrive at the show (after checking that your horse is still with you, alive and well), in case there have been any changes to the programme. Number cards are often supplied with bright white string threaded through reinforced eyelets, and the brightness detracts from the discretion of your turnout. Unless double knotted they frequently come undone and with the exertion of showing they can slip and fold, obscuring your number. This is serious because you don't want any confusion when it comes to identifying your horse as the winner, or any distractions while you are concentrating on showing the horse. Many people discard the string and use dressmaking tape in a dark colour which can be pre-cut to a suitable

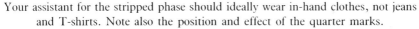

Your assistant for the stripped phase should ideally wear in-hand clothes, not jeans and T-shirts. Note also the position and effect of the quarter marks.

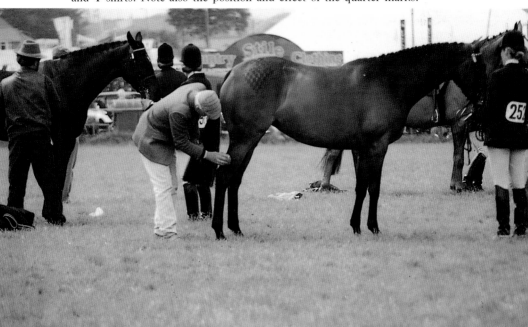

length. Any spare tape and scissors should go in the equipment box that you keep in your horsebox with all your showing requirements (see p. 12). If the string or tape is tied around the eyelet of the number card and knotted, threaded through the other side and tied again, it cannot slip or fold. If you are really particular you can wind one end of the tape around the button at waist level on your jacket and thread the other through the corresponding buttonhole so that the tape is tied on the inside of your jacket leaving no unsightly knots and bows.

You can also secure your number with safety pins. At the horse show different numbers can be worn on top of each other, in class order with the first class on top. All you have to do then is remove the number after it has served its purpose. Make sure that your breed society has not decided that numbers should be worn on the arm nearest the judge, or that the number is not worn on the horse, as in the case of heavy horse showing.

# TRIMMING

Once the horse is in good condition and on the road to show condition you can start to think about the little details that make all the difference to his appearance in the show ring. First consult the authority responsible for the rules under which your horse will be judged. In the first instance this may well be the breed society. Obtain a copy of the rules and a copy of the breed profile and read them. It would be heartbreaking to trim your native pony's tail out of kindness and then discover that the society is a stickler for natural condition. Some mistakes cannot be put right in a hurry.

The following guidelines apply to the types of horses and ponies seen at British horse shows of all levels of importance up and down the country from spring to autumn. On the whole they also apply to partbreds, with some exceptions like Anglo-Lusos (see Lusitano). For specific information relating to each breed see Part Three.

## Quality and substance

For all horses the object is to look as if they have quality and substance. This means different things to different people. To some people quality means lightweight bone structure and thin skin and is associated with Thoroughbred blood, but to others it means top-

The areas that will need attention are behind the jaw, around the muzzle and the edge of the ears. Controversially but frequently trimmed are the long hairs around the eyes and the insides of the ears.

class conformation with a kind of chiselled definition. Horses that possess it are thus the best of their kind, regardless of breeding. Substance provides the durability of conformation that makes the horse capable of performing its job day after day for its entire working life. Misinterpreted, 'quality' is sometimes accompanied by weak spindly legs with long cannon bones, whereas 'substance' can be associated with crude looks and coarse excessive hair, hence the expression 'a little hairy at the heel' to mean common. Quality to most people is seen most clearly in the head; substance, on the other hand, is looked for in the strength of the leg just below the knee, or 'bone', in addition to the overall impression, and should not be confused with an overtopped fat body on puny legs. In fact no breed has a monopoly on either quality or substance and neither is a substitute for good conformation that ensures long-term soundness.

45

Discreet trimming can do wonders for creating the impression of the ideal combination of both in the non-Thoroughbred. Bad Thoroughbreds are difficult to improve in this way because they don't grow much hair. They have to rely on fattening food, strapping and ringcraft, but nothing can disguise a lack of bone under the knee.

## Where to trim?

The areas that will need attention are behind the jaw and around the muzzle. Controversially but frequently trimmed are the long hairs around the eyes and the edges and insides of the ears, which protect the eyes and the ears. The mane may be trimmed underneath the headpiece of the bridle. If too much is cut in this area the plaits cannot start close enough to the ears and it can look ugly. The length of a bridlepath is a factor to consider in conjunction with your assessment of your horse, if it has a particularly long or short neck. Coarse hair may grow down the back of the legs and in the heel and sometimes around the coronary band. If a horse has a tendency to coarseness the chestnuts and ergots may be quite prominent too and these will also need careful tidying, perhaps after softening with vaseline, so that they don't give the game away.

## What to use?

For British showing, trimming is undertaken once the summer coat is established so there is not the profusion of protective hair that horses grow for the winter. This means that a subtle effect can be achieved by using sharp blunt-nosed scissors and a comb. Many people use electric clippers with good effect but in the wrong hands you can end up with a hard 'tide mark'. The Americans use clippers but vary the size of the blades according to which bit of the horse they are trimming. With one set of blades you can vary the length of the cut by using the clippers upside down so that the blades are further away from the horse. Usually you cut against the lie of the hair upwards, but with clippers upside down and going with the hair you can achieve a more subtle effect. It needs practice to get this right. With both methods you aim to reduce the long straggly hairs and whiskers to exactly the same length as the surrounding hair.

## The jaw

The jaw area is trimmed for most breeds with the exception of the tougher Mountain and Moorland ponies. It is officially against the rules of some societies. For the other breeds a closer and more obvious trim behind the jaw bones, sometimes right up into the gullet, can make a big difference to the sharpness of the outline. Similarly the whiskers around the muzzle and nostrils are removed.

## The eyes and ears

You need to think very carefully about trimming round the eyes and inside the ears, especially with youngstock, not only because of the protection they may need for the rest of the summer but also because of the stress factor. It is inescapable, though, that many of your fellow competitors will not hesitate because it undoubtedly enhances the look of quality. A kinder way to tidy the ears is to clasp the ear with one hand, closing it edge to edge lengthways, and then cut or clip the straggling hairs which protrude, against the edge of the ear. This has the advantage of leaving the inside of the ear intact but just sharpening the outline. Give some consideration to whether you leave the hairs at the extreme tip of the ear because these can make the ears look pointed which is desirable for some breeds and has a bearing on presence.

## The legs

The odd long hairs can be plucked out by hand over a period of time, preferably when the horse is warm after work and the pores are open. With a coarser horse that has too much hair in its heels and down the back of the leg a more efficient and less painful (and hence less risky) method is to use a comb and scissors against the lie of the hair.

For trimming down the back of the legs test where you have to cut the hair by combing the front of the leg first against the hair to see exactly how long this hair is when measured against the comb. You then comb the long hair at exactly the same angle, cutting the hair across at exactly the same place on the comb. Take care that the comb is held horizontally as you do it. After each cut comb the hair back into place to judge the effect. Don't panic if it looks as if it has

47

the moth at first; just keep combing and cutting and gradually it will become uniform. This is much better than using clippers – although the horse needs to be quiet – because you don't end up with a hard edge of cut hair which screams 'common' at the judge. If you leave a little tuft of hair around the ergot it looks as if this is all the horse grew naturally to help drain off the rainwater and not as if it has been trimmed at all. This is more important for breeds like the Irish Draught that are meant to grow a little silky hair but no feather, but is not permitted for breed society inspections.

*Remedial tidying/plucking*
If the horse is slightly tied in below the knee and the hair is thick enough here, you can pull out the hairs below this area to even up the appearance of the leg in profile. The area to pluck these hairs is evenly down the back of the leg against the tendons, but it has to be done with great care so as not to end up with a worse effect than the original fault.

## Cutting the tail

Tail length is generally decided by first lifting the tail, by resting the dock on the wrist to simulate the height that the tail is carried at during movement, and then running the other hand down the tail, encircling it, until you get level with the chestnuts. Then grasp the tail in the hand and cut off the end in one go so that the cut edge is even. Don't stop half way and start again otherwise the bottom of the tail will look as if someone has taken a bite out of it. It is possible to do this with the electric clippers so that the bottom of the tail is quite square across.

With this as with everything else the length of the tail depends on the faults of the quarters and hind legs and trying to minimise them. If a horse has weak trailing hocks they will be accentuated by a very long tail so it should be cut just below the hocks. Some people believe that longer tails do not flatter any horse.

## Cosmetic clipping

This applies more in the winter months than in the summer when coats are finer. Clipping along the lowest point of the belly can sharpen the outline, as can clipping around the quarters, near the tail, of some ponies.

# PLAITING

As with all aspects of turnout, plaiting provides an opportunity to improve on the overall impression of the horse. Slight faults of conformation can be disguised, or rather, the judge encouraged to believe that the horse conforms with his ideals. As these vary from breed to breed we can expect to see variations in plaiting style, from none at all in Mountain and Moorland classes, to very elaborate styles designed to show off the power of the neck for the heavy horses. So rule number one is understand the breed profile and the effect you are trying to create.

## The mane

Conventionally the riding horse should have an odd number of plaits along the neck plus one at the forelock, usually ten or twelve in all. In practice, providing there is an even number in total there can be many more than this, as it is considered highly desirable for the riding horse to show a good length of rein, an impression enhanced by lots of plaits. The most important thing is that they all *seem* the same size, in proportion to the horse, and that they stay in with no escaping wisps.

### Plan ahead

The secret of good plaits is the state of the mane before you start, which takes time. Long before the day, work will invariably need to be done on the mane so that it is a uniform length and thickness. This is where the real art lies, because the thickness of the mane decides the number of plaits, which may be crucial to the final effect. A short, thick mane can produce more, narrower plaits than a thin mane of the same length. Tastes vary as to the best length but usually this is around four or five inches (10–12.5 cm). Disaster can be guaranteed if the mane is long and thick. Although the convention is that manes are pulled it is the finished effect that is important, so if you have a horse that really does not like having its mane pulled it may well be better in the long term to thin and shorten the mane another way. Various equipment is available such as combs with a razor blade incorporated into them, thinning scissors and ordinary scissors. The only reason pulling is recommended is that cut ends growing out can stick out unattractively and a hard cut line to the

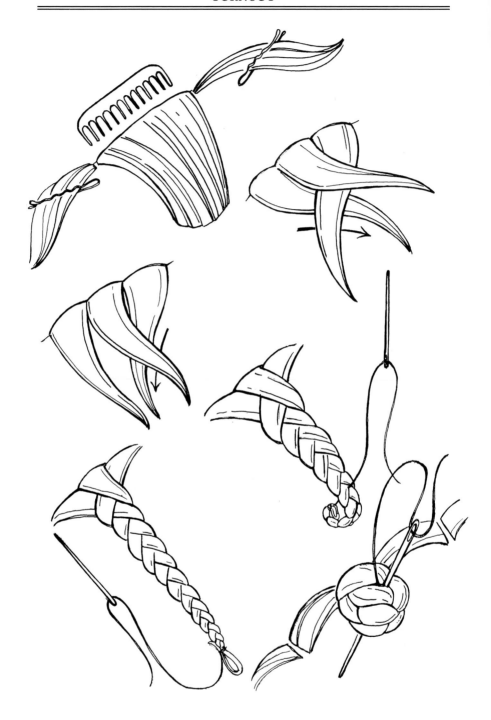

Mane plaiting.

mane is ugly. If you can use other methods carefully to avoid this by all means do. Judges do not hold mane-pulling inspections.

Ideally any pulling should take place when the horse is warm and when the pores are open, and only a few hairs should be taken at one time. Not only is this kinder to the horse as it is less painful, but it means you are less likely to sour the horse. It will then be more likely to stand quietly to be plaited, making for a better result and calmer nerves all round. The mane should be clean and tangle-free. Don't make the mistake of trying out new preparations on the day which may leave the hair so squeaky clean that it resists you, and remember that a freshly washed mane can be slippery to plait. There is much to recommend a dummy run or two!

## Equipment
Make sure that you have everything you could possibly require and in large enough quantities to cover all eventualities. The following is a guide:

Something firm and safe to stand on, e.g. a bale of straw or preferably an upturned box/crate.

Mane thread to match the colour of the mane (a more professional finish and more secure than elastic bands)

Several needles, the larger the better, securely attached to a piece of card by thread wrapped around in a figure of eight.

A mane comb or two. I find that a plastic one with short teeth is better for pulling manes than a metal one, which in turn is better for combing out manes and tails when wet to eliminate ringlets. As the task is to make a straight parting between plaits an ordinary human comb would do.

A pair of scissors that cut without pulling, preferably with blunt ends, which could then double for trimming whiskers.

Some hairgrips for separating the hair to be plaited from the rest.

A water brush or sponge (and a water container) for damping down the hair before you start to avoid escaping wisps.

Hair gel/spray (optional) for securing the finished plait. Hair gel is actually safer (no noise) and more effective.

## Some tips
1. You can plait the night before providing the horse can be prevented from rubbing the plaits out, e.g. by wearing a hood.
2. Before you start it is helpful to tie the horse up so that the light

will fall on the mane. If all else fails a single strand of binder twine tied around the hinge of the top door is useful and means that lasting damage is not caused should the horse pull backwards. It also gives the horse something to look out at and you can easily reach equipment more safely kept outside the door.

3. Make sure the neck and crest are ultra clean and dust-free on both sides beforehand, because grooming in this area will be restricted afterwards and it is difficult to remove dust from plaits. Damp the top of each section close to the roots before you start, especially if the mane is a bit flyaway. Some people use baby oil for this, which has the advantage that it does not dry out, but take care not to overdo it.

4. Before you start, thread a couple of needles with about eighteen inches of waxed thread, which will be strong enough not to need to be doubled but will need a firm knot at the end. Attach both needles to your jumper and secure them with a couple of figure of eight turns of the thread around them which can be easily released with one hand. This is most important as a dropped needle has to be found or the horse removed until the floor has been completely cleared (very tedious).

5. Work out an easy way of measuring the width of each plait which you have already decided upon, e.g. the width of the mane comb. Start at the potentially awkward but manageable areas first like the poll, proceeding to the forelock when the horse has settled, before the novelty wears off in case there is a tendency to fidget. Use the hairgrips to prevent stray wisps from creeping into the plait from the adjacent areas.

6. Plaiting away from you, in the opposite direction to normal (see illustration p. 50), makes for a tighter plait than form back to front, especially once rolled up. When you have plaited down as far as you can, secure the end with a stitch from back to front, wind the thread around the end a couple of times and sew again. If there is much hair at the end not plaited, lick the finger and thumb and then twist the whole end round tightly and double it underneath. Then wind the thread around again a couple of times and stitch again.

7. The secret of plaits staying tight is to ensure that the end is secured quickly and firmly at this stage. You can then be more relaxed about actually rolling them up. To avoid seeing the stitches afterwards stitch through from the back to the front of each plait right through the middle. As the plait is tightly rolled up, each turn is secured by a stitch and the thread is concealed underneath until

the final turn. The thread emerges at the top of the plait where, after another couple of stitches from front to back to front, it is pulled tight and cut off close to the plait. With practice you will find the method that suits you and your horse best.

## Remedial plaiting

If the horse has a short neck lots of small plaits can make it appear longer. If this is necessary, the mane can be slightly thicker so that the individual plaits are not ridiculously small. In a riding horse length of rein is very important, so the mane should not be clipped over the withers which can make a good neck appear shorter.

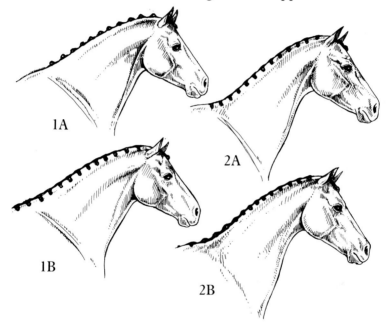

Remedial plaiting:

1A *A short thick neck* looks worse if the mane is clipped over the wither and there are large plaits along the top of the neck.

1B With many plaits set on the side of the neck the thickness is reduced and the horse shows a longer length of rein. If the horse rubs the mane over the wither false plaits can be made from the hair clipped (in the previous autumn) for a bridle path. However, a horse with this shape neck should not have a bridle path clipped out when it is being shown, because the neck looks even shorter.

2A *A weak neck* looks weaker with the plaits lying on the side of the neck accentuating the weakness of the top line.

2B The weakness in front of the wither is disguised by setting the plaits along the top of the neck at that point. By placing the others on the side of the neck the unevenness of the top line is reduced.

*Above* The goal is even-sized plaits and the impression of a long length of rein. Note how the plaits in the middle of the neck sit over one side, whereas those at the top and bottom are on top of the neck, evening out the level of the crest. Note also the smartness and discretion of the rider's turnout. *Below* 'Natural' tail length in Welsh ponies.

A weak neck can be made to appear thicker and stronger by raising the plaits so that they sit more on top of the neck rather than lying completely over to one side. Similarly if the neck is weak behind the head but gets stronger nearer the shoulder they can be graduated so that they are raised at the top of the neck and become more conventional lower down. To raise them all would just make the lower neck appear thick, which would not be attractive and would not flatter the proportions of the horse.

# The tail

There are very precise conventions for dealing with the tails of the different breeds and types of horses. They all have to be clean and tangle free.

The tails of Mountain and Moorland breeds are left completely untouched, not even cut to stop them trailing in the mud. The Welsh preserve the illusion of nature's way, but tails are very carefully thinned by strategic pulling to show off the quarters, and to appear to end 'naturally' just where it happens to be most flattering.

Hunter's tails are pulled and banged (cut) exactly as if they were going hunting, as are cobs, when they are shown under saddle. Don't forget that cobs are shown hogged, so a plaited tail would look ridiculous. Broodmares, youngstock, and stallions, whose tails are allowed to grow, are traditionally shown plaited, but as with other features, the deciding factor is the overall impression created and whether it flatters or not.

Hacks and riding ponies, as well as partbred ponies, often have their tails plaited rather than pulled, both in hand and under saddle, although the tails of children's ponies are increasingly pulled rather than plaited in ridden classes. Some judges prefer to see a pulled tail. It is a matter of personal choice and whatever suits your horse. Coarse tails can look clumsy plaited; fine ones, if they have grown sufficiently and are plaited by an expert, can look exquisitely elegant and can show off good quarters to perfection. Less good quarters can be made to look better by not plaiting (or pulling) all the way down to the end of the dock. A pulled tail needs to be damped and have a tail bandage applied frequently to lay and set the hair around the dock. The custom is that the hair is pulled from the sides but left down the centre of the tail. Like mane pulling it is best done by taking a few hairs out at a time when the horse is warm. You can be very vulnerable standing behind a horse!

*Plaiting the tail*

The easiest tails to plait have not been rubbed, which breaks the hairs. To avoid this, regular worming and lice inspections should be routine procedures. The tail should be clean and well brushed – with a soft brush to protect the hair – and then damped with a water brush. Before you start, thread a needle with mane thread (to match the tail) and secure it on your person, in the same way as for mane plaiting. You then take up the hair from the outside edge of the

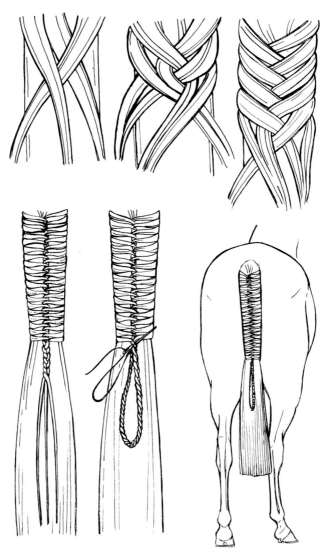

Tail plaiting.

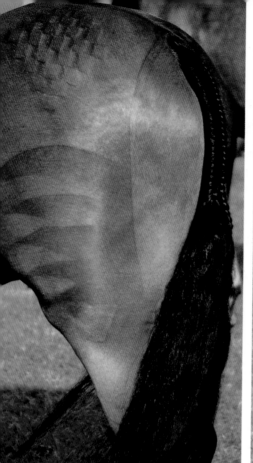

Fine tails, plaited by an expert, can look exquisitely elegant. Note also the quarter marks, shark's teeth and edging and their effect.

dock at the top of the tail on each side, and from the centre of the dock, and plait it down the centre of the tail. At each crossing of the plait, as you work down the dock, you take up another piece of hair from the outside edge of the dock on the appropriate side and plait that in too, but you do not take up any more from the centre. In this way you encase the tail in horizontal bands of hair taken from the sides with a plait running down the centre of the tail. At the end of the bone of the tail, or earlier if it is more flattering, you stop picking up hair from the sides and just continue the central plait right to the end, which you secure with the needle and thread in the same way as the plaits in the mane, doubling the end up behind the plait to the place on the dock where you last plaited in hair from the sides. Here you secure the end with a couple of invisible stitches and cut the thread.

# FINISHING TOUCHES

## Bathing

Your horse should now have a superb clean shiny coat and any mane and tail pulling and trimming (if permitted) should have been completed. If it is still in the field instead then it is time for the first of however many baths necessary before the last-minute preparation for the show. Don't forget that the object of bathing is to remove grease, so keep an eye on the weather and bring the horse in at least at night until the grease is replaced, which, without more bathing or body brushing, should happen within a few days. White/grey tails sparkle if rinsed in water made blue with old-fashioned blue bag, which can be bought from traditional hardware shops, but stained tails will need several applications to get them bright. Sometimes products for blonde women are used to great effect. Artificial shine products are not actually a very good idea for regular use, but are excellent for the one-off occasion. Some judges loathe them, especially for the native breeds, and they can be felt by running a hand over the horse, but I don't think this would seriously disadvantage you. Whatever you do, do not use them on the saddle area if you ride your horse because they can make saddles slip! The horse should not be allowed to catch cold whilst drying but should be led around.

## Quarter marks

These are the designs created by brushing the hair against the lie of the coat, usually on the top of the quarters on either side of the spine just in front of the tail, and also the flanks. The exact positioning of them depends on the faults of your horse and should be undertaken with extreme care.

Quarter marks proper take the form of a chessboard effect of small squares of hair brushed alternately with and against the lie of the coat. The chessboard can lie with the straight side parallel to the ground, at right angles to it, or somewhere between the two, to flatter the horse. Another form of quarter mark, very popular with the stronger-boned horses and ponies like hunters, cobs and hunter ponies, consists of large thick longitudinal and horizontal stripes.

Both sides of the horse or pony are patterned at the same height, and the marks are placed according to the shape of the quarters, the length of the back and the effect you are trying to create.

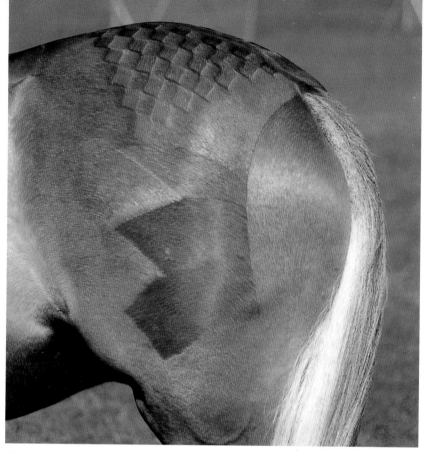

Tails do not have to be plaited. This one has the effect of a pulled tail achieved by using electric clippers on the sides of the dock – perhaps for reasons of personal security or speed. Note again the effect of the quarter marks, shark's teeth and edging.

## To apply

In years gone by the effect was created freehand by combing around a matchbox, having first brushed the area with the lie of the coat, and starting furthest away from you and working towards you. Nowadays plastic sheets can be bought with squares cut in them strategically. Both methods require practice. The sheet is placed over the coat and then the designs are created by brushing in the gaps against the lie of the coat. The disadvantage is that you can sometimes see where the sheet ended. If you are going to do it you might as well learn to do it properly because you can be more creative in the effect you achieve. Brush the hair with the lie of the coat and lay it well with a damp brush. Take a comb that has had its teeth doctored so that it is only as wide as the squares you want and then starting at the top of the quarters comb each alternate square against the lie of the coat, leaving the intervening squares to go with the lie of the coat.

Stripes are created by brushing 'freehand' alternately away from you and towards you. On the flanks they usually take the form of semi-circular brush strokes that intersect each other to make a sort of 'shark's tooth' effect, running from the flank down in the direction of the hock to enhance the look of the thigh. Sometimes they are finished off by making a brush stroke from the top of the tail in a shallow arc down to the top of the thigh.

Some people also try to fix quarter marks with hairspray but this is not really necessary. Whatever form yours take, the coat has to be exceptionally clean and shiny, preferably soft and fine, and very much in show condition. Coarse hair will resist you and will not stay put. Do not attempt any of this if you are going to expose scurf and dust when you rearrange the lie of the coat!

The entire concept of quarter marks and shark's teeth, which highlight the show condition of the coat, is anathema to the tough, hardy image of the Mountain and Moorland and native breeds and so quite unsuitable for them.

Hunters and cobs have chunky stripes if they have quarter marks at all and usually more in the ridden classes than in hand, although this is changing. They may have shark's teeth, too. The object is to give the impression of power and strength, so pretty squares are right out of the question.

Hacks, riding horses and riding ponies usually have squares or diamonds with or without shark's teeth, which, like the use of fine show bridles, are used to emphasise the aura of quality and elegance, and to distract the attention of the judge away from a weakness of conformation in this area. This is what the producers hope; judges think of both quarter marks and shark's teeth as irrelevant but attractive decoration!

## Oil

The finishing touches to your turnout involve oiling the hooves, passing a greasy cloth (baby oil or similar) lightly over your horse's coat and over the knees and hocks (but not below the knee), to lay the coat and sharpen the outline, and putting vaseline or baby oil around the eyes, nostrils and muzzle. Nowadays special varnishes can be bought that create the effect of hoof oil but don't wash off in the grass. Tinted varnishes are banned by some societies. They are

A gloss on the coat can be helped by applying oil to the body and around the eyes, nostrils and muzzle.

very effective but have to grow out and over a period of time damage the texture of the hooves, in the same way that wearing nail varnish constantly causes nails to split and break.

Before laying the coat you need to pass a clean cloth over the horse to remove any stray hairs and dust. Don't have too much oil on the cloth when you lay the coat or you will get streaks. If your horse tends to be light of bone be extremely careful around the legs because a fluffier coat texture can create an impression of strength. Some breeds and types really go to town with the oil around the eyes and even use cosmetics to darken the skin over the eyes. This is banned by the Arab Horse Society. As it used to be with eye makeup for women, the aim is to look as if you don't need it. Oil round the eyes is permitted but should be applied carefully so that it doesn't go in the eyes and cause irritation.

# CHAPTER SEVEN

# Ringcraft

The object of the exercise is to show your horse in the best possible way so that the judge cannot fail to notice it, whilst disguising any defects. The most important thing you have to remember is that from the moment you enter the ring and for every moment you are in it your horse is on show. Most people think that the competition is over once the rosettes have been presented, but it is not unheard of for a winner to be downgraded for bad behaviour, particularly in riding pony and hack classes where exemplary manners under saddle are as important as conformation and action. Anyone who has ever judged will tell you that there may only be one judge in the ring but there are at least twenty more looking on. There may even be someone watching who will be judging your horse next time out.

Although the competition is judged according to the performance and impression on the day in the opinion of that particular judge, judges are only human and can be influenced by past impressions too. An efficient and well-turned-out exhibitor can contribute to this impression just as much as the look of the horse, but unfortunately bad memories seem to linger, so don't give them any reason to remember anything bad about you or your horse.

There are two main systems of showing, the traditional British comparative method that everyone will recognise from showing classes at County Shows up and down the country, where the competitors are judged in comparison with each other, and the European system of showing, where the judges occupy different positions in the arena and the horse is sometimes lead around three sides of a triangle and marked by each judge, independently of the others, against an ideal standard, with the one gaining the highest marks winning. The procedures in the ring are different for the two methods, and there are American breeds and some Arab classes which are judged in a

*Opposite* All competitors are guaranteed months of hard physical work, but no one is assured of victory until they have left the ring.

manner midway between the two systems which I will explain in the sections dealing with those breeds.

With all systems of judging the competition can be broken down into a number of distinct phases. From the moment you arrive in the collecting ring you are under the orders of the judge as passed on to you by the stewards. It is very bad manners to leave the ring until you are dismissed by the judge. If your horse behaves badly or is discovered to be unsound, it is expected of you, with permission, to withdraw from the competition, as to remain may well result in your horse either being asked to leave or being placed last.

# TRADITIONAL BRITISH SHOWING
## The collecting ring

The art of show ring presentation starts in the collecting ring where your horse should be in the right frame of mind, having been quietly led around to settle, if excitable, and looking as good as you can manage. There is just time for a last minute wipe over with a soft clean cloth (avoiding the quarter marks if you have them, unless you feel able to redo them at the last minute) to remove stray hairs and dust, a touch up with the hoof oil by your assistant and a quick sponge of the bit and lips to remove bits of grass and dribble.

You will have been casting an eye over the opposition in the meantime and if you have the chance will have chosen the competitor to follow when you are instructed to enter the ring. If you have a free-going horse you may want to lead; if your pony is a bit close to the height limit you may want to follow another big one; if your horse lacks presence you may want to follow one that particularly lacks it, or alternatively follow one that looks as if it is excitable or badly behaved in the hopes that some of the enthusiasm rubs off (taking care not to get kicked). The collecting ring steward will have checked your number and any other documentation required against the entries list and will sometimes send you in in numerical order.

It is now particularly that presence is important, the well-known 'look at me' factor that everyone wants in a show horse. First impressions are very important and the minute you enter the ring the judge will be looking for the outstanding animals and getting a feel of the class generally with a view to choosing the first line up.

Before you enter the ring make sure that your horse is leading well with the degree of activity that suits it best, that you are level with its shoulder and have a good contact with its head, that your lead rein is held securely and tidily with no trailing ends and that your cane is held manageably so that you can use it effectively if necessary. Showing canes have no lumps and thongs so can be used at either end. Generally they are held in the middle, and can be held pointing upwards against the horse's nose to guide it round the corners, or behind the handler's back against the girth area to sharpen up a sluggish horse. Remember that you are aiming for a nice rounded top line and the horse's hind feet to be at least tracking up or over tracking. All should be to your satisfaction before the collecting ring steward is ready to start the class, when you then enter the ring.

## Entering the ring

In nearly all in-hand classes the leader goes on the outside of the ring and the horses circuit the ring in a clockwise direction. Allow plenty of space between your horse and the horse in front so that you are not forced to check your horse behind a slow-moving horse. Once all the competitors are in the ring you may circle round to find a gap if you find yourself getting too close to the horse in front, but do not impede the judge's view of the others. This is very bad manners and is a transparently obvious 'dodge' that the unscrupulous attempt, trying to force the judge to look again at their horse, but which can come unstuck. After about two circuits of the ring you should keep an eye on the steward next to the judge for further instructions.

Once the class is in progress some of the phases of the competition described below may be left out at the judge's discretion.

## The trot

In pony classes particularly, competitors may be halted on the track and asked to trot individually past the judge to the rear of the competitors. A lot depends on where the judge is standing and any faults that your horse may have as to how you deal with this.

Regardless of the type of class, at this stage the judge will be looking at the action in profile, for such things as knee action and engagement of the hocks, but he may be able to see the straightness of the action depending on the angle of view. Ideally you should ensure that your horse is alert and active the second you start to

*Above* At the trot it is important to maintain contact with the horse via the lead rein. *Opposite* Balance and head carriage are important at the trot. You must be level with the shoulder and be fast enough to keep pace. Note the use of the stick behind the handler's back to encourage activity.

walk forward, so that the top line is rounded and hopefully the horse is showing a reasonable length of rein rather than being overbent. At the trot it is more important than at the walk to maintain the contact with the horse via the lead rein. A beautifully balanced horse can trot down on a loose rein without any problem, providing it has good manners, but generally it is nice to have the horse going into its bridle and trotting with you. Less well-balanced horses need to be able to feel you in contact with them, helping them to balance, although they have to get used to this without getting upset. When you start to trot balance is everything, so you should still be level with the shoulder and able to run fast enough to

keep pace with the horse, rather than hanging back and pulling the horse's head round you, which can make it look as if it is throwing the leg nearest the judge. If there is any tendency for the horse's head to turn out you can hold the cane against the nose to push it straight, although this is best avoided by practice at home.

All being well you should trot on fast enough to show off the extension of the trot without becoming unbalanced or breaking into a canter, and keep going round the ring so that the judge can have a good look, then return to walk calmly before you approach the other competitors and halt quietly, until you are asked to walk on again by the steward. When you walk on the horse must be alert, active, straight and balanced and you have to watch the steward in case he tries, you hope, to catch your eye.

## The line up

Usually the judge will call in the best first but not always. You will be expected to line up facing the main block of spectators, off the track, and to remain halted until it is your turn to show your horse to the judge.

Pay close attention to the surface of the arena. Standing the forelegs in an almost imperceptible dip can be unflattering and make a correct horse appear immature and even back at the knee.

You must pay close attention to any little dips and mounds in the surface of the ring where you have to halt, and make all efforts to avoid standing your horse with its forefeet in a dip, because this will make the best of animals look back at the knee, or at the very least immature. When you see competitors bunched together and then large gaps in the line up this is sometimes the reason. It is unlikely that you will be made to stand on uneven ground to your disadvantage. Usually the higher the grade of competition the better the surface of the arena but as a rule of thumb you should try to walk downhill if a gradient cannot be avoided, so that you can trot, and halt, uphill to show your horse off to its advantage. Young horses tend to grow unevenly anyway, which, of course, judges understand, but if your horse is at the stage where the quarters are higher than the withers or if it really is back at the knee then you want to try and stand it so that it is standing uphill very slightly. If you are too obvious about this the judge will spot it. Most judges are wise to every little manoeuvre known to the showing world, but with any luck yours will have other things on his mind. Even if he realises how subtle you are trying to be, if the faults of your horse are never glaringly obvious at any time, unlike others with the same faults but less sympathetically shown, you should still be placed higher up the line.

It is unwise to keep nagging at a horse because it can only concentrate for so long, but keep an eye on the proceedings so that you will be ready to move forward when called.

If there are a lot of competitors don't be lulled into a false sense of security and let your horse go to sleep with hind legs resting, because the judge may not appear to be watching but somebody else might. On the other hand it is very unwise to keep nagging at a horse, because it can only concentrate for so long. Some judges find this irritating too because it is fussy and unnecessary. Teach your horse to stand properly as a habit and then allow it to relax briefly until it is its turn to exude presence. A fidgety horse can be calmed by being fed little tufts of grass picked by you. If the judge should glance round unexpectedly no harm will be done.

This phase is the same as the unsaddled or stripped phase in a ridden class. The difference is that there a correctly dressed assistant can enter the ring with a sponge for the bit and mouth, and a clean cloth, which is all you really need. If your horse gets very dusty under the saddle a body brush might be useful and at a pinch possibly hoof oil.

In either an in-hand competition or the same phase of a ridden class, you try to keep your horse reasonably alert and standing correctly without fussing it, especially in a large class, until it is nearly your turn, when you arrange the lead rein and whip ready for action and so indicate to your horse that something is about to happen. Then at a signal from you your horse walks forward smartly and doesn't need to be dragged away from a daydream.

## Standing up for the judge

When called, you walk forward away from the distraction of the other horses and halt in front of the judge. Strictly speaking this should be parallel with the track so that the spectators can see and facing the direction that you will be going when you show your horse's paces. You will have a few seconds to stand your horse up so that the judge can look at the general conformation.

The English traditional method requires the horse to stand with all four legs visible at once when viewed from the side. If the judge is standing still to one side, the legs nearest the judge should be furthest apart, but not exaggeratedly so otherwise the foreleg can look back at the knee. If you know your horse has a tendency towards cow hocks the hind feet should be a little bit apart and definitely not side by side. One can be a bit further back so that the two hind legs cannot be seen side by side from behind, but not stretched.

The British traditional method requires the horse to stand with all four legs visible at once viewed from the side. In this case, the near fore could be slightly back underneath the body. This pose would be subtle showmanship at work if the horse had a tendency to back at the knee or a straight shoulder. As the judge walks round there is no need to rearrange the legs.

The other foreleg away from the judge should be just behind the near one but not back underneath the body otherwise the shoulder on that side will look upright. Similarly the hind leg furthest from the judge should not be forward underneath the body which will make it look sickle (hooky) hocked. If the horse actually is sickle hocked then both hind legs should be further back, so that the angle of the hocks is as open as possible, but beneath the quarters and not exaggeratedly stretched. The feet should all be facing forwards. If a cow hocked horse turned its hind toes in this would be all to the good, but as this is virtually physically impossible, all you can do is try to stop it from turning them out which is the natural tendency with this particular fault. As the judge walks round to see the other side there is no need to rearrange the horse's legs accordingly.

Making the horse stand correctly is very much a matter of training and always insisting that it stands properly at home. This will develop the muscles and ligaments concerned and become more comfortable and easier to sustain. If the horse is used to having its stance adjusted one leg at a time by slight pressure on the shoulder (on the same side as the leg in question) pushing it backwards, standing it up correctly in the ring should not pose too many problems. It is better to nudge the horse backwards than to drag it

Successful repositioning of legs by using slight pressure on the shoulder on the same side as the leg in question.

forwards by the lead rein which can be misinterpreted as the signal to walk on and is too crude. It also balances the horse better, bringing the hocks under the body rather than pulling the horse on to its forehand, and so makes for a better outline. This is not to be confused with the general goal of forward movement at all times with young horses. You are only aiming to place the feet correctly. Once the legs are right the horse should be encouraged to reach forward slightly to show off the length of rein and then to prick its ears and look alert: the presence factor, again! This cannot be underestimated and is all the more important for a plainer horse. If the horse is utterly beautiful it just needs to be standing correctly without its head on the ground, and providing it is taking an interest in things will show itself without needing to be fussed.

Keeping horses alert at this stage is an art in itself and a variety of methods are used. The most popular is to pick a small tuft of grass, which can be thrown down quickly if necessary, and tantalise the horse with it by feeding it slowly. This will cause the horse to focus on the grass instead of gazing into space or fidgeting, and you can then dictate how much it stretches its neck and the height of the

Various methods of encouraging the horse to look alert and hold its head at a flattering height.

head. The short-fronted horse has to be encouraged to stretch out the head and neck. The plain horse needs to have the head slightly higher and to look up, with the neck slightly arched, and this will improve the outlook considerably. If County Show committees organised lawn-like arenas I sometimes think the whole system would break down. To be on the safe side you should have something in your pocket as well, like small sweets with papers that make a noise. I once saw somebody trying to feed the surface of an indoor school to a pony which wasn't fooled for a second. Rustling papers is better

The mechanics of encouraging flattering head carriage. *Above* Before. *Below* The result.

than actually feeding the sweets because you don't want your horse called forward just when it is trying to dislodge a toffee from the roof of its mouth. Rewards should be saved for later, otherwise they tend to lose their appeal, and in any case chomping jaws are not attractive! In the absence of grass a handful of the arena surface can be thrown a bit at a time over one's shoulder to attract the horse's attention, but preferably not when the judge is walking behind you.

Don't overdo the grass. However beautiful the face, chomping jaws are not attractive.

## The individual show

When the judge has seen enough at the halt you will be asked to walk away, turn and then trot back past the judge and return to the line. The judge will be looking to see if the action is correct. As you walk away he will be standing behind you to watch the hind legs for cow hocks and sideways movement in the hocks, as well as wide or close action. When you turn and trot back he looks at the action in front for dishing. As you go past he can check the earlier impressions of knee action and hock engagement, and as you go away he will stand behind you and look at the hind leg action at the trot and if you trot on right round the corner he can see the action again in profile.

This is where your assessment of your horse's weaknesses and strengths really comes into its own because your horse has the judge's undivided attention and is subject to close scrutiny. How you lead your horse is of paramount importance. If it has weak hind legs and action at the walk all you can do is to walk in a less than straight line and turn as soon as you can to trot back, remembering to turn the horse away from you so that it remains balanced and up together. Should there be any question of your horse being unlevel you should turn the horse in a generous semi-circle rather than in a sharp turn. If your horse is not free going enough, use the cane behind your back to drive the horse forward without dropping the contact with your right hand or checking the impulsion generated.

The judges will be looking to see if the action is correct as you trot towards them.

Bad behaviour can sometimes disguise action but if the judge is prevented from seeing your horse move you may well be asked to do it again, and subsequent failure will mean that you cannot be placed.

If your horse is wide behind this will become more apparent at the trot and the faster you go, so you should trot on well from the turn and then slow right down when you are level with the judge. Trotting down hill does not flatter any horse and dishing is accentuated, so again you should watch out for any dips in the arena and try to avoid them, while moving in a straight line from your turn if your horse has good action. If your horse has a good trot then you should make the most of it and carry on right round the corner to give the judge the opportunity to appreciate it.

Keep your eye on the steward.

## The final walk round

If the judge has difficulty deciding or wants to check something, some of the competitors may be asked to walk round the judge in a smaller circle. As before you should give yourself enough space so that your horse is not impeded or distracted by the others. If the judge is standing in one place looking at the competitors in turn as they walk past, it is in your interests to cut the corners on the 'blind' side where possible to try to bring your horse before the judge again as quickly as you can without overtaking other competitors, and without hurrying, which spoils the outline. At this stage you should be watching the steward beside the judge like a hawk, particularly once you have seen them conferring.

## Calling in and the final judging

Stewards often call in the winners simply by catching your eye, raising their bowler if they are wearing one, and saying 'Thank you'. You should then walk smartly to where you were previously lined up and turn to face the spectators again and halt. Keep an eye on the proceedings if you are not called in first so that you line up on the correct side of the horse called in before you. Stand up your horse immediately and concentrate on the presence factor for all you are worth while the judge walks down the line. Even if you are not the apparent winner you should not let up for a second because a pleasing aspect can sometimes result in a last minute change of place, and bad behaviour certainly can. If your horse is standing well but otherwise looking a bit bored a discreet flick of the finger on the cheek is more effective than use of the cane; otherwise it is the grass again.

## Presentation of rosettes

Whatever your final placing, when you are handed your rosette you should thank the judge politely and look reasonably pleased even if you are bitterly disappointed. There is nothing worse than a bad loser. Male competitors remove their hats. If you are thrilled don't be too effusive – remember all those judges in the stands. You can now give your horse a pat.

Don't forget to say 'Thank you'.

# PART TWO
# Ethical Considerations

# CHAPTER EIGHT

# Abuse or improvement?

From our very first riding lesson we never stop learning about horses and how to train them, ride them and care for them. It is the goal of every enthusiast to learn as much as possible from the specialists in the individual disciplines, and fairly early on you discover that in addition to the accepted wisdom of the textbook and training course there is a body of knowledge acquired by years of 'hands on' practical experience. One of the fascinating things about talking to traditional breeders, for example, is how closely their opinions based on generations of observation coincide with modern scientific thought. Even more fascinating is how their views, which might once have been considered old fashioned, suddenly regain favour in the light of new research. An example of this is the regular feeding of bran as part of the concentrate ration, which traditional breeders dismissed but which was later considered to be an important source of bulk, but modern thinking is that it should be fed only in conjunction with limestone flour because of its ability, when fed without it, to cause the excretion of important minerals and trace elements.

A distinction has to be made, however, between different viewpoints based on different perspectives that have developed from different expectations of the performance of the horse, and those that are based on the same perspective but differ only in the importance attached to the welfare of the horse.

In Britain we have traditionally valued fair play above winning, something which other countries sometimes find hard to understand and even amusing. We are also known as a nation of animal lovers with a reputation for sometimes preferring them to children. Most British people view with repugnance the prospect of abusing horses in order to gain an unfair advantage. It is inescapable, though, that the spread of showing to new corners of the world, the increased

*Previous page* It is important to choose the right speed at the trot to show your horse at its best.

demand for show stock, and various other social and economic factors have made the difference between a first prize and a second prize considerably more significant than even twenty years ago.

One can argue that there are aspects of ringcraft that are on the borders of sportsmanship but there are few people who would resort to cruel cheating which gives showing a bad name and destroys the sense of achievement of winning. In the course of my travels to write this book I have been told some remarkable things, which may or may not be true, about the lengths that some people will go to in order to win in the show ring. At the same time it was explained why these practices are considered harmful by some people. Bearing in mind that many people do not go on to produce their horses under saddle it would be charitable to assume that they do not realise the long-term harm they might be doing to the ability of the horse to perform later to the best of its ability, either physically or mentally, and their actions are the actions of the ignorant and incompetent. On the other hand who is to say that certain widespread practices unpopular to modern thinking do not fall into the category of traditional practices which are based on a wisdom grounded in generations of observation? I thought it would be interesting and perhaps helpful to subject some of these practices and opinions, which I think of as allegation and counter-argument, to the scrutiny of a farrier and a veterinary surgeon to see just how far they correspond to the latest thinking. Do they represent pragmatic observation or the black side of the art of showing? Are they abusive to the horse and should they be discouraged?

# ALLEGATIONS AND COUNTER-ARGUMENTS
## Presence and the bold eye

Apparently all sorts of things have been attempted in order to influence presence according to the various requirements of individual breeds. One example from the USA was the blood letting of Quarter Horses just before a competition to make them lethargic as a sign of good temperament, but the most extraordinary tale I heard, also from the USA, involved inducing cocaine addiction in the horse, which was withheld for a couple of days before the show, then placed in the glove for the show ring where the horse could smell it and followed the glove with its nose. This was for a breed that required a sparkling presence in conjunction with a rather forced, high head carriage.

There are certain breeds that are renowned for the boldness of their eyes and sometimes for the high spirit of their character which, as with people, is shown by the expression in the eyes. I have been told that one way of inducing this effect is by severe discipline, 'taught' at home and sometimes reinforced by the use of whips and electrical gadgets. One notable artificial aid is a particularly severe showing bridle. The use of these methods has the effect of pushing the horse to the limits of its tolerance which cause it to develop an aggressive look or one of sub-terror, where the trainer just has to move and the horse almost shakes. The confidence of a horse in its trainer, so essential for any demanding performance, takes a long time to become established and once effectively destroyed is almost impossible to regain. There are warning signs and minute clues to this practice once suspicions are aroused, including tiny singed patches sometimes where electric current has burnt the horse. One advantage of expecting horses to walk quietly into the show ring rather than storming in flamboyantly is that it provides one less reason for hyping the horse up outside.

Concern for correct interpretation of the rules, aroused by Arab showing practices in America, prompted the Arab Horse Society (AHS) to create a Disciplinary Committee and to ensure the presence of a member of this committee at every Class C show where European qualifiers are held. If abuse is suspected a deliberately public inquiry takes place with sanctions for the guilty, because the AHS takes the view that a strong stand must be taken to prevent abuse succeeding, and hence gaining a foothold. In this country the consensus is that a system that prevents abuse, even if it allows unfit amateurs to take fat horses out of fields, bathe them, show them and win, is preferable.

In the past people have been known to put drugs in the eyes to dilate the pupils, and also to cut the eyelashes, whose function is to protect the eyes from grit and foreign bodies, again to achieve a wide-eyed look. This was particularly prevalent with Arabs until the practice was banned.

Another more subtle way of producing a bold eye, which appears just as abusive, involves shutting a horse up in the dark for some days before a show, even loading it in the dark with the ramp against the stable door, and then unboxing it seconds before it is due to go in the ring. This, I am told, also does wonders for the exuberance of a dull animal and is a trick employed with Arabs and Welsh Cobs. It may, however, have a lasting adverse effect on the temperament. A horse, which is after all a herd animal, probably on a high protein diet, is shut in the dark in the midst of the excitement of a show. It cannot see what is going on, will not eat properly and gets anxious. This can lead to box walking, crib biting and weaving, difficult if not impossible vices to cure, and to a distrustful attitude.

## Trimming

The whole issue of quality heads and bold eyes leads on to the subject of trimming which is quite controversial, especially the trimming of ears. The hairs inside the ears have evolved to protect the sensitive inner mechanisms of the ear. Fine hairs prevent the entry of insects and foreign bodies and expel anything that gets inside. The hearing of the horse is particularly acute and hair also insulates the hearing from very loud noise.

The tactile hair or whiskers around the nostrils and muzzle, which are almost routinely removed for the show ring, are associated with a complex system of nerves that enable the horse to be aware of its environment in the areas it cannot see. The ones around the eyes are there to protect the eyes from hazards outside the line of vision. The close association of these hairs with the nervous system has a bearing on the development of young animals. Work with brain-damaged

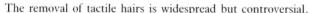

The removal of tactile hairs is widespread but controversial.

children on stimulating the passage of neurological information along these kinds of networks is the basis of the famous Peto Institute and the reason for the remarkable physical progress of children who have learnt to do things they were thought to be incapable of, like walking. Whilst there is a limit to the parallels that can be drawn between two very different kinds of mammals it does provide food for thought.

## Stabling of youngstock

The horse is an animal of the grasslands of the world and it is well known that foals and young horses need to be able to exercise freely for the development of healthy reflexes and strong muscles and limbs. Even when turned out every morning for exercise show stock spend a large part of every day confined to the stable, in some cases twenty-three hours and more.

## Early weaning

Early weaning of foals is also controversial. American producers believe that there is no nutritional benefit to leaving the foal on the mare after three months. This is in contrast to those who believe that the foal's large intestine is unable fully to digest fibre effectively until it is seven and a half months old. There are other benefits which can be overlooked, the main one being the socialisation of the foal that is disciplined by the mare and learns so much from her by example. Apart from this, as herd animals young horses gain confidence from each other and particularly from their mothers.

## Top line and head carriage

Equally controversial are the methods used for developing the top line and the correct head carriage. Fixing the heads of show ponies is based on a theory that the horse is incapable of placing the fore feet in advance of the nose, so if the head is fixed and the pony ridden forward the result is the moment of suspension of the fore feet in the air associated with the extravagant action of the 'daisy cutter' as the pony tries to place its feet and stay in balance.

Then there are the alleged abuses involving the nicking of neck muscles to ensure a lower head carriage for American Quarter Horses, and tying their heads up very high for long periods before entering the ring so that the neck muscles are tired. They all have consequences for the long-term ability of the horse.

Dressage enthusiasts will argue that correct head carriage is a question of correct hock engagement which comes with gradual development of the back muscles and the general athletic ability of the horse. They see this as best achieved by progressive schooling on the flat that strengthens the muscles by stretching them in the course of performing various movements like loops and circles; that forward movement is an attitude of mind taught from day one by expecting the horse to use its back at all paces without restricting the head. They argue that stretched muscles are ultimately capable of greater contraction so the horse is encouraged to stretch the top line with the hocks engaged under the body and the correct head carriage will follow naturally. Thus if the head carriage is raised or lowered artificially it will affect the ability to use the back, and hollow backs, trailing hind legs and poor hock engagement will be a consequence, all of which impair the ability of the horse to develop its paces or to jump.

Also concerned with improving the outline is the reported practice of inserting silicone implants to boost the natural tissues in areas that need it, such as around the loins where strapping should not be carried out. Hollywood's 'Dream Factory' is only now finding out to its cost the true price of this procedure in humans, with migrating silicone and serious ill health.

Lungeing young horses has to be undertaken with extreme caution because it places considerable strain on immature hock joints. This is more important when you are dealing with big, slow maturing horses that should eventually be capable of performing at national level or higher. It follows that over-enthusiasm for winning in hand with a big sloppy yearling or two year old could have the effect of producing an adult horse that is an underachiever over fences and incapable of real collection. How much more damage can be done by regularly lungeing foals, a practice advocated by American producers? Lungeing in small circles also places uneven strain on developing limbs, which can cause permanent unsoundness in later years.

## Improving characteristic action

Some bohemian 'training' methods to develop characteristic action were reported which may be widespread but perhaps are of doubtful efficiency. Welsh Cobs have been known to spend time with chains trailing on the ground from straps around their pasterns, which are removed just before the show. The unusual noise and interference causes them to snatch their feet up when moving, in order to exaggerate the distinctive knee action expected of the breed. This practice is criticised on the grounds that it may be associated with hollow backs and trailing hind legs, because developing the back appears to the ignorant to be unnecessary. Of equally doubtful efficiency is the practice of putting hacks' knees in Plaster of Paris to keep the action low.

Another aspect of this which causes concern is the practice of shoeing sometimes quite young Welsh ponies and Hackneys with heavy shoes for the same purpose, which is believed by some to affect the healthy development of the limbs and the hooves. A possible explanation for the development of this practice is the effect observed when two opposing sets of muscles are concerned with the movement of a limb and one set is put under uneven strain. When the weight/pressure is removed the other set responds involuntarily, resulting in the movement of the bone/joint concerned. However, the effect can only be observed momentarily until the muscles readjust. The certain consequence of wearing heavy shoes for any length of time is the development of the leg muscles, as in working out with weights. The difference is that weight lifters do not have weights superglued to their hands!

Also concerned with demonstrating perfect action is an alleged but clearly abusive practice of blistering frogs which become sore. The rationale for this is making the horse delay putting its feet to the ground for as long as possible to make the stride bigger and rounder, or in other circumstances putting the weight on the heel.

## Show condition

The conditioning of youngstock is at last a matter for public debate, with judges' panels being instructed not to favour the over-fat. Young horses are not meant to be heavy when they are growing because of the strain it places on growing limbs and feet. I was told that cracked joints and degenerative joint disease are just two consequences and that the young horse that has been overconditioned starts life with a predisposition to foot, limb, liver and respiratory problems. A practice that was mentioned was feeding concentrates ad lib to youngstock in the belief that they only take what they need. Not only is it apparent to the observer that animals vary in their attitudes and enthusiasm for food, but there is research to indicate that those fed ad lib, amongst a group of young horses related genetically and kept in the same environment, had a higher occurrence of conformational and musculoskeletal abnormalities as a result of developing faster.

# Height

Making the height for the all important height certificate is another area of alleged potential abuse. Horses are believed to measure shorter when they are relaxed, because, the lay thinking goes, the bones in this area are supported by ligaments and not fixed rigidly, and this can be an invitation to some people to work them to the point of exhaustion before they are measured. Others don't leave it to chance and have the withers operated on, risking infection including the very serious fistulous wither and all the problems associated with the drainage of this area.

# Surgery

Operations may also be resorted to for lumps and bumps like splints, which once formed don't actually harm the horse unless close to a joint, but can be deciders in a competition.

The role of the vet generally in showing is quite interesting because these and other practices, like operations to influence tail carriage in certain breeds, and the previously mentioned silicone injections, may involve their assistance, and raise issues of professional integrity.

If someone is determined to obtain drugs the veterinary profession does not necessarily have to be involved. In this respect the authorities of the showing world are above reproach. I am referring to the banning of the administration of steroids as growth promoters, tranquillisers and painkillers, practices that must be common enough for the various authorities to have instituted dope testing procedures at major shows. Just how are drugs obtained and what sanctions exist to prevent general abuse outside the show ring? There is not enough discussion or information about these issues which would in themselves deter the ambitious, ignorant but generally well-meaning owner. If there were severe and more widely published sanctions by the veterinary profession for clinically unnecessary treatment the incidence of cases would reduce.

These are the alleged practices and the counter-arguments. Who is right?

# THE VETERINARY SURGEON'S VIEWPOINT

## Bold eye and presence

*Administering eye drops to dilate the pupil is extremely dangerous and can result in permanent damage to the retina from exposure to sunlight.*

*Shutting a horse in the dark and then exposing it to sunlight causes constriction of the pupil; the brighter the sun the more constricted the pupil becomes. The effect of this practice on the behaviour of the horse is unknown.*

## Trimming

*The most important thing about the removal of tactile hairs is the protection of the eyes. Around the muzzle it really doesn't matter but the long tactile hairs around the eyes and anything associated with them is terribly important, because they are early warning systems for anything approaching the head. Under no circumstances should they be removed from around the eyes if the interests of the horse are considered. The hairs in the ears are not very important other than preventing the small flies from entering the ear. There is no way of measuring the horse's hearing to my knowledge, so this allegation cannot be evaluated scientifically.*

## Stabling of youngstock

*Stabling youngstock and turning them out for about three hours is common practice. It is unnatural for the horse but it is common practice.*

## Early weaning

*Weaning at three months, if it is the practice of an individual stud, managed with care and in the interests of the foal, then I see no harm. But if weaning at three months is used to force feed a foal then that is malpractice and an effect will possibly manifest itself later on in life, particularly if it is used with anabolic steroids.*

## Administration of drugs

*A drug should not be administered to a horse unless it is in the course of reasonable therapy, directed to the benefit of the horse. Any drug that is used to control the horse should be to assist the veterinary surgeon or the farrier or people clipping the horse to do whatever they have to do with reasonable safety, both to the horse and to themselves. However, no sedation, antibiotics or drugs, even equipalazone/butazolidene, may be administered to a horse without the direct involvement of the veterinary surgeon. If they don't actually administer it they should be present when it is administered, or they should be in attendance on the horse, recommend its use over a period of time and then re-examine the horse.*

*As far as steroids are concerned it is bad practice to administer anabolic steroids to enhance growth. It is not professional practice. I know it is done but it should not be done. It unbalances the normal hormone system of the body which can result in its permanent maladjustment. It is possible that it could damage the immune system and it can result in malformation of the skeleton.*

*The administration of any drug that is not for the direct benefit of the horse is immoral and under all circumstances should be banned.*

## Improving characteristic action

*Putting a metal shoe on a horse is an unnatural thing to do anyway. It is done so that the horse may be used on ground that might, if the shoes weren't there, wear out the feet. They are also put on the horse so that it may grip better in the fields. The weight is important. In racehorses, for instance, they use aluminium shoes to reduce the weight as much as possible. Big heavy shoes are unnecessary and, in a show horse, in my opinion, they should be as light as possible while still protecting the feet. Providing the shoes are not excessive and providing they are put on by a qualified farrier and the shoeing doesn't harm the horse, then I would not describe this as a malpractice. Whether it actually produces an effect or not is difficult to say.*

*Blistering frogs is nonsense because the frog is so thick with hard skin that if it weren't well protected it would be raw. Blistering heels is unlikely to achieve any change in the natural action of the horse, is unnecessary and abusive of the horse.*

## Show condition

*Over-condition is a very important and much discussed situation. In other words, showing in hand is showing fat and not conformation. One of the most important things that can happen is that when the horse, at youth, is overweight the growth plates at each end of the long bones become compressed and the horse does not grow to its full height and in a proper manner. Obesity in a young horse is really very harmful and can result in malformation of the skeleton.*

*Every case of osteochondrosis, however, is not an obese young horse. They can have osteochondrosis and not be obese at all.*

## Surgery

*The part of the anatomy around the withers, far from not being rigid, supports the head. The withers are the anchor to the huge ligament that holds the head and neck up. It is possible for the ligament to slip off, or the wither to fracture causing pain. Removing the dorsal spines at the withers surgically to reduce the height of the horse is absolutely disgraceful and grossly abusive of the horse.*

*The bony* splint *(exostosis) is there to help anchor the splint bone to the cannon bone and removing it for cosmetic reasons is not in the interests of the horse. If it has been operated on and any part of the splint bone has been removed that horse cannot be described as a sound horse. It has to be stated quite clearly if the horse is offered for sale. There is nothing unnatural about a splint. Surgery at best is unnecessary; at worst it is harmful.*

*The practice of inserting silicone implants in the horse is quite unworthy of any sort of discussion at all. The people who do that should be attacked with every vigour.*

*In all activities where the horse is used and enjoyed the welfare of the horse should be considered first.*

# THE FARRIER'S VIEWPOINT

*On the subject of heavy shoes to encourage a certain kind of knee action, a shoe weighing a pound and a half is an incredibly heavy shoe. I have been asked to put them on but I have always refused as I don't consider it necessary. A good Welsh cob that has been bred properly will have the action anyway and it really doesn't make any difference. In fact it is more likely to impair the action. With any well-moving horse, regardless of breed, the less you have on its feet the better it will move. If there is a slight fault in the action there is a possibility of injury. The idea is that the heavy shoes are used to work the horse until the morning of the show when a light plate is put on and the horse reacts to the change of weight. Over the years it has*

'A good Welsh cob will have the action anyway', including good hock engagement and a rounded top line, which come from correct training.

*always been done and no matter what you do you always get people who think that what has been done in the past is best, until somebody comes along and eventually convinces them it is not the best way forward.*

*Shoeing youngsters that are still growing, all the time, will restrict the growth of the foot to a degree. Yearlings are still babies and the bones are still developing. There is no reason to shoe a horse until it is working. A large proportion of what happens to horses' feet for the show ring lies with educating the owners of the horses.*

*Showing needs to modernise itself in line with what we know now. Attitudes in farriery have changed so much in the last ten years because we know so much more now, such as when you can, when you can't and when you need to alter the feet. For example we used to get a lot of foals, particularly in Thoroughbred studs, that used to come up on their toes, and this was thought to be a conformation fault. We now know that it is to do with the way they were fed. They were stuffed with food to get big yearlings and the high levels of protein played havoc with the muscles, drawing them up. When you stop feeding them everything relaxes again. This was only discovered within the last five years. Corrective shoeing has been gone into and they are now finding that deviations in the limbs at birth or shortly after birth, in nine cases out of ten correct themselves if left alone. In other cases growth around the chest area causes splayed front legs to straighten naturally. They have also discovered that while a horse that toes out is a disaster, if a horse toes in it doesn't matter because they all do it naturally and it is the action of the muscles, which are on the outside of the leg, that straightens them and can account for slight deviations. In this case, providing you can get the correct limb balance and the weight is distributed correctly it doesn't matter what it does at the bottom. If it needs to toe in to be correct and keep the horse sound then so be it. What they have got to get away from is that a judge will look at a horse standing straight in front of them with its feet turned in and they will disregard it, but they cannot see if the horse needs to do it, whether it is a bad fault or part of the horse's make up. Given a choice of two horses the one with straight feet will be put up but it is not necessarily the soundest horse or the straightest mover.*

## OTHER 'TRICKS OF THE TRADE'

In addition to the professional opinions, I asked a hack judge about *plastering the knees* of hacks to improve action. 'A load of nonsense' was the short reply. He reinforced the other opinions when he said that 'good action is natural and can be improved by hard work and good horsemanship, but there are no short cuts or substitutes for experience and skill. Any changes achieved in this way would only be of very short duration and not enduring enough to influence a competition.' His comments sum up the opinions of the vast majority of showing enthusiasts and all the experts consulted. It is just unfortunate that hard work and dedication are not sensational and do not make the headlines.

## CAN PRODUCTION STANDARDS BE TOO HIGH?

Quite apart from obviously abusive practices there is a fundamental question about showing which is rarely if ever addressed, but has been referred to obliquely by the highly respected judges consulted for their opinions. Bearing in mind that the show ring is the main platform for assessing breeding stock, to what extent should the appearance of the horse be interfered with at all?

There is an unspoken assumption, especially amongst producers, that by using the full range of their techniques they can fool the observer into choosing a horse that may well be incapable of passing on genetically its apparent perfection; that better horses can be

High production standards for the show ring give much pleasure to the spectator,
but do they assist or hinder the evaluation of breeding stock?

overlooked if not produced to the same standard. This is endorsed
tacitly by the breeders who have gradually stopped showing, discouraged by the apparent importance judges attach to production
and showmanship. On the other hand there is almost universal
agreement amongst experienced judges that a good horse can be
spotted irrespective of presentation, and the customs of show ring
turnout are simply a reflection of good manners and respect to the
judge, the show and the general public.

As a means of assessing breeding stock and youngsters, the show
ring and its methods of evaluation are actually quite limited. The
horse is asked to stand, walk and trot obediently in hand and its
conformation and action are assessed. The visible features, in other
words, which are certainly very important, can be scrutinised, but
not the myriad of invisible features that provide the essence of
the breeds and types. Intelligence, willingness to learn and work,

temperament and performance can only have the merest assesment. Other features like stamina, hardiness, food conversion ability, fertility, whilst hinted at by their association with conformation and appearance, may be overlooked. There is a danger that increasingly sophisticated methods of producing show stock and an over-reliance on show ring results could result in the production of 'toy horses' that conform ideally with visual criteria but lose sight of the qualities for which the various individual breeds are revered.

Over-enthusiasm for breeding animals that conform to a man-made ideal may even go so far as to harm important natural functions. An example that comes to mind is the show ring desirability of a certain type of head that has resulted in the breeding of stock with insufficient room for the teeth, and this in a native breed that is assumed to be able to live rough on indifferent grazing. The same emphasis on quality heads for hunters has resulted in the systematic diminution of bone not only in hunter classes but in the judging of the stronger breeds that produce them, where once the need was merely to ensure that a riding horse bred from a farm mare had a head that was light enough not to tire easily. It is in dealing with issues such as these, clearly, where the breed societies and the various regulatory bodies have a tremendous responsibility and the evidence is that they are aware of it and take it very seriously.

It may be no coincidence that at a time when methods of production have 'advanced' so significantly, the breed societies are developing ever more rigorous evaluation procedures of breeding stock, including performance testing where appropriate, and repeat inspections during the lifetime of stallions in the light of the qualities and faults of their progeny. However much of a pleasure it is to see a horse produced to the peak of its beauty, character and condition, in the final analysis it is only by assessing performance, progeny and the prepotency of breeding stock to pass on all their good qualities that the horse can truly be evaluated.

*Opposite* Properly dressed for a small show or a big show.

94

# PART THREE

# Breed and Type Classes

# CHAPTER NINE

# British Types and Breeds

The advice in Part One applies most directly to the competitions covered in this chapter, which includes hunters, hacks, riding horses and cobs of various sizes and weights, as well as the Cleveland Bay and the Hackney. It also applies to show ponies, which have a chapter of their own.

## THE HUNTER

In Britain when people think of traditional showing it is usually the hunter classes that they have in mind, whether it is the in-hand youngstock classes, the elegant ladies riding side saddle or the high profile ridden heavyweight classes. They would probably be surprised to know that the whole concept of hunting and the horses it requires is more or less unique to Britain and Ireland. There are a number of packs of hounds in France and America, but for social and geographical reasons the demands of their hunting fields have not had such a profound influence on the types of horses bred for the commercial market.

The hunting field calls for the same qualities in its horses that competitive riding is increasingly demanding of breeders. In many ways it makes even greater demands, because the horses have to be strong and sound enough to gallop and jump all day long, as well as for short bursts of energy, and to sustain this year after year with time off for summer breaks. They also have to be confident and clever enough to think for themselves when faced with unusual terrain and obstacles. The sheer numbers of people both keen to and capable of riding across country following hounds accounts for the availability and outstanding success of British and Irish horses and riders in international competition. As European performance horse breeders keep pointing out, correct conformation is essential for successful competition, but it always was essential for the best seasoned hunters. It is hardly surprising, therefore, that hunter classes, in addition to the combined showing and jumping working hunter classes, continue to be keenly contested and observed by professional breeders and competitive riders. Recent years have seen the addition of hunter pony and more recently working hunter pony classes for the younger rider, although these are run under National Pony Society rules quite separately from the adult hunter classes. All of them are the nurseries for the star performers of the future. Far from becoming an anachronism, hunter competitions are gaining in significance. This is reflected in the numerous opportunities to show hunters both at affiliated and unaffiliated shows, most commonly in ridden classes.

Hunter classes are run according to the rules compiled by the National Light Horse Breeding Society (HIS), which used to be called the Hunters' Improvement Society (HIS), and with whom the horses usually have to be identified, particularly at the larger affiliated shows. Identification and height certificates (if relevant) have to be submitted with entry forms for these shows but not for the unaffiliated shows. This should be confirmed by close examination of the show schedule, and in any case the rules should be obtained and read. They define a hunter as follows:

> A hunter should be capable of carrying its designated weight regularly for a full day's hunting. It should have substance, quality and a calm, bold temperament. It should have the conformation to produce high performance with sustained soundness. It should be alert, and have four athletic natural paces.

As with other types and breeds of horses, classes are for brood mares, foals, yearlings, two year olds and three year olds, all of which are shown in hand. Once the young horse reaches four years of age the classes are for ridden hunters, and are subdivided according to the weight of rider (plus equipment) that the horse (mare or gelding) must be capable of carrying. Two- and three-year-old brood mares, and colts other than yearlings, are not allowed to enter in youngstock classes. Brood mares must have their own foal at foot. Mares which have not yet foaled or that have lost their foals are not eligible to enter. To be eligible for hunter foal classes a foal must be the progeny of a mare entered in the previous class and must be at least three weeks old on the day of the show.

Small hunter youngstock, which are defined by being estimated not to reach over 15.2 hh at maturity, are judged before the open in-hand hunter classes so that they can be transferred to them if they

The vast majority of the best mature hunters are non-Thoroughbred.

exceed the height limits. A horse which is registered as a small hunter cannot compete in an Open Weight class. No horse may be entered in both a hunter and hack or riding horse class at the same show.

## Producing the show hunter

There are many opinions and preferences regarding the breeding of the best hunters, some of whom would be totally unsuitable if moved to a different kind of terrain, and one of the paradoxes is that although the vast majority of the best mature hunters are part Throughbred, a much higher percentage of winning, in-hand, young hunters seem to be full Thoroughbred. The most obvious explanation is that big horses take longer to mature whereas the Thoroughbred, bred and expected to race as a two year old, has the edge in the early years. Another factor is the action, and the degree of knee action in particular, which tends to be lower in the Thoroughbred, whose principal pace is the gallop, rather than the heavier horses whose principal pace is the trot. Lower action is more eye catching for the show ring, although many people believe that slightly more robust action is safer for some of the more rugged hunting terrains. Don't forget, though, that winning is about being the best on the day!

Production methods obviously have a large part to play. Since there is an in-hand element to ridden competitions as well as for youngstock, these will be touched on where relevant.

The stripped phase of a Ladies' Hunter class. In a big class, many judges call out the competitors two at a time so that one is preparing for the judge's inspection while the other is showing its paces.

## The producer's viewpoint

*A lot of people make the mistake, particularly with youngsters – yearlings, two year olds and three year olds – of not starting early enough. Six weeks before the show is too late! With youngsters, feeding and gradually building all the muscles up takes a long time. You need to start at Christmas by bringing them in and feeding them three feeds a day. Actual quantities of hard food have to be worked out on an individual basis. Some don't have such hearty appetites as others and need to be built up more slowly. Fattening foods like boiled or micronised barley may well be an important ingredient, as well as protein, depending on the needs of the horse. Experience is really only gained by trying it out yourself. A young two year old would need a bit of everything as well as plenty of good hay. We always like to turn them out every day, even if it is only for a couple of hours, regardless of the weather, and we find that it keeps them a lot more settled and sensible. From about March they can be rugged up and groomed. There isn't much point before then because young hunters usually have some Thoroughbred blood so they don't grow the same kinds of coats that Mountain and Moorland ponies grow. You don't have the same problems of getting the winter coat out for the first shows in May.*

*Basic training starts when you lead them in and out of the field every day. You have to make sure that they are holding their heads in the position you want them to be in [see Part One Chapter 3] and*

99

*they have to walk up beside you, not dragging back behind you with their heads down. At some point on the journey halting correctly is good practice too. You have to get them used to halting with their legs positioned correctly so that it becomes automatic. Some youngsters learn quickly; others can get a bit wound up, especially when it is cold and wet. They have to have a bit of spark in them to help their presence if they need it. Some youngsters don't achieve their peak until later in the season despite your efforts. They can change very dramatically in a short period of time and this is difficult to predict.*

*Driving can be a good thing for horses that are too young to lunge, because it gets them to walk on their own and you can see how they are going and insist on them tracking up and consequently developing their top line. At home they can be driven off a cavesson rather than risking the mouth by attaching the reins to the bit. It should not be attempted by the inexperienced, however. We never lunge young horses until they are three. If the ground is hard we wouldn't lunge them then. Generally young horses move better without shoes, but if the ground is hard they would go better with them or with just front shoes. If they have a tendency to turn their toe in they might need careful trimming to help the feet to develop correctly.*

*Trimming is necessary around the muzzle and in the chin. We trim inside the ears as well at the outer edge because it tidies the appearance of the head. It gives them a bit more quality.*

*Tack consists of a leather bridle, usually brass mounted, and a bit with a long leather lead rein. For my yearlings I usually use a small rubber bit. After that, if they aren't too strong they can stay in the rubber bit, otherwise they move on to a straight bar bit. On the whole it is sensible to use a bit although you get the odd quiet one that doesn't need one. The bigger colts can get quite strong and they need a little more control. Three year olds I like to see in a double bridle because it suits them better. It does help a little with the control and the head carriage too. If they don't take to it then it would be better to stick to the lead rein, taking care to have it a good length.*

*You have to be quite strong with youngsters, because like children they have to know who's boss, otherwise they will walk all over you, and they are stronger than you are. They have to know what 'whoa' means. There is quite a lot going on at some of these shows for them to take in at once.*

*Foals are shown in a nice leather headcollar. Make sure it is fitted properly, not halfway down its neck. If this is a danger then a plain browband should be fitted. I don't like to see foals plaited, although*

100

*this happens more with ponies. It is quite unnecessary and quite stressful. They need feeding, but this is quite easy because they feed when their mothers feed. If necessary put in two feeding bowls so that they both eat at the same time. Quantities, again, depend on the temperament of the animals concerned and the condition of the grazing. Some mares, regardless of whether they are being shown or not, may need extra food or minerals when they are rearing a foal. Don't forget that foals can miss going out in the field every day if you travel to shows any distance from home, which can be quite problematic. Travelling long distances can be quite a strain on their limbs, too.*

*Quarter marks depend on the maturity of the animal and the effect you are trying to create. They are usually put on two and three year olds rather than the very young animals. [See p. 234 for an illustration of hunter-type quarter marks and their effect.]*

## The judge's viewpoint

*You can always tell the professional producers because their horses' heads are always carried at the right height. You see some real sights with amateur producers, particularly with the way their horses go. I try to help them but if a horse plays up you can only judge what you can see.*

*Conformation is everything and you never see a perfect horse. Choosing the winner comes down to personal preference. I look for long low action which makes for a more comfortable ride.*

*Turnout has got to be top class and immaculate. I don't like to see foals plaited and generally hunters have pulled, not plaited, tails and of course plaited manes. If I see a long tail I look more closely to see if it is trying to conceal bad hocks. With regard to tack they are all shown in leather bridles, foals are shown in leather slips and without too long a lead rein – you don't want them to get too far away from you because they are harder to control. I don't like to see double bridles on young horses because they take some getting used to and it is a lot for a young horse. When you do see them it is usually on a horse that has been broken in, and very often professional producers will show in a double bridle, perhaps with a broad noseband if the horse has got a large head. A showing bridle with a bit is quite sufficient for a young horse.*

*I do have strong views about the clothes the people wear. Tweed jackets are essential, with bowlers for men and riding hats for women. Jeans can look quite smart. The handler should carry a rigid leather stick or cane. Anyone coming into the ring must be well turned out or it is an insult to the judge.*

*I don't like pot hunters and do not like to see professional producers at local one-day shows. I very much dislike people coming up to me about a week before a show who don't normally talk to me. The best horse has to win.*

# SHOW HACK, COB AND RIDING HORSE CLASSES

These are run under the auspices of the British Show Hack, Cob and Riding Horse Association. As with hunters there are many more opportunities to compete in ridden classes than in hand, particularly at unaffiliated shows. The big affiliated shows have classes for all categories and sizes, but in-hand opportunities for cobs in particular are limited.

The rules of the Association should be obtained and read, but they contain the usual prohibitions with regard to doping, and they also penalise or ban horses which have been fired or hobdayed.

## Hacks

As the Association defines them:

> The Hack must be a pleasure to ride and have excellent manners, self balance and ride light to the hand; show conformation with the emphasis on quality and elegance. The latter stems from a well set on head and neck combined with a good length of shoulder, and the movement should be smooth and graceful with a true pointing of the toe. To achieve these qualities the Hack must be extremely well schooled.

The handlers and owners of in-hand horses are not obliged to be members unless they qualify for the Association's National Championships, in which case they have to become members within two weeks. Horses shown in hand do not have to be registered with the Association. Stallions and colts in hack breeding classes do, however, have to be registered in their respective Stud Books. For example, stallions have to be of 'Hack type suitable to breed a Show Hack'. As the Association explains in its rules, 'The ideal breeding

The movement should be smooth and graceful with a true pointing of the toe.

for a Show Hack is the thoroughbred, the small Hack tends to have some pony or Arab blood to keep the height down', so stallions may well be registered with Weatherby's as Thoroughbred or with the Arab Horse Society as Anglo-Arab.

In-hand classes are held for stallions, brood mares, foals, yearlings, two year olds and three year olds. They are subdivided in each category according to estimated height at maturity. Stallions classes and brood mare classes are subdivided into Small Hack, those exceeding 14.2 and not exceeding 15.0 hands, and Large Hack, exceeding 15.0 hands but not exceeding 15.3 hands. Foal classes are open to the progeny of the mare classes.

Yearling, two- and three-year-old classes are also subdivided into Small Hack, filly, colt or gelding to make between 14.2 and 15.0 hands at maturity, and Large Hack, filly, colt or gelding to make between 15.0 hands and 15.3 hands at maturity. *On the day* they must not exceed the following heights:

Yearlings:    Small Hack 14.1 hands
              Large Hack 15.0 hands

Two year olds:  Small Hack 14.2 hands
                Large Hack 15.1 hands

Three year olds:  Small Hack 14.3 hands
                  Large Hack 15.2 hands

The rules emphasise that 'For shows held after 1st July an additional ½ inch should be added to the height on the day.'

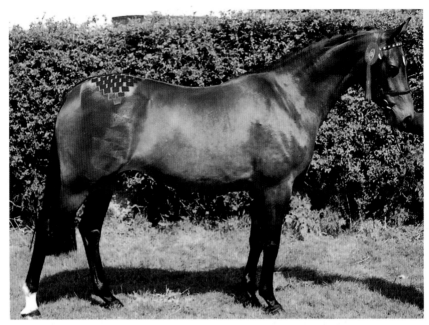

'Basic conformation is fundamental, but with elegance, temperament, quality and action...' Note the position of the quarter marks and their effect.

### Hack judging

The judging of hack breeding classes for youngstock in hand bears in mind the criteria for judging the ridden hack classes. Once again basic conformation is fundamental, but with elegance, temperament, quality and action as additional essential factors. With regard to turnout, quite simply no effort is spared, with plaiting and the frequent use of quarter marks and shark's teeth. Tack, also, should reflect the supreme elegance and quality of this type.

The rules for judging ridden hacks state:

The following method of judging is adopted:

40% for conformation, presence, type and action in hand.
60% for ride, training test and manners.

All hunters, including ladies and small, are barred from entry in Hack and Riding Horse classes at the same show and vice versa.

## Cobs

The Cob is a type rather than a breed. A short legged animal exceeding 14.2 hh with a maximum height of 15.1 hh, it has the bone and

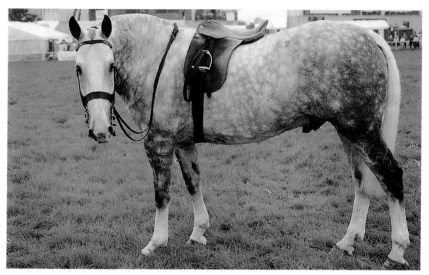

An Irish Draught cob showing the conformation, temperament and weight-carrying qualities required. Note the hogged mane, pulled tail and clipped legs, as well as the rugged tack to match. Note also the suitability of the saddle which not only flatters the shoulder but seats the judge as close as possible to the horse, counteracting any possible impression of shortness of neck or low wither to which cobs are prone.

substance with quality of a heavyweight hunter and is capable of carrying a substantial weight. They should be well-mannered and ideal for nervous or elderly riders. Cobs have sensible heads, sometimes Roman nosed, a full generous eye, shapely neck, crested on the top, with hogged mane, well defined withers, and clean, strong hocks, and all the attributes of a good hunter, low movement, comfortable to ride and should not pull.

## Cob judging
'Cobs should be judged as hunters, but they should be well schooled and particular attention should be paid to manners.'

Cobs are generally shown under saddle, which does not concern us, but as their style of turnout is unique it is mentioned, as it would apply if they are ever shown in hand. Whiskers and heels should be trimmed, manes hogged (frequently − no designer stubble!) and tails pulled and not too long to flatter the quarters and hocks. Tack should be plain and sensible to suit the rugged image. Quarter marks if worn should be stripes rather than squares, and possibly, but rarely, shark's teeth, to enhance the impression of strong quarters and second thighs. (As with hunter classes riders wear tweed jackets.)

# Riding horses

The Association recommends that a Riding Horse should have quality, substance, good bone, correct conformation, presence and true action. It should be a horse best described as something between what is generally recognised as a true Hunter and a true Hack, that is to say, while it does not require the substance of a Hunter or the elegance of the Hack it should, nevertheless, be up to sufficient weight to carry an average adult: at the same time to be a comfortable ride and show ability to gallop.

Ridden classes are for mares or geldings and are subdivided into Small Riding Horse exceeding 14.2 hh and not exceeding 15.2 hh, and Large Riding Horse exceeding 15.2 hh. Turnout and tack have to reflect the above recommendation.

In all three categories, hack, cob and riding horse, the in-hand phase of the ridden competitions of the Association may differ from purely in-hand competitions in one respect. In the interests of saving time competitors are frequently called out two at a time so that one is preparing while the other is running the horse up in hand (this frequently happens in ridden hunter and pony classes as well). Once again no effort is spared with regard to presentation and turnout.

# The judge's viewpoint

*My advice on producing hacks, or any other horse, is to watch the best people and try and produce the best standards. The only way to be successful is with a great deal of hard work. Something people find very difficult to come to terms with is that producing horses is like playing the piano or painting, some are talented and are successful and others aren't. You don't even have to like horses to be talented at producing them whereas others may love them and can't do it.*

*When judging hacks you look first of all for a near perfect animal and then for elegance, movement and manners, which are very, very important. If a hack behaves badly it is sent out of the ring. The distinctive action of the hack is bred in them and firstly has to be straight, and nothing will alter it if it isn't. Basically good action can be improved and the professional producers are very good at it. If you can afford it, go to them for lessons or send your horse to them for schooling or just ask their advice, most are very helpful. Otherwise watch what they do and persevere.*

*It may be unpopular but I would say that, by the way people dress you can predict with almost 90 per cent accuracy if they can ride or not. My overwhelming message is don't overdress because this is what distinguishes the amateur from the professional. You should aim to be neat and unfussy. It isn't a fancy dress competition but a showing class. You are only there to steer the ship, not to dress up like the captain.*

*Looking neat, well dressed and unfussy applies equally to showing in hand and in both cases you should carry a leather covered stick.*

*For in-hand showing the correct tack is leather showing bridles with brass mountings and a leather or webbing lead rein. I don't like brass browbands at all, and coloured browbands, in my opinion, are another instance of the jazzing up of the amateur riders, who go in for them more than the professionals. Once again the emphasis is on being neat and well dressed and conventional. The more professional you are the less flashy you look. Manes are plaited, and tails, in my opinion, should be pulled and not plaited, although many people do plait tails, but I think this is the mark of the amateur. I would almost prefer to see a full unpulled tail than a plaited tail. Quarter marks and shark's teeth are really only decoration and don't fool the judge.*

*You can improve the look of a plain horse by making it fatter. Fat covers a lot of faults which is why we see so many overfat hunters. The most important thing about condition is that the horse should be in good health, when you could almost prepare it just by rubbing it over with a damp cloth. You can't do away with class; if it is there it will shine through regardless.*

*There is no substitute for hard work. There are no short cuts.*

# THE CLEVELAND BAY
## Early history

According to the society:

When the Cleveland Bay Horse Society was formed in 1884, the Clevelands – then known in their native Yorkshire as Chapmans – already had a history going back 150 years and were, even then, as fixed in type as any British breed of horse has ever been. They were strong and short legged and capable of carrying great weight, and were extensively used in hilly areas on the farm and as pack animals. Each was reputed to have been able to carry 600 lbs of iron ore out of the mines in the North York Moors.

# Official breed profile

HEIGHT   16.0 hh to 16.2 hh, but height should not disqualify an otherwise good sort.

COLOUR   Cleveland Bays must be bay with black points, i.e. black legs, black mane and black tail. Grey hairs in mane and tail do not disqualify. These have long been recognised as a feature in certain strains of pure Cleveland blood. White is not admissible beyond a very small white star. Legs which are bay or red below the knees and hocks do not disqualify, but are faulty as to colour.

BODY   The body should be wide and deep. The back should not be too long, and should be strong with muscular loins. The shoulders should be sloping, deep and muscular. The quarters should be level, powerful, long and oval, the tail springing well from the quarters.

HEAD AND NECK   The head characteristics of the breed should be bold and not too small. It should be well carried on a long lean neck.

EYES   Eyes should be large, well set and kindly in expression.

EARS   Ears tend to be large and fine.

THE LIMBS   Arms and thighs and second thighs should be muscular. The knees and hocks should be large and well closed. There should be 9 inches upwards of good flat bone below the knee measured at the narrowest point on a tight tape. The pasterns should be strong and sloping and not too long. The legs should be clear of superfluous hair and as clean and hard as possible.

THE FEET   One of the most important features of the breed; the feet must be of the best and blue in colour. Feet that are shallow or narrow are undesirable. *'No foot — no horse.'*

ACTION   Action must be true, straight and free. High action is not characteristic of the breed. The Cleveland which moves well and which is full of courage will move freely from the shoulder, and will flex his knees and hocks sufficiently. The action required is free all round, gets over the ground, and fits the wear-and-tear qualities of the breed.

The Cleveland Bay is frequently shown in a strong adjustable leather headcollar with a bit and bit straps, and, as here, a plain leather browband.

By the mid 19th century the Cleveland's ability to produce an unsurpassed carriage horse when crossed with the Thoroughbred led to the pure-bred Cleveland becoming threatened, and the Society was formed to protect the pure breed. This remains its principal function today. When entries were taken for Volume I of the Stud Book, there were several mares with eight generations of back breeding shown on the dam's side and it will be noted that this is still the way that a pedigree is shown in the modern Stud Book.

Nowadays the Cleveland is frequently crossed with the Thorough-bred and the progeny can be seen competing successfully in all the different spheres, at all levels, in addition to their continuing popu-larity in the hunting field.

## The judge's/producer's viewpoint

*To all intents and purposes the Cleveland Bay is shown in the same way as the hunter. The mane is plaited and the tail is either plaited or pulled. At present quarter marks are not employed. I think they would be an unnecessary distraction, although we are starting to see them with some competitors in hunter youngstock classes. Showing is an individual art and the Society does not have hard and fast rules regarding turnout. Brood mares, as in hunter classes, are often shown in double bridles in hand. Big strong youngsters tend to be shown in strong, good quality headcollars that can be adjusted at the nose and throat, with bits and bit straps, rather than thin-strapped bridles, because they are safer and also more flattering.*

*The Cleveland Bay is supposed to have a long lean neck which can* be helped by good plaiting, but it also has a fairly heavy crest so heavy pulling of the mane is not a good idea because you can end up with a bottle brush effect when it starts to grow out. It is kinder and more practical to shorten the mane by other methods, especially for youngsters that can be soured by over pulling, so that the plaits are not too bulky.

They don't grow much hair on the leg so this area can be tidied with scissors. They have fabulous coats so they are very easy to 'do'. They only need to be washed clean to get that lovely dappled look.

The handler is expected to wear standard British showing clothes, and the procedure in the ring follows the conventional pattern for showing hunter youngstock.

They have tremendous fronts which can make the back seem long to the uninitiated, but you only have to look to see where the saddle should go to realise that it isn't long at all. They should track up really well and cover the ground well with no knee action. I like to see a bold eye and width across the forehead. In times past they occasionally had Roman noses but you just don't see this nowadays in the show ring. They must have at least nine inches of good flat bone. In the past there have been incidences of boggy hocks so I always look for flat hard hocks.

As a carriage horse the Cleveland Bay was the crème de la crème and had the conformation for the high reining that was popular with the fashionable Victorians. This is comparable to the kind of head carriage demanded for dressage nowadays and the Cleveland Bay can achieve this with a snaffle, in contrast to the racehorse that evolved to be capable of stretching the nose forward to reach the winning post.

# THE HACKNEY

Nowadays, with the virtual disappearance of horsedrawn transport, it is easy to underestimate the importance of the role the Hackney has played. With this breed more than any other one thinks of parallels with the top-selling cars on the market, which invariably combine style with performance, and even today this is reflected in the standards expected in the show ring.

A steady demand for a superior breed of trotting horses led, in 1883, to the creation of the Hackney Stud Book Society. Its aims were 'to improve the breed and to promote the breeding of Hackneys, Roadsters, Cobs and Ponies; to compile and publish a Stud Book;

and to hold shows of such horses'. The first show was held in 1885.

Three hundred people joined the Society in the first year alone including some extremely influential and wealthy people, like William Burdett-Coutts and Walter Gilbey. The latter was a prolific writer on equine subjects who used his influence extensively to promote the interests of the breed, such as persuading the Congested Districts Board in Ireland to import expensive Hackney stallions to 'improve' the indigenous horses after the failure of the potato crop, although this policy was subsequently discontinued following the report of the Royal Commission on Horse Breeding in Ireland in 1897. Other members of the Hackney Stud Book Society wrote extensively on their belief in the superiority of the Hackney for army purposes. The Society changed its name to the Hackney Horse Society in 1891.

Although, like other long-established working breeds, numbers are now considerably reduced through force of circumstance, the Society is still going strong and so is the breed. There may be fewer opportunities to show purebred Hackneys, particularly in hand, but their style and performance is undiminished and they remain one of the more spectacular and entertaining breeds to be seen at horse shows today, not least because the customs of production are so different from riding horses.

## Guidelines on the showing of Hackneys

These are provided by the Hackney Horse Society from the *Hackney Horse Society Year Book*.

### *Judging of Hackney classes*

Hackney Classes are divided into horses over 14 hands and ponies not exceeding 14 hands. The major Shows divide the classes further, e.g. not exceeding 12.2 hh, over 12.2 not exceeding 14 hh, over 14 hh not exceeding 15 hh, over 15 hh.

Although Hackneys are mainly shown in a four-wheeled vehicle known as a show wagon, the official guidelines indicate the criteria for judging them in hand.

The action must be fine, the leg raised and thrown forward to cover the ground. The legs must go 1-2-3-4 and be straight and true.

Presentation is important. A good animal badly presented, will be beaten by a lesser animal that is produced well. A horse or pony requires that 'look at me' attitude combined with elegance... Entrants should have good manners and are judged on conformation and action. Straight correct action is desirable which should be high and progressive and not 'up and down'.

Hackneys should have small convex heads, with small ears and large eyes. A long well formed neck with powerful shoulders and low withers. A compact body with good depth of chest, tail well set on and carried high, with strong well let down hocks.

The Society offers the following guidance for handlers:

### Handlers. In-hand classes. Male and female

Long trousers; shirt with collar and tie; plimsolls or clean comfortable walking shoes. A coloured waistcoat and cap may be worn if desired.

The Breed Show is, effectively, the main venue for the in-hand showing of Hackneys. At other shows the emphasis is on driving. Not only do entries have to be registered with the Society and the property of or formally leased to the exhibitor, but there are strict rules regarding excessive shoeing and 'cording'. Almost uniquely amongst breed societies exhibits are examined not only for unsuitable tack but for soundness before being allowed to compete. It is claimed that this has had a significant effect on the elimination of hereditary problems in the breed. An extract from the Breed Show rules give an indication of this.

### Excessive shoeing, cording horses etc.

The Judges, Stewards, and the Veterinary Inspectors will receive directions from the Show Executive Committee to disqualify any animal which is 'corded', doped or faked in a manner, which, in the opinion of the committee, is discreditable to the exhibitor or his servant, and report same to the Council. ['Cording' refers to an outmoded method for controlling over-exuberant horses, involving string in the mouth. Its use incurs instant disqualification.]

The Veterinary Inspectors are empowered to subject any horse to a special examination and to take such samples and any such tests as may be necessary for this purpose. Any horse may be subject to re-examination at any time. These rules will be strictly enforced. Before entering the ring, animals will be liable to examination for cording, doping, faking and excessive shoeing.

The society offer the following guides to the weight of shoes permitted.

Hackney – Yearling – 12 oz maximum.
All other Hackneys exceeding 14 hands – 2 lb maximum.

Hackney Ponies – Yearlings – 8 oz maximum.

All other Hackney Ponies not exceeding 14 hands – 1 lb 7 oz maximum. If in the opinion of the officiating judge, any shoe exceeds the prescribed weight he will have the power to have such shoes removed by a veterinary surgeon or farrier appointed by the Society, and if found to exceed the weight specified the horse will be disqualified.

Schooling of Horses/Ponies with boots, hobbles, and/or other devices will not be allowed on the showground.

The sort of penalties imposed for infringements are barring from the whole of the show for both doping and schooling with boots etc. Please note that abuse of the role of handler can also result in disqualification:

Assistant trailing an exhibit will disqualify the exhibit from the class in which the incident occurred.

## In-hand classes

a. Classification

The Society's Annual Breed Show provides a full classification for both horses and ponies with separate classes for yearlings, 2 y.o., 3 y.o., and 4 y.o. and over, males and females.

b. Veterinary Examination

All exhibits entered in the Breed Classes at the National Hackney Show will be examined on the Showground with the exceptions of colts and stallions holding a Stallion Permit issued by the Society. Any animal rejected as unsound by the Veterinary Inspector shall be ineligible to compete.

c. Showing

Yearling colts to be shown in a halter, bridle or tack, 2 y.o. colts and over to be shown in tack, yearling fillies to be shown in a halter or bridle, mares 2 y.o. and over to be shown in a bridle.

d. Judging of In-Hand Classes

i. Exhibits will be judged on conformation, type, quality, and turn out which shall count 60% and performance, manners and way of going which shall count 40%.

ii. Exhibits to be walked in the Ring until instructed to the contrary by the Stewards.

iii. Each exhibit will be pulled out and stood up in front of the Judge/s to be adjudicated for conformation and turn out.

iv. Assistants trailing an exhibit are not allowed.

v. Exhibits arriving late will be penalised.

# The judge's viewpoint

*In-hand classes are held at the breed show for breeding stock but occasionally geldings are shown as well at other shows.*

## Tack
*The main difference in the tack is that in hand they wear an open bridle, usually with a horse-shoe type of bit, rather than one with blinkers. They also wear a leather roller with side reins and a crupper. The roller is made of brown leather in two pieces, the top, which is reinforced over the withers and has two girth straps, and the girth which has brass buckles. The side reins are made of flat leather with hooks on the bit end and buckles fastening to the roller. The purpose of side reins is to aid the head carriage, action and control, so their fitting depends on the individual Hackney. Some have natural head carriage while others need the rein to assist.*

*Bearing reins, made of cord, can also be fitted to a plain-mouthed, straight-bar bridoon bit which is worn above and in addition to the horse-shoe bit, and these are attached via a loop just behind the browband back to the top of the pad. Their use is based on an expert trainer's opinion, and actually very few, above the age of yearlings, don't wear bearing reins. The overall effect is like stallion tack, but everyone wears it.*

*Yearlings can wear just a bridle without the pad and crupper but some wear the roller. Two year olds, however, definitely wear the full turnout. Strictly speaking fillies and mares have coloured browbands whilst colts and stallions have brass browbands. Very old traditional in-hand bridles have a chain link design with brass rosettes at each side. For both sexes the lead rein tends to be leather with a chain which either clips or buckles to the bit. Personally I think buckles are safer than clips because they are less likely to come undone.*

*Mares with foals at foot are shown in either a white webbing halter or a leather in-hand showing bridle with a bit. Quite a lot are shown with just the long cheeked curb of a double bridle with a curb chain and lip strap, the coloured browband, and ordinary riding reins. As with other showing the aim is to match the weight of the leather to the head.*

## Feet
*Good Hackney feet are longer than other horses' feet and sand papering them carefully makes them look nice. They have blacking on the black parts but nothing on the white parts which are left natural. Never put*

Hackney stallion in 'tack'. Note the fitting of side reins, bearing reins and the traditional browband for male Hackneys.

*hoof oil on Hackney feet. The reason is that oil darkens white feet so the action can not be highlighted to the same extent. For the same reason white hair is chalked.*

### Plaits

*Every Hackney is plaited for showing, sometimes including foals. The technique is slightly different from other horses. Instead of sewing plaits you plait in lengths of dishcloth cotton, usually yellow or old gold or cornflower blue. You then knot it once, turn it under and tie, then turn it under and tie on top of the mane where the ends are knotted and cut off. The aim is to have the plaits, about eleven or twelve depending on the size of the mane, sitting on top of the mane, and they should be small and tidy. This means that the mane should not be more than three or four inches long maximum.*

### Tails

*The cruppers worn cause the tail to be carried fairly high and are known as tail sets or spoon cruppers. The tail has to be dressed to flatter this arrangement. It is parted down the middle so that the hair falls each side to hide the crupper. Sometimes there is special bandaging around the dock depending on the look of the horse. Tails are never pulled or cut square but can be trimmed at the bottom with scissors to appear to end naturally. The goal is to emphasise the silkiness of the tail.*

### The handler

*Handlers really have to be able to run so they wear a shirt and tie, long trousers, soft leather shoes or white plimsolls but definitely not trainers. A waistcoat and cap are optional but hair must be tied back tidily. Very often there are two handlers for each Hackney so that the activity of the breed, which may be too tiring for one person, can be shown to advantage. The second handler joins the main handler once they are first lined up. When there were very professional handlers about some of them showed the horse on the side away from you, leading from both sides to give you a clear view. Very few are capable of this nowadays but if they did it would be quite correct. Speed may well be a factor that accounts for handlers on the inside of the ring nowadays.*

### Judging the Hackney

*The first appearance in the ring is very important and successful Hackneys must demonstrate a 'look at me' attitude. They enter the ring at the walk, on the left rein, with the handler on the inside. The walk is a very bouncy walk even when collected and I like to see them up on their legs with a clear 1-2-3-4 rhythm and not breaking their stride.*

*They are asked to trot individually down the stand side but not all the way round the ring because that would be very hard on the handlers. First impressions come together fairly quickly so I call them in quickly in roughly the order of preference.*

### Standing up for the judge

*They are then called out to stand in front of me, sideways on, with the side reins and the top rein undone so that the conformation is not obscured. They should stand four square and parked out but not exaggeratedly so. The front legs should be at 90 degrees to the body and the hind legs at about 45 degrees to the body. I inspect for conformation, soundness and turnout.*

### Shoes and action at the trot

*I like to see what sort of shoes they are wearing and occasionally pick up a foot, but with youngsters I ask the handlers to do this if it is likely to cause a problem. If it is a 12.2 pony wearing a 2 lb shoe this is an enormous amount of iron. It shouldn't be more than 1 lb, but to comment there and then would be difficult so I would bear this in mind. Hackneys need to have the best possible action. Some are happier with no weight, others need it to get the action. With some the effect is mental only and not just a physical reaction, whereas others are completely lost if the heavy shoes come off and they resort to almost a kind of swimming action. It is all part of the art of production and there are no rules. Some have been ruined by weight and others go better with less than their handlers imagine they need.*

*After standing still they walk away and I stand behind to check that they are not dishing or showing bad front or hind leg action. They trot back and usually trot away from you which is why you have two handlers per animal so that you can see the action from both angles. They then return to their place while your opinion is formed. Sometimes they are sent out again to make the final decision.*

*I look for progressive action and not the kind that has an enormous amount of front action coming down in the same place. They have got to use their shoulders, bend their knees and round their feet. The hind end has to follow through so that it is underneath the body and not trailing behind. The trick is to get them to bend their backs. If the back is stiff the hocks trail. They have got to be supple in their backs. High head carriage can help if the conformation is correct. If the head and neck are in the right place they should bend their backs which will bring the hocks underneath. If the back is stiff and the neck looks as if it is upside down then the hind legs will trail.*

## Producing the Hackney

*The more you work them in long reins the more supple they get. Some people stand them in their boxes tacked up but they can lean a bit if this is overdone. Nearly all Hackneys have very good limbs and it is very rare to see unsoundness or blemishes unless they are man-made splints and curbs. You do get some that go wide behind, or not quite straight in front. This can be man-made because of trying to develop the action. Some stallions in the old days were shut in the dark and came out stepping sky high. Many bad old practices have been cleaned up, like standing them in pillar reins all day. Amateurs don't have the time to do things like this. The biggest abuse is 'the boots' as a muscle developer. You can see it in the action, which is very false. There are various methods loosely based on weights and pulleys. In the right hands five minutes once a week can be helpful but an hour every day can be very dangerous. A little bit of knowledge can be a dangerous thing. The experienced trainer will know what to do, how often and for how long. Horsemen are born and not made.*

*My advice is go and watch. There are all sorts of different methods, some better than others. Training is a matter of discretion and common sense. With young horses it is not so easy to develop muscle and they can be ruined before they ever get in harness.*

## The producer's viewpoint

*It is not possible to breed Hackneys without showing them because premiums for breeding stock are awarded on the basis of show ring performance to individual, championship-winning horses and ponies and, by association, to their sires and dams. Breeders receive payment from the society if they breed from premium stock. An intrinsic part of the show is the veterinary inspection of competitors before the competition, when they are examined for unsoundness, banned equipment and overshoeing. This examination has replaced the breed society inspections which involved too much travelling for members, and is the first opportunity the competitors have to see the opposition.*

*Before the price of special shoes made it virtually impossible, Hackneys used to be shod with heavier shoes until the day before the competition when they were changed for lighter ones in order to show off the action. Nowadays we like them to grow a bit of a foot and shoe them with more weight in the toe. A longer toe can help the action and in this case the foot appears more oval in shape. More weight in the toe helps if the action is a bit up and down, but if the action is basically all right but not high enough then we shoe with shoes that are heavier all round. The horse has to have the ability to step in the first place, however.*

*Part of the training of Hackneys involves teaching them the 1-2-3-4 rhythm of the distinctive Park Gait which enables them to achieve high speeds without striking their legs. Various gadgets can be used, which are not allowed on the show ground, but they only help them to time their movement because they have to be able to step naturally. This is an extremely skilled procedure that can only be learnt from an expert, initially by observation. If it is done badly their legs can be ruined.*

*Turnout has to be to a very high standard. Because of the emphasis on quality, ears are clipped right out, as is the hair around the nostrils and jaws, as well as any white patches and feather on the legs. Some people even clip out foals' heads and all foals are plaited. Any white*

118

The 'H' shape of the Hackney, aided by the carefully fitted spoon crupper, side reins and top reins. Note the plaits which sit on top of the neck ornamented by the cotton threads that secure them.

*hair is chalked, white feet sandpapered and black feet blackened with black shoe polish. All horses and ponies are plaited with coloured threads, sometimes to match the cream lining of the show wagon, plaited in and tied around the plait, so that the plait sits up on the neck to flatter the individual.*

*The overall outline of the Hackney aims to be like a letter H with the head up, the tail up, and the body in the middle. In-hand showing is only part of the process of becoming a driving animal and for this reason the selection of the correct width and angle of the crupper to fit the dock is so important when 'tack' is worn. This consists of the roller, crupper, side reins, top rein and bridle. If the dock is too high, the horse is uncomfortable and tense all along its back which may become hollow, and the head carriage may suffer. The action of the hind legs can suffer too, becoming crab-like or skipping as well as trailing. The pad of the roller is worn as far back as possible to show off the front and not to cut the elbow.*

*During the class itself, the exhibits are led anti-clockwise in single file, and when they trot they all trot together. When we are showing we have a relay of handlers in the ring. They watch very carefully and take over from each other before the handler tires enough to slow the horse down. They do this at the trot so as not to spoil the show of the horse. This is necessary because the judge may want to compare the final shortlist, and this takes place at the trot, so it would be impossible for one person to show a horse throughout a competition.*

# CHAPTER TEN

# Show Ponies

Classes for ponies, namely show ponies, show hunter ponies and working hunter ponies, are run under the rules of the British Show Pony Society, an organisation with considerable experience of dealing with a highly competitive area of the showing world. The rules are, not surprisingly, extensive and once again need to be obtained and read very carefully. Classes for youngstock are also run under the rules of the National Pony Society, again with an extensive rule book which needs to be consulted.

Showing children's ponies was a fiercely competitive and, for the winners, lucrative activity when some of the foreign breeds being shown today had not even been heard of in this country, and when others were being shown in halters with the mud knocked off them. Considerable expertise has been acquired over the years in training and presenting these ponies to perfection – much more than can be adequately represented here. You have to face the fact that to win at the top level is immensely difficult and increasingly a professional activity. Standards are extremely high and so you have to be prepared to pull out all the stops with regard to preparing the pony not only to a high standard of turnout but with the correct outline.

Good conformation and an exemplary temperament are the basic requirements and nowadays the placings are often decided on the more elusive qualities of presence and action. Conformation details are standard and the same as one would expect for most ponies in Britain, minus the idiosyncratic features that distinguish the individual breeds. This means that you are looking for conformation that will enable the pony to be a comfortable, manageable ride and to remain sound during its lifetime, for the age and hence size of child suitable for it. Highly practical reasons dictate the basic conformation features required; such as a reasonably but not too narrow pony that a child can sit astride comfortably, with a good length of rein and a neck that is not so thick and strong that the pony can overpower its rider, a wither high enough that the saddle remains in place behind a sloping shoulder which gives a comfortable ride, and

Considerable expertise has been acquired over the years in training and presenting these ponies to perfection. They have sometimes been criticised for becoming miniature Thoroughbreds.

obviates the need for a crupper. Legs and feet obviously have to have correct conformation so that the pony can join in all the usual activities and remain sound.

As standards of conformation have risen over the years the winners of these classes have at times been criticised for gradually becoming miniature Thoroughbreds in the relentless pursuit of quality, so striking the right balance between the 'look at me' factor and the temperament you would trust your child with is an appreciably skilled task.

## Height guidelines for youngstock classes

Annual J.M.B. Height Certificates are not required until the pony is four years old. The National Pony Society offers recommended heights for 'on the day of the show' (Rule 21) for riding pony breeding classes, as shown in the table. In addition to the young-stock classes, there are also classes, as one would expect, for colts, stallions, brood mares and their foals as well as barren mares and geldings.

| Height | Yearling | 2 year old | 3 year old |
| --- | --- | --- | --- |
| 12.2 hh | 11.3 hh | 12.0 hh | 12.1 hh |
| 13.2 hh | 12.3 hh | 13.0 hh | 13.1 hh |
| 14.2 hh | 13.3 hh | 14.0 hh | 14.1 hh |
| 15.0 hh | 14.1 hh | 14.2 hh | 14.3 hh |

At shows staged on or after 1 July each year half an inch may be added to these heights. It is stressed that the above heights are recommended for 'on the day of the Show'. Half an inch may be allowed for shoes.

'To win you have to have good conformation and straight action in equal quantities...'
*Above* Riding pony stallion.   *Right* Riding pony mare.

## The producer's viewpoint

*Breeding show ponies is unpredictable and it is rare for top-class winners to breed top-class winners. Significantly, it is also very rare for top-class winners in hand to go on to be top-class winners under saddle. A possible reason for this is that in order to win producers believe that they need to make the yearling, two year old and three year old look almost a year older than it actually is, which is achieved with feeding and condition. This is despite directives to judges not to favour over-fat youngsters. Excess fat is not good for developing youngstock, and many producers are reluctant to put a lot of condition on their ponies so continue to show in hand, because it is good training, but do not go all out for the condition that seems to win. These producers settle for being further down the line and concentrate on bringing their ponies out under saddle as four year olds.*

*To win you have to have good conformation and straight action in equal quantities, even if the action isn't exuberant, because it can be worked on and helped.*

*As with other breeds you have to find someone who really knows what they are talking about and get them to help you assess your pony's strengths and weaknesses, and to decide which classes to enter. Classes are broken down by height: riding pony breeding classes are*

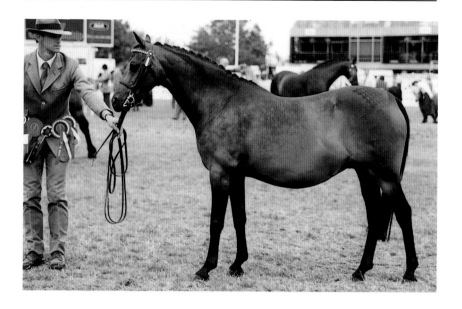

*aimed towards producing ponies with heights at maturity of 12.2, 13.2, 14.2 hh and under respectively, hunter pony breeding classes are aiming for the height categories 12.0, 13.0, 14.0 and 15.0 hh and under respectively. The main distinction is that hunter ponies have more body and substance in exactly the same way that hunters differ from riding horses. The classes for them, and the way they are shown, mirror those for horses.*

*The main shows start in May so you have to start getting ready at the end of January at the latest. After Christmas they should be brought in and wormed and then wormed again, rugged up, teeth checked for two year olds and older, and then fed with gradually increasing quantities of food. Feeds should be as bulky as possible with initially small amounts of protein which can come from a variety of sources such as corn – oats (the best), barley or maize – nuts, mix, one of the alphas (varying protein contents) to suit your individual pony's temperament and size. Bulk is ensured by feeding a combination of sugar beet and chaff or mollichaff. The main thing is to know your animal and the food that agrees with it. Start off with two bulky low protein feeds a day and pay close attention to the way the pony reacts to them with regard to health (no rashes?) and behaviour. Over a period of two or three weeks the protein content and the number of feeds can be increased gradually. Hay or special silage for horses can be fed ad lib, and spring grass when available. By the end of March*

123

they should be looking right and if not the feeds and the grass should be increased. Grass should be controlled. On average about three hours of good grass is sufficient and provides relaxation as well. An average daily programme would start with a morning feed followed by three hours of grass wearing a New Zealand rug, then they would come in, be fed and wear a summer sheet. At night a night rug would go on over the summer sheet and this not only helps the coat but also keeps the condition. This is all part of the overall programme of work and grooming based on the individual pony's needs. Depending on the age of the pony work may be walking in hand or lungeing, loose schooling and riding.

Strapping may be a very important part of the preparation for most ponies, but not all. This may be needed on the neck or the hind quarters or both areas. It has the effect of hardening them off and gives a better finish to the top line of the animal. It shapes them up and makes them look hard and strong. You have to look hard at them and decide where they look weak. You use a proper leather strap and need to use it daily 25–50 or 100 times each side.

The pony has to have manners and respect for you and this includes in the stable too. Moving over and standing still when asked should be expected and when you lead out you should carry a crop in one hand. It should walk and trot in a straight line without trying to bite you or the hedge. I also let it stand in a bridle with a rubber snaffle with elasticated side reins attached to a roller to develop the muscles on the neck. It shouldn't be too tight, just enough so that the pony is bending its neck with the poll in the right place for a couple of hours a day every now and again depending on how bad the head carriage is. This can be done with yearlings. If it is overdone you can have problems later at the riding stage. From two and three years light lungeing also can help to make it fit and not fat.

Winners have to be good looking and smart, pretty but not excessively so, have correct conformation but above all they really have got to move. Action or lack of it, assuming all the other qualities are present, can make the difference between County and local standard. Production makes a lot of difference and well done ensures a good top line. Nowadays ponies ooze quality, perhaps even lacking a little bone, especially now that we have the hunter pony classes catering for the ponies with bone. Providing the action is straight with a bit of elevation good production can improve it to show standard.

When the pony is stood up, the judge is looking at the conformation. We were always taught to walk ten strides away and then trot ten strides back, when the judge is looking to see if the action is straight.

124

*To disguise faults remember to place the hind legs one in front of the other if the pony is a bit cow hocked, or don't let it turn its toes in if pigeon toed, etc. Blemishes like broken knees need disguising with black boot polish on greys, for example. Splints or curbs can't really be helped.*

*Some ponies don't wear shoes. It is a question of how well they travel and move, but if worn light shoes are the best, sometimes just in front, sometimes all round. I keep shoes off as long as possible and then when road work starts use lightweight shoes. Heavy shoes do not enhance the movement. Plates are used for the show ring.*

*The days of counting plaits are long gone and it is now a question of flattering the neck. Elastic bands, if used, must not be seen and the final rolling of the plait must be secured with thread. Know your animal and what suits it is the rule.*

*In leading rein classes the mothers dress up and they aim to coordinate their outfits with the children's clothes and look very smart. Sometimes this can be a bit excessive but is very attractive. In hand it seems ridiculous not to wear a hard hat when leading young horses which can rear, kick and strike.*

*I would advise anyone wanting to show their pony to start locally and then if they want to aim higher to get some help.*

## The judge's viewpoint

*You can only judge what you see in front of you on the day. Manners are the most important feature as far as I'm concerned, especially with the ponies for the younger rider.*

*I like a quality pony, not a weedy boneless pony, but one with a nice bit of bone and quality. Other people like a stronger pony but a lot of these have gone on into the show hunter pony section which has become extremely popular now, more even than the show pony section because if the pony has a jump in it they can eventually do the working pony classes as well with the same pony. The pony has to be a good mover with presence but not gassy.*

*All ponies are shown in leather bridles both in hand and ridden. Turnout has to be to the highest possible standard of grooming with quarter marks and shark's teeth if appropriate. These don't apply to greys because they don't show up. Some people really go to town with hair gels and sprays but a damp brush is effective. Clever shark's teeth can distract the attention from a poor second thigh, but need practice. Quarter marks are best put on with a comb and you have to work out the best place for the diamonds and the gaps between them*

'In leading rein classes the role of the leader is just to be there to restrain the pony if necessary.' Note the leader's right hand which is near but not touching the lead rein.

*and how wide they should be. You have to keep standing back to see the effect. Most ponies have pulled tails nowadays, and plaited manes, of course.*

*Lead rein classes are something else again! These can be done sensibly with the leader wearing a nice light skirt, or culottes which are brilliant for running, sensible shoes, a jacket and a nice small hat that won't blow off. There is no need to match the child's clothes. The object is to look smart and elegant and coordinated. When I am judging, the leader's clothes don't influence me at all, but often the ones with the smart turnouts have the better ponies too, because they know all the way down the line what to do and how to do it. The first impression is when you think, 'That's nice, I must remember that', whereas if it slops along past you you aren't impressed. First impressions are very important.*

*The role of the leader in these classes is just be there to restrain the pony, if necessary, at the end of the lead rein, but you don't always see this. You see all sorts of things like hanging on to the pony by the noseband etc. There may be leading rein show hunter pony classes in the future because the blood ponies, whilst attractive, sometimes do not have the temperaments of the stronger ponies. Manners are very important. This means that the winner could be a quite plain pony compared to the rest of the line but with very good manners.*

## 12.2s

These are expected to have more presence and be better moving because they are more capable of it, but are basically a larger version of the same thing. Manners still are important because the riders will not be very old – up to thirteen. The same is true of 13.2s.

## 14.2s

Character is important in this section because they are getting closer to the hacks in size so must have definite pony character.

Judges vary in the type of pony that they go for and this applies in all the categories. Quality is not just a question of head and action, it is the overall impression and does not mean matchstick legs which often go with over-narrow bodies. The degree of bone must be suitable for the size of pony. A good conformation pony can be blown up to any size because it is in proportion: a good 13.2 could be imagined as a good 14.2 or even a 15.2. Some judges object to splints, others only if it interferes with the action. Curbs are obviously more serious but are very unusual with ponies and can be missed.

### Show hunter ponies

These should be like miniature hunters and so are beefier than the show ponies. Some pony judges are not used to this outline. Handlers, riders and ponies are turned out as in the full-size hunter classes, i.e. tweed, plain leather bridles to flatter the size of pony, plaits, pulled tails, shark's teeth if necessary and a few stripes over the quarters if appropriate, but nothing excessive and no diamonds or squares by way of quarter marks.

The show hunter pony should be like a miniature hunter and is turned out accordingly.

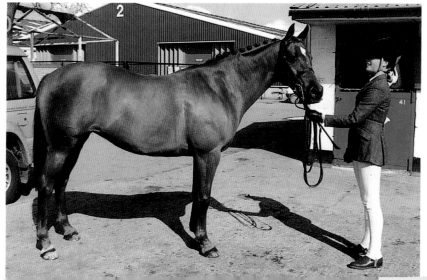

The in-hand phase of the ridden competition.

## The in-hand phase

*This follows the usual format of walk forward, pose for the judge, walk away, trot back and return to the line. The trot phase is not long in ridden classes because the trot will have been seen under saddle. The object of the in-hand phase in a ridden class is to see the straightness of the action coming towards you and away from you. Getting the child to come straight at you is not always that easy, especially if they have something to hide, but that's showmanship!*

*Over-schooling can make ponies sour but if they enjoy themselves and do a bit of everything at home it is easy to keep their interest in the ring. There is a difference between gross fat and condition. Gross fat is dangerous to the health and soundness but is rare, especially with ridden ponies that have to be worked regularly. Fixing heads to develop top line in youngstock can cause hollow backs which reduces their usefulness in later life. Correct schooling on the flat can improve the action and involves learning to ride properly so that the rider's legs are used correctly to get the hocks properly engaged and the top line can then develop naturally. It is a question of knowing what suits your pony.*

*When in doubt ask someone who knows and does it themselves. You can learn as much by going and watching at shows. When you compete yourself, don't forget, a smile can work wonders!*

# CHAPTER ELEVEN

# Mountain and Moorland

Most but not all shows with classes for native breeds are run according to the rules of the National Pony Society (NPS), and those that are not do not deviate to any great extent. The rules are periodically reviewed and updated so it is essential to obtain a copy and read them carefully.

## Eligibility

The rules state that 'All ponies exhibited in Mountain and Moorland Classes must be registered with the National Pony Society or their appropriate Breed Society and entered in the name under which they have been registered.' To compete in the major NPS championships the exhibitors must also be members, and to be awarded NPS

Fell ponies demonstrating their consistency of type.

Silver Medal Rosettes membership cards have to be produced in the ring.

# Ponies

In all Riding Pony Breeding and Mountain and Moorland Classes brood mares must be four years old or over.

All foals must be at least three weeks old on the day of the Show and must accompany their dam into the ring and be led alongside the mare as much as possible.

All stallions and colts, two years old or over, must be in possession of a current Ministry of Agriculture, National Pony Society or appropriate Breed Society Licence. For Shetland, Highland and Dales ponies this rule is extended to three years old or over.

# Tack

NPS rules state that:

in Mountain and Moorland classes:
(a) *Youngstock* may be shown in a halter, leather head collar or snaffle bridle.
(b) *Brood mares* may be shown as above or in a pelham or double bridle.
(c) *All stallions and colts* two years old or over must be adequately bitted.
(d) *Foals* MUST only be shown in a halter or leather head collar.

# Turnout

The rules require that everyone, whether exhibitor or groom, who enters the show ring must be 'neatly and smartly dressed'.

Show canes are the only canes permitted. A show cane is described as 'a plain or leather covered cane with no additions or embellishments'. They must not exceed 30 inches. The rules also state that 'in *all* Mountain and Moorland Classes, Ridden and In-Hand, ponies must be shown as recommended by their Breed Society rules and are restricted to the height limits laid down by their appropriate Breed Societies'.

Clearly there is close cooperation between the breed societies and the NPS and, while it is not obligatory for ponies to be registered with the NPS to show at breed society shows or for the exhibitors to be members, it is a good idea. If you are going to go to the bother of preparing a pony that you are proud of you might as well be eligible for all the glory that might come your way.

130

# THE CONNEMARA PONY

As one would expect of wild ponies that roamed free among the bogs and mountains of Connemara in the rugged West of Ireland, respect is paid to Mountain and Moorland traditions in the show ring. Although technically a foreign breed, the Connemara Pony is

## Official breed profile

CHARACTERISTICS   Good temperament; hardiness and staying power; intelligence and soundness; surefootedness and jumping ability; suitable for child and adult.

HEIGHT   133–148 cm high [13–14.2 hh].

COLOUR   Grey, bay, brown, dun with occasional roan, chestnut palomino and dark-eyed cream.

TYPE   Compact, well-balanced riding type with depth, substance and good heart room, standing on short legs covering a lot of ground.

HEAD   Well-balanced pony head of medium length with good width between large, dark kindly eyes. Pony ears, well-defined cheek bones, jaw relatively deep but not coarse.

FRONT   Head well set on to neck. Chest not over-loaded and neck not set on too low. Well-defined wither and good sloping shoulder giving a good length of rein.

BODY   Deep with strong back. Some length permissible but should be well ribbed up with strong loins.

LIMBS   Good length and strength in forearm, well-defined knees and short cannons with flat bone measuring 18–21 cm [7–8¼ inches]. Elbows should be free, pasterns of medium length, feet well shaped of medium size, hard and level.

HIND QUARTERS   Strong and muscular with some length, well-developed second thigh and strong low-set hocks.

MOVEMENT   Free and true without undue knee action, but active and covering the ground.

firmly established in the Mountain and Moorland category at British shows because of the close links between Britain and Ireland for so long. Historically Ireland always sold the bulk of her young horses to Britain, and included among them, indubitably, were Connemara ponies, the native pony of Ireland. There are, consequently, many opportunities to show them both in hand and under saddle, at the breed society shows, at county level and more locally.

# The judge's viewpoint

*Over the years the Connemara has improved from the little animal that successfully scrabbled about in the very varied country of Connemara, but a tall animal of 15 hands with long cannon bones and everything which that implies is not suitable for that sort of terrain. The fact that it is not commercial to have these little animals any longer has nothing to do with the fact that the ponies were bred to live in those surroundings, and I think it is sad to change them. We chose the Connemara pony because we liked what it looked like then, twenty or thirty years ago, although there were things that needed improving and there have been improvements – the shoulders are better and they move better. After the war the English went to Ireland and bought show ponies that were very successful, including Pretty Polly and My Pretty Maid. They were by a famous Arab stallion out of a mare called Gypsy Gold who was probably partbred Connemara. This encouraged the breeding of partbred Arabs for the English market. A stallion was brought into Connemara for the purpose who was half Arab, half Connemara. The Connemara buyers didn't want show ponies and it had a bad effect on the ponies, because the Arab cross does not have the toughness of the Connemara. If you are going to cross them you get much better results with a Thoroughbred. Unfortunately people got the idea that you need a much bigger, more showy animal and it was a pity. Then they got bigger, which they did anyway when they were taken out of Connemara and into the better land in the middle of Ireland. They have been very carefully selectively bred to be bigger in America – 15 to 16 hands, with pedigrees that are just as worthy as our pedigrees.*

*There is a tendency with other breeds – less with the native breeds – to breed quick maturing animals for youngstock classes which peak when they are very young and tend not to be heard of again. If you want to you can show foals every week of the season and the winners*

The mane and tail of the Connemara pony are trimmed, unlike other native breeds.

*can show a quick return for their breeders, but it can be a tremendous strain on the joints. A limited amount of showing is good for them if they are going to be shown later, because the show ring can be a tremendous shock to the system if they are plunged into it much later. If you have a very good yearling perhaps you will show it as a yearling and perhaps as a two year old, and then turn it out as a three year old, but not expect it to spend all its summers going to shows.*

*Other than the obvious benefits of showing, such as learning to be groomed, travel and have the feet picked up, the benefit is having your stock looked at and assessed by somebody else. Without showing breeders have no guidelines. It is very difficult to be critical of your own stock. A well-trained pony is going to have a much better life than a badly trained pony because people want it. A well-schooled pony that does all that is expected of it in the show ring is going to be a well-schooled ride for a child anywhere.*

### Presentation
*I quite like a sharp outline. I like them to be trimmed out under their chin and most people do that now in all the native breeds. The Fells and Dales don't and neither do the Exmoors or the Highlands, but the others do. With the kind of head that the Connemara has, a strong pony head, you have to show it. With the Fell and the Dales part of their attraction is the hair in every direction, but it isn't with the*

Connemara. Some of them are clean limbed anyway; they don't have much hair down there, just a tiny little bit. I usually tidy them up down the backs of their legs. With very young stock I would leave the hair in the heel, but with the ridden you have to do what the others do. Different people do different things, but as far as the Society is concerned you can do what you like apart from plaiting the manes and tails, which is not allowed. People don't pull the in-hand ponies' tails, but they thin them a bit to show off the quarters and they would put on a tail bandage for travelling to help this, as well as for protection. If they are white they have to be washed until the bubbles come white. I don't take off the whiskers around the nostrils but some people do, but you don't trim inside the ears apart from the greasy bit that sticks out at the bottom. Connemaras don't get the kind of coat that needs the belly clipped to sharpen the outline. Manes aren't pulled as such, but are groomed vigorously so that they end at the level of the neck that is most flattering. Tails have to be levelled off square to suit the hind quarters. Cut it off half inch by half inch until you have what you want, because once it is off, it is off.

## Tack

You have to experiment to find the right kind of bridle to flatter the head. The ponies do vary and some of them are quite strong in the head. You don't want a very fine bridle; with a lot of them you want a fair amount of leather about the place. The bridle would be plain leather with no brass or velvet browbands, although stallions very often have a brass rosette on the browband. Nobody uses stallion harness any more.

Youngstock are shown with a standard showing bridle and bit but brood mares look better in a double bridle, unless they are young mares in which case they would wear an ordinary snaffle, but still not a showing bridle. Some people use a horse-shoe shaped stallion bit on their youngstock but it isn't right. You've just got to see what the pony goes best in. Some go best in a rubber snaffle, some in a vulcanite snaffle, some like a jointed snaffle, some a straight bar. For the very young pony some use a light nylon bit, as long as they don't chew it. You mustn't be hidebound, because things can change and you have to adjust accordingly. Things can be splendid and then suddenly the pony needs more control and starts taking advantage of you. You can't punish a pony in the show ring so you have to be very well organised before you get there.

*Training*
*Your pony has got to learn to walk beside you and go in front of you,*
*which is not as natural as following you as head of the herd, so needs*
*careful training. They have to look cheerful and they have to use their*
*hind legs and quarters. When we started we didn't long rein etc. in*
*order to build up the muscles, but now you really have to do it because*
*the standard is so high. There is very little you can do leading in hand*
*to make them track up. Some of them will do it naturally if they are*
*well made and well balanced. It is the ones that are not so good that*
*you have to put a lot more work into. The best way of learning how to*
*do these things is to watch other people.*

*Judging the Connemara pony*
*Thoroughbred conformation is the nearest to classic horse conformation.*
*If you read the description of any breed of pony in a magazine they all*
*sound the same regardless of the breed. Good bone should not be like*
*scaffolding poles — round; but should be shaped and oval with all the*
*tendons and ligaments laid beautifully behind. A lot of people say it is*
*difficult to pin down the Connemara type and in a way it is, but when*
*you look at a map and see how diverse and separate the different*
*areas are where they were bred it isn't surprising. They would have*
*been performance tested to do different things in these areas too. They*
*were all driven, but down on the coast with its flat sand dunes they*
*were bred to be faster because they were raced. The mountain ponies*
*were inclined to be straighter in front and had different feet — some*
*people call them donkey feet — and these were much more sure footed.*
*I would never say 'Ah, donkey feet, this is bad'. Connemaras don't*
*have flat round feet. Blacksmiths always know exactly what a Con-*
*nemara foot is like — basically very hard with good quality horn. Big*
*flat feet are fine for clomping around in bogs, but the smaller narrower*
*mountain feet are often associated with better action because the*
*mountain ponies have got to be much more active. People talk too*
*much about flat action in the native breeds; they really shouldn't*
*because they should be picking their knees up — not like a Hackney,*
*but active. They have got to be Land Rovers, they have got to do*
*everything, smart enough to go to church and basic enough to do all*
*the hard work.*

*Connemaras have quite a lot of white about them. A lot of them*
*have white socks and white on their faces and there is no problem over*
*that at all. They shouldn't have white anywhere else, like white*

*splashes on their stomachs or anything like that. They should be whole coloured.*

*They need to be long in the back because of the food they eat, mountainous food, which is very rough and they've got to take in a tremendous amount in order to survive on it, not like an Arab that has a very short gut and can live on the very high protein food it was given. The long gut helps them to get the most out of it. People say things like, 'I like my animals short in the back', and then they say, 'I do like a long length of rein', but you can't actually have long vertebrae in the neck and short vertebrae in the back. If a pony is short in the back the chances are it will be short in front.*

*You have to be terribly careful when you are breeding to improve horses' heads because of the problem with the teeth. Teeth size does not vary with breeding but the length of bones in the face do, particularly the nasal bones below the eye and the jaw bones, and you can have the problem that the Welsh ponies encountered of overcrowded mouths leading to bony lumps in the jaw, like teething lumps. The problem stems from trying to breed what is in effect a foal's head — tiny faces with big eyes — in a breed that lived on rough grazing and consequently had big teeth. This is why a head shaped like a coffin is much sounder really because there is room for the teeth to be properly laid out to cope with the food.*

*When the ponies come in the ring, immediately your eye is caught by particular ponies and you start to sort them out in your mind, but you are not vetting them and you only have about half an hour to judge about fifteen ponies, so you can't go into absolutely everything. Immediate impressions are very important, which is why they have to be clean, interested and that sort of thing because that is what catches the eye. You don't really look at the handlers very much unless they are unsuitably dressed. I'm always very worried about people who wear very unsuitable shoes, like sandals and high heels.*

*The ponies that catch my eye are the ones that look well balanced, move well, look happy in themselves and nothing immediately strikes you as being bad, or not looking like a Connemara. Basically when I'm judging if I'm not sure if it is a Connemara pony or not then it is probably not a good one. This is particularly true of mixed Mountain and Moorland classes. Sometimes you can wonder if it is a grey New Forest or a Connemara, and then you know that whatever it is it isn't particularly good, because they are different enough. The Connemara is basically longer than a New Forest and their necks and heads are put on differently. The New Forest neck is basically shorter and more triangular in shape, the Connemara one is longer with more of a curve and with a more refined jowl line. The Connemara has better bone than the New Forest because of the terrain they come from.*

*You line them all up and make them trot and then if a pony moves very, very wrong for a native pony – like a tremendous daisy cutter or if it picks its knees up too high – then you'd discount it. You bring them in in the order you want them which is important and needs a good steward not to muddle them. You then start looking for unsoundnesses and faults. I'm very fussy about the drop of the front leg – all horses are prone to offset front legs; I don't think Connemaras are more prone than anything else. A lot of them are not strong enough in the hind leg and I do penalise them for that. The Connemara used to have a very good hind leg until they put the Arab blood in, which was not a good move. If they had only penalised the ponies with bad hind legs twenty years ago we wouldn't have any kind of a problem now.*

*I don't touch the ponies because I think it is not my business and if you touch one you have to touch them all. Injuries do not affect the placings for brood mares but may in a straight beauty competition, e.g. Connemara pony four years old and over.*

*I do not like to see hind feet not following in the tracks of the front feet, which may stem from back trouble or wide action behind or close action behind. If they are going to dish or plait I would rather they dished because plaiting is dangerous.*

*I do think that people have to decide why they show and should use showing as a tool to breed better animals, putting what they have bred against other people so that they don't make the same mistake twice. You should try to breed ponies with the best conformation so that they lead useful and happy lives and aren't constricted by faulty conformation, which is a terrible abuse of an animal. Showing shouldn't be an end in itself.*

## THE DALES PONY

Apart from breed society shows the main opportunities for showing Dales ponies are in mixed Mountain and Moorland classes, although, at County Show level, there are, as for the Fell, classes for breeding stock. Sometimes the classes for the two breeds are combined.

To be shown in Dales classes ponies have to be registered with the Dales Pony Society. This has to be done before the age of two, although exceptions to this rule will be considered by the Council.

# Official breed profile

*Origins*

Native to the upper dales of Tyne, Allen, Swale and Tees, the Dales pony stems from the pennine pony, with infusions of Scotch Galloway, Norfolk Trotter and Wilson pony blood. Bred specifically for the Pennine lead industry as pack ponies, they were famous for their ability to get over rough country under heavy weight, at a good speed and for distances up to 200 miles a week. With the advent of railways and better roads, the ponies found a niche on the small farms of the inhospitable upper dales, where owing to their strength and surefootedness, they were capable of doing all the work of small hill farms where larger horses were at a disadvantage. They carried the shepherd and burdens of hay for great distances on the fells. Stylish and fast in harness they were also successful in the trotting races of the day and, when harvest was over, were capable of giving their owner a good day hunting. They also served with the Army as pack and Mountain Artillery ponies.

*Conformation and type*

These very hardy ponies are up to 14.2 hands, colours predominantly black with some brown, grey and bay and rarely roan. They are renowned for the quality of their hard, well-shaped feet and legs with beautiful dense, flat bone. Their action is straight and true, they are good movers, really using their knees and hocks for powerful drive. They have tremendous stamina, an iron constitution, high courage and great intelligence, combined with a calm temperament.

The head should be neat, showing no dish and broad between the eyes. The muzzle is relatively small, no coarseness about the jaw and throat and incurving pony ears. A long foretop, mane and tail of straight hair. The muscular neck of ample length for a bold outlook, should be set into well laid, sloping shoulders. Withers not too fine. Stallions carry a well arched crest. The body should be short coupled with strong loins, with well sprung ribs. Short, well developed forearms are set square into a broad chest, quarters are lengthy and powerful with very muscular second thighs above clean, broad, flat hocks, well let down. The cannons should display an average 8−9 inches of flat, flinty bone with well defined tendons. The pasterns should be of good length with very flexible joints, the hooves large, round and open at the heels with well developed frogs, and with ample silky, straight 'feather'.

## The judge's viewpoint

*A Dales pony should be shown without any trimming. The full tail, long mane, foretop (forelock) and feather is necessary survival kit for Dales winters. Even when the tails were docked a good length of hair was left and tied up with ribbons for shows. However, the pony should be clean and well groomed.*

*Traditionally, for in-hand classes, mares and youngstock are shown in white halters. Mares can also be shown in a plain riding bridle and bit or an in-hand bridle. Licensed stallions (from the age of three years) must be in full stallion tack and bit. This is optional for one- and two-year-old colts. All Mountain and Moorland ponies should be shown without cosmetic additions, plaits or ribbons. In the days when Dales ponies were docked it was the custom to dress the tail with ribbons, which can still be seen on some Dales ponies and are not prohibited by the Dales Pony Society. When Dales ponies became rare, they were usually shown in combined classes with Fell ponies and tail ribbons were retained to mark the breed. Most down-country judges had little experience of judging Dales and, particularly in the case of smaller ponies, they were very often mistaken for other breeds. Most Dales ponies these days are shown without ribbons. Many Dales exhibitors have been awarded breed rosettes which should have gone to a Welsh Cob, Fell, Highland and even Exmoor, by mistake, though this is becoming rarer as more ponies are coming into show rings all over the country.*

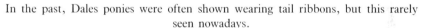

In the past, Dales ponies were often shown wearing tail ribbons, but this rarely seen nowadays.

*Judging the Dales pony*

When the pony first appears in the ring, the judge will be looking for a compact, alert pony with a high head carriage and long-striding, energetic walk. Viewed from the front there should be a distinct look of 'a leg at each corner', broad chest, well-muscled forearms, broad, flat knees, fine quality cannons and large feet. The quarters are lengthy and muscular with very muscular second thighs, broad well-defined hocks with the same good legs and feet. The foretop should be long, the mane up to a yard long, and the tail, which is well set but not high, should reach the ground. The feather should be straight and silky, curtaining the coronets in front and falling from above the fetlocks over the heels. Coarse, curly feather is not required.

A Dales judge will start the inspection from the feet up, looking for large, dense, round feet, open at the heels with an elastic well-shaped frog. The hooves will be slate blue (unless on the end of a white fetlock in which case they will be a tawny colour). The pasterns should be of a good length and the fetlocks very flexible. These ponies are reputed to have the best feet and legs in the British Isles so small boxy feet go to the bottom of the line. [See the Breed Profile.] Judges unfamiliar with the breed may put up a pony with a great deal of bone but often overlook another which seems to have less, whereas the latter has a better quality, flat bone with the same inches. The cannons ideally show $8\frac{1}{2}-9$ inches of flat, knife-like bone with well-defined tendons rising from a larger, shield-shaped knee and well-defined, well let down hocks. Bone of high quality is sought, not round, coarse bone, however much there is of it.

The shoulders should be well laid back and well muscled, the back short and the quarters muscular and lengthy. The body is deep with well-sprung ribs. Some ponies have a high croup. In America this is known as 'the trotting pitch', the sign of an exceptional trotter, and it is no coincidence that such a feature is also known as the sign of a good jumper. Natural high steppers are usually good at jumping. Good Dales ponies are active and willing across country under saddle, and are extremely fast, stylish trotters in harness.

The head is usually considered last. It should be neat but long enough to accommodate a strong set of teeth to deal with poor quality fodder. Ears should be pony-like and eyes bright and almond shaped. The profile is straight and may have a Spanish-looking, sub-convex curve from below the eyes but is never dished. There should be a good breadth between the eyes which tapers to the narrow, mobile muzzle with nostrils which can close in bad weather (no Arab influence). The

140

*neck should be of a good length to give the pony a bold outlook. Short necks and straight shoulders do occur but are considered a fault. The withers are not very fine and may be rather flat – 'harness topped'. On the other hand these ponies are all-rounders and should be able to haul a ton as well as they can trot fast, and also give a comfortable ride. A mare should have a sweet expression, the stallions should be very impressive with considerable crests when mature.*

*When judging for action, it is customary for the pony to be walked out of the line away from the judge and back into the line and then trotted in both directions. The judge looks for tracking up and a long active stride at the walk, with the full face of the shoe and sometimes even the toe clip being shown with every lifted foot. The trot is THE Dales pace and trotting away the judge will look for POWERFUL, HIGH, HOCK ACTION with, if possible, a flick of the hocks, the hindlegs being taken well under the body with each stride. Trotting back the judge will expect STRAIGHT, HIGH KNEE ACTION with rhythmic timing and a rounded, fast, workmanlike movement which gives the impression of a pony on wheels. A good Dales pony can accomplish twenty miles per hour or more and keep going for hours. There is no energy-wasting extension of the fore-limbs and should be no sign of artificial, trained action. Any pony with high action and little forward movement would be put to the bottom of the line, as would any sign of daisy cutting, dishing or plaiting. Movement at all paces must be forward going and free.*

*Traditionally Dales ponies were only shown under saddle at a walk and trot, now they will also show at canter and gallop. Some may have a heavy plunging action which usually means they have not been schooled properly or have spent their life as brood mares, rarely looking through a bridle. A well-schooled pony should do everything to a good standard. Because they have such a muscular back and such flexible limbs, the ride is very comfortable and the ponies are up to great weight. During the last war they were used as Mountain Artillery pack ponies carrying guns weighing 22 stone and packs up to 240 lb.*

*Fat, overdone foals rarely mature well and are often never seen in the ring again. A bonny active foal showing intelligence and spirit with good limbs and straight action should top the line.*

*Youngstock which are well furnished often end up as coarse when mature. If the feet and legs are of good quality and the action straight and energetic, the youngster should get into the ribbons, however gangling and awkward. A Dales pony is in its prime at about eight years old, when fully furnished. This should be taken into account when comparing*

141

*a four year old with an older pony; the youngster will appear narrower across the chest. It is said that the chest should be wide enough to 'take a dustbin through the front legs'.*

*Dales ponies can be black, brown, bay, grey and roan, and most carry white markings. These are preferred as a star or snip and white on the hind legs, up to fetlocks only. White as a blaze or on the fore feet have been downgraded into Section B for the last 30 years, but this does not preclude them from classes. A good pony with wrong markings can win above right marked ponies and may get a Championship, but at the breed shows Section ponies have their own classes. Height may come into question, as many over 14.2 ponies are shown in performance and other classes. Where the regulations require exhibits to be under 14.2 hh the rule applies, but where over-height Section D Welsh Cobs are allowed to be exhibited so are Section B Dales. Until 1964 all Dales mares had a height limit of 15 hh, stallions 14.2 hh. There are still many over 14.2 hh Dales ponies but these are retained as the Dales pony is a rare breed and needs the full use of this gene pool.*

# THE DARTMOOR PONY

The Dartmoor Pony Society in its literature reports that:

The earliest reference to the Dartmoor Pony appeared in 1012 in the Will of a Saxon Bishop, Aelfwold of Crediton. Much later during the heyday of tin mines on Dartmoor, the ponies were used extensively for carrying the tin to the Stannary towns. When this finished they were left to roam free apart from those required for work around the farms.

In 1898 the Polo Pony Society (now the National Pony Society) set up Local Committees to produce descriptions of each native breed. Apart from the heights the original description is almost identical to the present Breed Standard. Five stallions and 72 mares were inspected and entered into the first Stud Book by the Local Committee. The height limits then were 14 hands for stallions and 13.2 hands for mares but very few ponies came near to them. The biggest stallion was Brentor Confidence at 13.1 hands. Two mares reached the maximum height. Both were registered by the Director of Convict Prisons, Dartmoor, and were probably two of the ponies ridden by the warders as they escorted convicts to and from their work outside the prison. In fact the warders continued to ride ponies when escorting prisoners until the early 1960s.

Less than twenty years after this good start the breed was hit very hard by the First World War. About this time too the Duchy Stud, owned by the Prince of Wales, began buying Dartmoor ponies to use in a breeding programme aimed at producing an all round saddle horse. One stallion used with success was a desert bred Arab, Dwarka, a bay with a real pony head...

The 1920s were an important time for Dartmoors. A Breed Society was formed in 1924 with a large Council and a paid secretary. The height limit was finally fixed at 12.2 hands. Several of the breeders known to exhibitors today started their interest in breeding and showing Dartmoors around this time, and some of the most influential bloodlines of today first attracted attention in the 1920s and 1930s. Unfortunately the Breed Society failed about five years later but was reformed with Miss Calmady-Hamlyn as Hon. Secretary, a spot she continued to hold until 1960 when, through ill-health, she reluctantly retired...

The 1930s were a period of consolidation for the breed ... In 1931 the first Dartmoor Pony Show run by the Dartmoor Pony Society was held at Brimpts, above Dartmeet in the heart of the moor...

The breed came out of the Second World War with very few registered ponies. Registration by inspection was introduced, and prizewinners at various selected shows were automatically eligible for registration. Despite the difficult times there were some bright moments for the breed during the war years with the arrivals of Jude (1941), Quennie XX (1943), John and Linnet (1944) and Jennie VII, Betty XXI, Chymes and Honeybags (1945), all destined to play their part in putting the breed back on its feet again...

The memberships and registrations gradually increased and by the end of the 1950s the breed was in much better heart. So much so that registrations on wins or by inspection finished in 1957, with all registrations in the Stud Book in future coming solely from ponies whose parents were already registered. By now the breed had spread over the country with the main strongholds outside the South West being in the South East, the Midlands and the North East of England. There were also a few breeders in Scotland, and some ponies had been exported to the United States.

At the beginning of the 1960s there was a great upsurge of interest, and membership and registrations increased sharply. Inter-breed Championships at the National Pony and Ponies of Britain Shows were won on many occasions ... Ponies were exported in considerable numbers to the Continent, principally to Holland, Denmark and Germany, while a few went to the United States, mainly to previous importers. The 1970s brought a slight setback to registration in line with the general trend, though inter-breed successes at the principal shows continued ... Exports continued on a lower key though further afield than before, and Dartmoors could now be found in Denmark, Holland, Norway, Sweden, Belgium, Germany, Italy, Switzerland and the United States, Canada, Eire, Australia and Malta...

Dartmoor ponies are very versatile, and are renowned for their wonderful temperaments, and suitability for young children to ride. Results in the ridden classes are excellent when compared to the number of ponies registered, and success has been achieved all the way up the ladder to the National Pony Society ridden Mountain and Moorland Championships at Olympia ... Recently, Dartmoors have gained an increasingly good reputation in the Mountain and Moorland Working Hunter competitions ... Dartmoors have also achieved considerable success in driving classes ... Whether you want to ride, drive, show in-hand, take part in Pony Club activities or just have fun you will derive enormous pleasure from owning one of these kind and affectionate ponies.

# The producer's viewpoint

*I have a mare from a line that came from my mother's side of the family and can be traced back to a mare an uncle had in 1877. He used to go to all the top shows at the time like Okehampton and Lydford, and they had to lock the ponies in the night before because some of the people who were scared of being beaten would let them out the night before so that they couldn't be taken to the show. I've been showing and breeding [Dartmoors] all my life since I was a boy. The Dartmoor farmers were fiercely proud of their breeding, and in different parts of the moor there were different types of pony according to their particular likes. There was one type that was dun with a stripe over its back. The mares didn't go to any stallion but were kept off the moor until they had been covered. There was agreement over the features of the breed, though, like the importance of small ears. They didn't like chestnuts and these wouldn't have been shown, or a pony with a white foot. They wouldn't judge a chestnut years ago. There's always been a certain amount of chestnut in the ponies but they wouldn't have it. Dark bays, brown and blacks are all right but they don't like the rich bays. There were always greys on Dartmoor but a lot of them tried to say that grey wasn't a Dartmoor colour. They were tolerated but not the chestnuts.*

# Official breed profile

HEIGHT  Not exceeding 12.2 hh.

COLOUR  Bay, brown, black, chestnut, roan. Piebalds and skewbalds are not allowed. Excessive white markings should be discouraged.

HEAD  Should be small, well set on and bloodlike, with nostrils large and expanding and the eyes bright, mild, intelligent and prominent. The ears should be small, well formed, alert and neatly set. The throat and jaws should be fine and showing no signs of coarseness or throatiness.

NECK  Strong, but not too heavy and of medium length. Stallions have a moderate crest.

SHOULDERS  Good shoulders are most important. They should be well laid back and sloping, but not too fine at the withers.

BODY  Of medium length and strong, well ribbed up and with a good depth of girth giving plenty of heart room.

LOIN AND HIND QUARTERS  Strong and well covered with muscle. The hind quarters should be of medium length and neither level nor steeply sloping. The tail is well set up.

HIND LEGS  The hocks should be well let down with plenty of length from hip to hock, clean cut and with plenty of bone below the joint. They should not be 'sickled' or 'cow-hocked'.

FORELEGS  Should not be tied in, in any way, at the elbows. The forearm should be muscular and the knee fairly large and flat on the front. The cannon should be short from knee to fetlock with ample, good, flat, flinty bone. The pasterns should be sloping but not too long. The feet should be sound, tough and well shaped.

MOVEMENT  Low, straight and free-flowing, yet without exaggeration.

GENERAL  The mane and tail should be full and flowing. The Dartmoor is a very good looking riding pony, sturdily built yet with quality.

*If there was a chestnut stallion running out on the moor they'd go out and geld it. The early breed society had good stallions running on the moor and you had to pay a shilling a colt. With all of us then breeding ponies was a hobby, not a business, and the rivalry of showing the ponies was part of the pleasure. They were ridden but this was not as important as showing them in hand. The conformation was kept up because of the quality of the showing. It was something you were thinking about all the time, planning ahead. Years ago they weren't supposed to be off Dartmoor more than a few weeks a year, but in fact showing ponies were on the farm all the time to avoid getting crossbreds. Widdecombe was the last show and if we knew the mare was in foal then she could be turned out so that the herd learnt to stay on the same area of the moor and not stray. Young ponies learnt from the older ones which areas to stay on. If they were sold away they would manage to get back to the part of the moor they knew.*

*Since those days the showing hasn't changed that much, except that ponies get put up that wouldn't have years ago, like breedy ones with a bit of blood in them. They wouldn't have dared to put one that wasn't fit in the first three but you'll see that today. In those days 11.3 hh was the size of them even when kept on good ground, but you see them bigger today. On the other hand you did see them with low backs (saggy), especially if a mare had had seven or eight colts, and sometimes this was in the breeding, but this has been bred out of them now. A good Dartmoor had a fair hard neck, good loins and a straight back. They also had manes to their knees and tails sweeping the ground. On the moor their manes stay long. Dartmoor ponies should have absolutely untouched manes and tails although the whiskers on the jaw will be trimmed, if it suits the pony. When leading them at home keep them up together and make them stand right and then they will do it in the ring naturally. Every day make sure that the mane is hanging over to one side which will train it. They don't need special food. Years ago father used to let the weaned foals have fresh milk from the cow. I always like to see a pony on its toes a bit. In the ring you should stand about two feet away from them, in front of them, not to one side talking to other people. It is important to be correctly dressed, too, otherwise it is an insult to the judge. Never lose concentration if you are not pulled in first because the order can change.*

*Things changed in the early 1950s when people outside the farming community started breeding ponies and thanks to them more are kept. They also take the trouble to register them. It is not just adults who buy ponies to show, because there are a lot of ponies now being ridden and driven.*

## The judge's viewpoint

*I like to see them with a tidy head but not light of bone. They must not have long ears. My father used to grasp the ear in his hand and did not like to see the top of the ear protruding from the top of his hand. Ponies with long ears and light bone are not typical Dartmoor ponies. A thick short ear is a sign of hardiness and constitution in ponies and is what I like to see for the moor and for foundation stock. The modern riding type pony is narrow and light boned and could not live out. A good hard colour is bay or black, although there are actually more greys on the moor than anything but these are not Dartmoors at all. There are a couple of subsidy schemes running at the moment to improve the quality of the wild ponies on Dartmoor and their progeny will be eligible for registration in a couple of generations but not yet.*

*As with other animals, like sheep and cattle, it is not the show winners that produce the best stock. A problem today is that a lot of people can't spot a good typical Dartmoor pony unless it is shining with a rug on. I'd sooner see them in their natural condition. It is very difficult with the Dartmoor breed, especially in the early part of the year if they aren't produced specifically for the early shows. They don't shed their coats naturally until later in the year. The judging of ridden classes can be difficult too because it should include the way that the pony goes as well as its conformation. In-hand classes are judged on conformation.*

### Tack

*Mares and youngstock used to be shown in white halters but now it is all leather bridles with brass mountings. Females used not to be shown in bits, which are for stallions. Even yearlings are shown in leather bridles now although if mares, foals and yearlings came before me in white halters I would quite like to see it. Narrow leather in a bridle can make a lot of difference to a head, though. In the last ten years things have changed tremendously and now we see mares and stallions wearing all sorts of fancy bits, and brass and coloured browbands (but not elaborate velvet ones), although these tend to be concealed by the forelock. There are no hard and fast rules.*

147

The Dartmoor pony. A short thick ear is a sign of hardiness and constitution and a good hard colour is bay or black.

## Trimming

*They can be trimmed around the jaw and under the chin to tidy up the head but I wouldn't like to see anything else touched. People are more conscious of turnout these days. A typical Dartmoor pony with a fair amount of bone will have some feather and I like to see it. It should not be trimmed, pulled or damped because it makes them look lighter of bone. Manes and tails should be washed, combed and tidy. A tail bandage is all you need to show off the quarters because it sets the hair around the dock. Tails should not be cut off square at the bottom but grow quite long and thick. A good thick mane and tail shows the constitution of the pony.*

## Faults

*The old-fashioned Dartmoors were prone to thick, fat, flat withers but this is more of a problem for ridden classes when I might think of sweating it off. A good head, good bone and a good colour are what I look for and each gives an indication of toughness. I don't like to see white fetlocks and feet. Black skin resists the bad weather better. Even white on the head is to be avoided in breeding stock.*

*When a pony comes in the ring I look for them to walk on well, nice and freely and straight. Pasterns need to be reasonably upright but not too much. A lot of ponies lately seem to go wide behind at the trot with a short stride in the hind leg and appear to waddle [not tracking up]. I would put them down for this.*

*Clothes*
*Standard English showing clothes — no bowlers, except for the judge.*

No Devon farmer's smocks!

# THE EXMOOR PONY

To talk about the Exmoor pony in the context of the show ring is to place yourself firmly on very thin ice! One of the oldest and purest of our native breeds, it is considered to be more the product of evolution and natural selection than any deliberate management by Man, the usual function of breed societies. Enthusiasts maintain that as a consequence even the term 'breed' is inappropriate to the Exmoor which could more correctly be thought of as a species in its own right. As the show ring is all about opinion and choice in the light of commercial demand there is a potential conflict here, which is reflected in the resistance of traditional judges to any practice that suggests a beauty contest rather than fitness to survive. They are shown, however, and not just at their breed shows but in their own classes and mixed Mountain and Moorland classes at national, county and local levels.

In the words of the Exmoor Pony Society:

> The ponies have been on the Moor since ancient times, and the Moor shapes their size, their characteristic hardness, their independent spirit, and that native intelligence which gets them out of trouble in difficult conditions. Although Exmoors are now being bred throughout the country, the Moor pony is the foundation stock of this unique breed from which outside breeders can replenish their stock.

It should be noted that only those ponies with a brand are purebred Exmoor ponies.

The Exmoor Pony Society in its literature provides further explanation of the distinctive features of the Exmoor pony listed in the official breed profile, as follows:

*Colour*

This along with uniformity of type is the most distinctive feature of the breed. Colour ranges from a special kind of dun unique to Exmoors to bay or brown with black points. There is a mealy colour (light buff) round the eyes, on the nose, inside the flanks and under the belly. Note: No patches or collections of white hairs or white markings whatsoever are permitted as these are thought to indicate foreign blood.

---

## Official breed profile

HEIGHT   Stallions and geldings not exceeding 12.3 hh (129.5 cm) at any age. Mares not exceeding 12.2 hh (127 cm) at any age.

GENERAL APPEARANCE OR TYPE   Definite 'pony' character; hard and strong; vigorous and alert and symmetrical in appearance; mealy muzzle; 'Toad Eyes'.

HEAD AND NECK   Ears short, thick and pointed; clean cut face; wide forehead; eyes large, wide apart and prominent (Toad Eyes); wide nostrils; mealy muzzle; clean throat; good length of rein.

SHOULDERS   Clean, fine at top, well laid back.

CHEST   Deep and wide between and behind forelegs; ribs long, deep, well sprung and wide apart.

BACK   Level; broad and level across loins; tail neatly set in.

LEGS   Clean and short, with neat hard feet; forelegs straight, well apart and squarely set; hind legs well apart, nearly perpendicular from hock to fetlock with point of hock in line with pelvis bone; wide curve from flank to hock joint; legs free in motion with no tendency to sweep or turn.

ACTION   Straight and smooth, without exaggerated action.

COAT   Close, hard and bright in summer.

COLOUR   Bay, brown, or dun, with black points; mealy colour on muzzle, round eyes and inside flanks. No white markings anywhere.

QUALITY   Alert expression and general poise indicating balance and symmetry of movement; fine clean bone.

---

## Size

Large ponies would find it difficult to survive the winter on the Moor. Suitable shelter is not available, so they would find it hard to withstand the cold wind and rain. Food is scarce. Thus the height of the Exmoor has become established at up to 12.2 hh for mares and 12.3 hh for stallions and geldings. Very small ponies are not favoured.

## Action

The Exmoor is a sturdy pony with good bone and is up to great weight in relation to his size. The action, though, due to a well-proportioned frame and good shoulder, is that of a lighter type of animal, the stride being long, low and smooth giving a balanced comfortable ride. The Exmoor is well proportioned, well balanced and extremely sure footed.

## Coat

To withstand the prevailing winter conditions a special coat has evolved. An undercoat of short wool-type hair is topped by a longer greasy coat. This repels the rain which simply runs off. Whorls of hair strategically placed help to direct water away from sensitive parts of the body. So important is the quality of the coat and the positioning of these whorls that research has shown that ponies without this correct coat structure do not survive well. The correct two-layered coat retains the body heat so well that snow can lie on the pony's back for days. So little heat is lost from the body that the pony remains warm and dry and the snow stays frozen.

## The Exmoor head

In many breeds a tiny pretty head is desired. Having evolved for survival and not for fashion the Exmoor has a large well-shaped head allowing plenty of space for the essential functions of thinking, breathing and eating! The nostrils are wide to allow inhalation of a liberal supply of air and this is warmed while passing over the generous area of mucous membrane before reaching the lungs.

## 'Toad eye'

The eyes are large and dark and appear to stand out, being surrounded by the rim of light hair. They are protected by a heavy ridge of bone above the eye.

## Teeth

The jaw is long and deep and so can support long, strong molar teeth which are set at an angle enabling the pony to survive on poor grazing. The teeth meet exactly and cut off the grass without damaging the roots. Purebred ponies with faulty dentition are not accepted for registration.

*Temperament and character*

Accustomed to looking after himself on the Moor the Exmoor has developed a quick-witted independent attitude to life. His very survival depends on his ability to think and act for himself quickly in all circumstances. It takes those born on the Moor a little time to acclimatise to the ways of man. Once his confidence has been gained he becomes an active and dogged performer.

A particularly interesting feature of the Exmoor pony which has evolved to resist the harsh climate of Exmoor is the coat structure and the way that the hair grows on the body. Close examination shows that the hair grows in a pattern or hairstream to direct water away from the sensitive areas of the body so that it can drip off fringes of long hair in key places, like the chin, down the mid line under the neck, the back of the thigh (helped by the lateral hairs of the tail when tight to the body), the back of the cannon and the fetlock. Changes of direction in the water flow are effected by the precise position of the circular whorls, which keep water away from the eyes, the breast and the flank in front of the thigh. The curious thing is that although the double coat referred to above is shed in the summer and does not affect showing, foals are always born with the degree of coat that their mothers have at the time of their birth. Seen in the context of survival the rules concerning trimming make perfect sense.

## Official breed show rules

(a) All ponies exhibited in Exmoor Pony classes, with the exception of driving classes, shall be shown in 'natural condition', i.e. tails not cut, no trimming except washing and/or brushing.

(b) All ponies exhibited in 'riding' and 'performance' classes shall be four years old or over.

(c) A member shall not knowingly exhibit a pony bred, leased or produced by the judge, his/her immediate family or his/her employer.

## The judge's viewpoint

*Although very localised geographical variations exist within certain breeds, of the Mountain and Moorlands, the Fell, the Dale, the Highland and the Exmoor are the only ones with a good type left. Of the others, if some of them were turned out in traditional natural conditions they would not survive the winter, because their metabolisms have gradually changed, as a result of a change of environment, even though the external appearance might not have changed so much. Brood mares should be fit not fat. Keep them moving. It is an error to think of a native breed in a show ring context. You have to go back to basics and think of the place where it evolved and remember that it has got to live there. Then you have to think of the purpose for which it was used in that area, and then find the animal that will fit that. Most breed points must have a purpose. The Exmoor must have a big prominent eye, not because it looks beautiful but because it is expected to live in open country and needs to see the wolves before they attack it. The New Forest has to run amongst the trees so needs to be lighter and faster than for example the Fell, which is stronger because it lives on steep ground and was used as a pack animal.*

*The value of an animal is not what it has won but what it leaves behind, because that is the succession. An exhibitor has to see his animal through a judge's eyes, not an individual judge's personal preferences but their search for correct conformation, which is bone structure, basically, covered by muscle and flesh. The wrong conformation means the animal will not be able to work either practically or in a breeding context. After correct conformation the judge will look for minor variations related to the most common purpose of the breed. We tend to see this operating in reverse nowadays, with judges looking first for an example of the breed and then looking for*

Exmoor pony stallion in a show bridle with a bit.

correct conformation. One consequence of this has been the loss of bone in some breeds. Some features like head shape, colour and size have been decided by men in pubs.

The really gifted stockman will look at their animal very, very closely before they bring it out. The task is to hide the bad points and accentuate the good points. Within the walk and particularly the trot, for in-hand classes, every horse has a pace where it is at its best. Too few people have ever had somebody watching, or they themselves watching, while the horse moves at different paces until they find where its action is at its best. Too often they lead it at the same pace that they led Dobbin last year! The true stockman does his homework. It is too late when you get to the show, and it is this that is the most important aspect, rather than polish or finish which may make a pretty picture.

Within the Exmoor breed there are three main types, the Ashwick ponies on Winsford Hill, the Withypool ponies which are the biggest of the three, always light coloured with nice shading underneath, coming from a grass fern moor, and number twelve herd from Dunkery, the coldest, highest part of the moor nearest the sea where the vegetation is the sparsest with dark heather. These ponies, not surprisingly, are the smallest and the darkest in colour of the breed. [After inspection, registered ponies are branded with two brands, the herd number on the near shoulder and the individual pony's number within that herd on the nearside hind quarter.]

Traditionally the Exmoor was used for shepherding and as pack horses. Sledges were used in preference to carts for crossing heather. The average weight is 10 hundredweight which is a lot for a 12.2 and they are very compact. They were also used in the drift mines of the Forest of Dean.

*Training the Exmoor*
This is rather different from other breeds because they are foaled on the moor so have to become accustomed to people rather quickly. It has to be remembered that frequently the pony is physically mature before it has been halter broken. The Exmoor Pony Society organises training sessions for new owners to teach them the techniques, which consist in part of using rope halters with rings rather than rope loops so the rope can slide easily (in the same way as correctly fitted choke chains on dogs) and with particularly long ropes. Conventional headcollars, especially nylon ones, are quite unsuitable because they press on the poll in action and cause the pony to rear.

## Showing the Exmoor

*The same principle applies with showing the Exmoor that needs to be helped to show its best pace, by using a lead rein of sufficient length, so that the leader doesn't stifle the action by over-concentrating on hanging on to the front end. Schooling with long ropes like plough lines can help. Initially the pony may pull away, but can run to the extent of a long rope and will be quickly checked by a pull on the halter. With time and practice the length of the rope can be reduced.*

*Cannon bones should be exceedingly short, as should the pasterns which should not be sloping. There should be a good hand's width between the forelegs, especially for stallions. The point of the hock should be below the widest point of the quarters, not stretched right out when posed. Exmoors have huge heads but they should be in proportion to the rest of the body which is quite substantial. Manes do not lie over on one side until the mane has grown quite long. Forearms should be powerful, as should necks which may look short and thick because of their immense strength but which still have a very good length of rein in comparison with the length of the back. For this reason the ponies have traditionally been ridden by men on Exmoor.*

*Exmoors must be shown in natural condition and this used to mean straight out of the field, but nowadays they are bathed and groomed, but they must not be trimmed or with their tails cut. This is hard on someone who has hunted their pony all winter and cut the tail for practical purposes, because they are penalised, sometimes quite drastically. Tail maintenance is actually not all that difficult because while still wet the bottom of the tail can be dunked and swished about in a bucket of cold water without wetting the dock, to good effect. Out on the commons of Exmoor tails are sometimes cut to raise the end from the ground, because it has been known for snow to ball up on the tail and a valuable stallion was lost like this once. The traditional method, which is now rather old fashioned, was to brush the mud off with a dandy brush and then polish them with a cloth which leaves the grease in the coat intact. The wording of the rules (washing or brushing) does not allow for synthetic shine products and some judges will object to their use, which can be detected when they run their hands over the pony.*

## Tack

*For in-hand competitions there is nothing better than a leather, brass-mounted headcollar with a lead rein. Stallions may need a show bridle with a bit but not a bridle, but many can be controlled with a headcollar to which a fairly long lead rein, with a length of chain at the end nearest the head, is attached by a clip. It is a mistake to use a bit for the first time at a show when the pony is more comfortable with a headcollar. Traditional judges prefer to see a white webbing halter on youngstock.*

# THE FELL PONY

The main opportunities for showing Fell ponies, apart from the breed society shows, are in the mixed Mountain and Moorland classes the length and breadth of the country. The County Shows generally have specific classes for breeding stock.

## Breed society regulations for turnout and ring procedure

Ponies are shown in their natural state, as they are a mountain and moorland breed. Therefore, they are shown unclipped and untrimmed, with manes and tails left to grow long and unplaited/braided. Traditionally ponies were and still are shown in a white cotton rope halter. However, it is equally correct to show in an in-hand bridle, or riding bridle if broken under saddle. Traditionally ponies both in hand and ridden were only required to be walked and trotted before the judge, whilst this is still true of in hand, riders are now usually asked to give a full show under saddle.

---

### Official breed profile

HEIGHT   Not exceeding 14 hands (142.2 cm).

COLOUR   Black, brown, bay and grey, preferably with no white markings, though a star or a little white on the foot is allowed.

HEAD   Small, well chiselled in outline, well set on, forehead broad, tapering to nose.

NOSTRILS   Large and expanding.

EYES   Prominent, bright, mild and intelligent.

EARS   Neatly set, well formed and small.

THROAT AND JAWS   Fine, showing no signs of throatiness nor coarseness.

---

NECK  Of proportionate length, giving good length of rein, strong and not too heavy, moderate crest in case of stallion.

SHOULDERS  Most important, well laid back and sloping, not too fine at withers, nor loaded at the points – a good long shoulder blade, muscles well developed.

CARCASE  Good strong back of good outline, muscular loins, deep carcase, thick through heart, round ribbed from shoulders to flank, short and well coupled, hind quarters square and strong with tail well set on.

FEET, LEGS AND JOINTS  Feet of good size, round and well formed, open at heels with the characteristic blue horn, fair sloping pasterns not too long, forelegs should be straight, well placed not tied at elbows, big well formed knees, short cannon bone, plenty of good flat bone below knee, eight inches at least, great muscularity of arm.

HIND LEGS  Good thighs and second thighs, very muscular, hocks well let down and clean cut, plenty of bone below joint, hocks should not be sickle nor cow hocked.

MANE, TAIL AND FEATHER  Plenty of fine hair at heels (coarse hair objectionable), all the fine hair except that at point of heel may be cast in summer. Mane and tail are left to grow long.

ACTION  Walk, smart and true. Trot well balanced all round, with good knee and hock action, going well from the shoulder and flexing the hocks, not going too wide nor near behind. Should show great pace and endurance, bringing the hind legs well under the body when going.

GENERAL CHARACTER  The Fell Pony should be constitutionally as hard as iron and show good pony characteristics with the unmistakable appearance of hardiness peculiar to mountain ponies, and, at the same time, have a lively and alert appearance and great bone.

SCALE OF POINTS

| | |
|---|---|
| Height and colour | 5 points |
| Head, nostrils, eyes, ears, throat and jaws, neck | 10 points |
| Shoulders | 15 points |
| Carcase | 20 points |
| Feet, legs and joints, and hind legs | 25 points |
| Action | 25 points |
| General characteristics | 100 points |

Perhaps the most easily recognised type is the big strong black Fell pony that is up to height with lots of substance.

## The producer/judge's viewpoint

*The Fell pony is one of the purest of the British native breeds, breeding very true to type, a number of which are identifiable and acceptable. Perhaps the most easily recognised is the big strong black Fell pony that is up to height with lots of substance. Then there is the smaller lighter type and, regarding colour, dark browns and bays are more frequently seen in the north nearer to the home territory. Grey Fells are attractive but rarer and consequently further from the generally held view of the typical example of the breed. For someone setting out to buy a sure winner in the show ring it is wiser to avoid the unusual, although the rarer types and colours are perfectly acceptable if included in the breed standard.*

*The most important feature of the Fell pony is its pony character and presence. They must not be insipid but must sparkle. As a breed they usually have a lot of personality and the pony temperament which is never dull. They are often wise and sensible, occasionally mulish or* stubborn, very rarely unpleasant and usually have a well-developed sense of fun. Physically this feature is enhanced by the obligatory pony head, which should be short with a broad forehead and small ears. Fells must be useful crossing any kind of terrain and this is refected in their movement, which should show a certain amount of knee action. Although most showing takes place at a time of the year when the longer hair has been cast, care should be taken not to allow assessment of the limbs to be confused by the presence and movement of the longer hair, which can make the limbs appear tied in and the action unstraight.

Although the breed description refers to the round ribs and square quarters associated with the weight carrying/pulling breeds, this is slightly misleading because the quarters should appear well rounded from the side. The tail should not fall away sharply from the croup (goose rump) even though the Fell carries its tail fairly low, a feature that has developed over the centuries and is associated with strength of back and heat retention. It is from the rear where, like most breeds, you are looking for strong quarters and second thighs which give a square impression. The Fell is not the ideal shape for a riding pony because it is a strictly multi-purpose pony with the emphasis on work rather than riding alone. Although traditionally driving ponies had a straighter shoulder than riding animals, nowadays they are expected to have the sloping shoulder of the riding animal, which makes all the difference to the comfort of the rider but does not stop the pony from driving efficiently. As you look at the pony you should ask yourself: could it pull a trap to market, could it carry 16 stone in panniers, could a man shepherd on it all day long, could I hunt it and could my daughter take it to a pony club rally? The overall impression should be one of latent energy and power and the pony should look ready to go off and work. In a ridden class they have to go well for their rider but the typical pony has to have strength as a consequence of its conformation. It is worth bearing in mind that they really were used to carry up to 16 stone in panniers, and although pony sized themselves frequently take a hunter size in girths and have a bone measurement that would not disgrace a much bigger animal.

## Rearing and feeding
In the traditional habitat the Fell pony is expected to foal out and live out until the following spring. Any concession to the climate might take the form of being brought down to a lower pasture in the winter. Apart from during very bad weather there would be no supplementary feeding and even then it would only be hay. The single most important

*factor, therefore, in preparing a Fell for the show ring, is not to let it get too fat. Five acres of rich pasture is equivalent to fifty acres of moorland. There is the ever-present worry of laminitis and the possibility of the breed gaining in height. Judges have even been instructed not to put up overfat stock, as it is widely recognised that obesity is a danger to the wind and heart as well as putting extra strain on the limbs. This is easier said than done, though, because the Fell is, not surprisingly, a very efficient converter of food. One of the differences between native breeds and Thoroughbreds is that excess food is converted into fat rather than energy.*

*Preparation for the show ring, as with all breeds, starts at birth with basic handling. Foaling often takes place at the time of year when mares are still coming in at night, if they are not kept in the traditional manner, and this makes it more convenient to handle the foal at once, and to get it wearing a foal slip within the first couple of days. This is the ideal time to practise picking up feet and leading. After weaning at six months they resume living out and the first winter need feeding and good quality hay as well as access to a mineral block. It is a good idea to add cod liver oil to the feed which is best in the form of a balanced mix. Fells do not as a rule need more than grass unless it is to give them a bit of sparkle and presence. Like all horses they need regular worming.*

*The Fell pony is physically mature at seven years and mentally mature at nine years. A good regime for the pony with access to good pasture would involve grazing one or two hours a day on the good pasture, being worked for about an hour, standing in the stable for part of the day and being turned out on sparse to bald pasture for the rest of the time. To ensure a healthy coat and sparkle for the show ring an average supplementary feed would consist of molassed chaff, hay mix, enough soaked sugar beet to damp the feed, a handful of pony nuts, a handful of oats, garlic powder for the wind and breathing (keeps flies away too as well as vampires!) and cod liver oil for the feet, hair and eyes. In addition some limestone powder should be added. The rule, as always, is to feed according to the character, location and work of the pony. If working hard the pony can have a few more oats but Fells do not really need more than maintenance feeding, which should be well balanced.*

*Training*
*As with all horses you have to insist on an acceptable standard of manners and these are best taught gradually, consistently and preferably by example.*

160

## Tack
*The first year the Fell is shown in a show headcollar but if the temperament tends towards fussiness then a bridle with a small rubber show bit is preferable and offers the pony something to play with. Mouths should be treated with care and for this reason couplings should be fitted so that they work primarily off the noseband, not the bit, avoiding the danger of a bit injury and a one-sided mouth. Again the voice is the principal aid. It should be noted that Fells tend to have shallow mouths so care has to be taken with couplings that they don't pull forward and get hooked up in the mouth.*

## Turnout
*The Fell pony should not be trimmed under any circumstances and this includes not squaring off the bottom of the tail. Most shows take place in the summer when the longer hairs are cast anyway. The coat should be very well groomed to show condition so regular grooming, with a body brush and a curry comb, has to start fairly early, particularly if the pony has been clipped for hunting when the problem will be getting the coat out before nature intended. Rugs help here; a New Zealand rug will keep the coat clean when turned out and a light rug keeps the coat flat. After exercise a sweat rug can be used although sweating in itself is good for controlling the fat. Attention should be paid to the fitting of rugs so that they don't rub the shoulders. As the winter coat is shed grooming increases and the mane can be brushed occasionally with a body brush and laid with a damp water brush.*

*The leader should be turned out in the traditional English manner.*

## Ringcraft
*The walk is very important and often underestimated. You should aim for a medium walk. Maintain a light contact with the bit, not a loose rein, because this helps to show off the top line which should be rounded, and the pony should at least track up if not overtrack. In other words you want the hind feet to exceed the footprints of the front feet or at least to step in them. During the individual show after standing the pony up in the traditional English manner you walk away from the judge straight, turn and rebalance the pony then trot towards the judge at a steady regular working trot that is not too fast. Maintain a straight line because at this moment the judge is looking for correct action. In native pony classes you are expected to carry on round the ring and to go faster to show off the shoulder action and length of stride. At this point you are trying for lengthening at medium trot.*

# THE HIGHLAND PONY

Once again the main showing opportunities are at the breed shows, and County Shows for breeding stock, other than mixed Mountain and Moorland classes generally.

## The judge's viewpoint

*The Highland pony was used on the crofts in the Highlands of Scotland. It was dual purpose in that it was used on the farm and it was also used by the farmer as a trap pony and riding pony. They were also used for bringing the deer down after stalking. So probably in those days it was a draught animal and had a rather more upright shoulder than would be desirable in a riding animal. They are now being ridden very much more for pleasure than they were, and much more in England, and people now look for a much more sloping shoulder for this. Recently people have started driving them a lot and they are doing this very well and also in recent years they have been exported a lot, to France in particular. They are now much more active too. They are not seriously used for farm work now. Registration of stock is greatly on the increase. The pony is very useful because it is big enough for father and sensible enough for the children so makes an ideal family pony that is capable of performance when fit. They are very good doers so have a tendency to fat and need a lot of work, so are ideally suited for riding and trekking centres.*

*Presentation in the show ring*
*As a Mountain and Moorland breed they must not be trimmed or have their manes pulled or plaited. The tail must not be cut off square although very discrete reduction in the length for practical purposes would probably not be penalised, but they are expected to have a fair length of tail. The top of the tail should not be tidied because it is there for a purpose, to assist the drainage of rain water and to protect against bad weather. Sharpening of the outline around the head is officially not permitted although some people surreptitiously tidy the chin. The ears should not be trimmed inside or even along the outer edge but probably have the tuft that sticks out clean and tidy.*

*Tack*
*White halters are traditional for mares and youngstock, particularly in Scotland but less in England where there is no prejudice against*

162

---

### Official breed profile

HEIGHT   13 hands to 14 hands 2 inches.

HEAD   Well carried; broad between alert and kindly eyes; short between eyes and muzzle; muzzle not pinched, nostrils wide.

NECK   Strong, not short; good arched top-line; throat clean and not fleshy.

SHOULDER   Well sloped. Withers pronounced.

BODY   Compact; back with slight natural curve; chest deep; ribs well-sprung.

QUARTERS   Powerful; strong, well-developed thigh and second thigh.

LEGS   Flat, hard bone; forearm strong, knee broad; short cannon, pasterns oblique, not too short; well shaped, hard dark hooves. Forearm placed well under the weight of the body; hocks clean and flat. Feather silky, and not over-heavy, ending in a prominent tuft at the fetlock.

MANE AND TAIL   Hair should be long, silky, and flowing, not coarse. Tail set fairly high and carried gaily.

COLOURS   Various shades of dun: mouse, yellow, grey, cream, fox. Also grey, brown black, and occasionally bay and liver chestnut with silver mane and tail. Most ponies carry the dorsal eel stripe and many have zebra markings on the forelegs. Apart from a small star, white markings (blazes, socks, etc.) are disliked and discouraged.

---

*leather showing bridles. I personally don't like coloured browbands but a plain showing bridle is all right, more so for a stallion. A lot of stallions wear stallion harness but it doesn't suit all of them — a long back can look even longer. Mares can also be shown in a double bridle, especially if they are going to be competing in a ridden class later on. Foals can wear leather foal slips. Yearling colts should wear bits because they can be strong. Longish lead reins are a good idea.*

*Clothes*
*An increasing number of handlers wear kilts to show Highlands but they shouldn't unless they are entitled to by being Scots and a member of a clan. This wouldn't matter to me because I am judging the pony.*

White halters are traditional for Highland ponies in Scotland, but less so in England where there is no prejudice against leather showing bridles. Kilts should only be worn by Scots belonging to a clan.

*If they do it is very nice. At the Royal Highland Show they always had to wear white coats if they didn't wear a kilt. In England the rule is not enforced.*

### Judging the Highland pony
*First impressions count and handlers should look neat and tidy which is a compliment to the judge. As they go round the first time something will hit you as being nice and that should stay with you, and you have*

*to make sure you don't miss anything to make you change your mind when you inspect them closely. How they come into the ring is important and the order they come in; some people make a point of coming in late to create an impression but that does not go down well with me. They should be there in time for the class with the others and they shouldn't keep you waiting. I wouldn't put them down because of it, though.*

*In England they walk round and then halt on the track and trot in succession past you, then you bring them in rough order before seeing them individually. In Scotland they only walk and do not trot until the individual show, when they walk away, walk back, trot away and trot back and then stand up for the judge. At the Royal Highland the youngstock classes can be colossal. In England they stand up for the judge first in the individual show and then walk away and trot back, but it depends on the judge.*

*Some people will try and conceal bad action by not trotting straight back to you and they will be made to do it again. Others aren't very good at leading ponies and they lead them with their heads pulled round towards them, which does not let them move freely and they do themselves a lot of harm like that. I usually ask them how old the pony is.*

*In years gone by the Highland was shown quite fat and their trot was not good, but nowadays especially in England they are expected to trot on well when they are shown. One thing you used to get in the Highland, but you don't see so much now, they used to dish but the action has been straightened out quite a lot. They used to say that it was easier for them to go through the heather if they dished but that doesn't apply now. Dishing puts more of a strain on the joints. It isn't anyway nearly as common as it used to be.*

*If it is going to carry a saddle you do want a decent wither. When they were very fat you had a job to see the wither, and to get a saddle to stay in the right place, but that was not just common to the Highland but to a lot of pony breeds. Another tendency was a thickness through the throat which made good head carriage difficult. When looking at the head you don't want a narrow head but a broad muzzle and mouth because they are bred to live in hard conditions and need a wide mowing machine to take in enough food, but not an ugly head.*

*Similarly you don't want a narrow chest but one with plenty of room and width between the legs. Otherwise they haven't got the heart and lung room to enable them to breathe properly to get up and down the hills at high altitudes. Pasterns should not be upright because that would make them uncomfortable to ride, nor long because they have to work in hard conditions on rough ground and long pasterns would put too much strain on the legs.*

*Colours are mainly dun of one kind or another, i.e. variations on a grey or beige theme. They must not have white feet which tend to be soft.*

# THE NEW FOREST PONY

Apart from the breed shows the main opportunities for showing New Forest ponies are in mixed Mountain and Moorland classes, other than specific classes at some County Shows.

## Presentation and turnout

There are no fixed rules for presentation because many ponies compete in a variety of competitions both ridden and in hand. Plaiting, when permitted, often does not suit New Forest ponies. They are normally shown trimmed but unplaited unless they run the Forest, in which case they need all the protection nature provides and so are shown in a natural state. This is the ruie for classes specifically for ponies running the Forest.

With regard to tack, a bridle with a bit or just a white halter is the only requirement. Hind shoes are not permitted.

# Official breed profile

VERSATILITY Its native virtues of strength, intelligence, speed and agility, coupled with a calm and willing temperament make the New Forest pony an ideal riding pony for any member of the family. Most jump very well indeed and they are naturally good at gymkhana events and mounted games. They make excellent harness ponies, the forest-bred animal being particularly useful for this, as he has no fear of traffic. New Forest ponies have been successfully trained for dressage, polo, long distance riding, cross country events and carrying the disabled. They have always been raced locally, and are surprisingly fast, especially over rough terrain. The New Forest pony is also fertile and breeds easily. The stallions are easy to handle, and most are ridden outside the breeding season. New Forest mares may be put to Thoroughbreds or Arabs to produce useful small riding horses of around 15 hands, capable of competing in any sphere.

HEIGHT The upper height limit is 14.2 hh (1.47 m). There is no lower limit, but New Forest ponies are seldom under 12.0 hands (1.2 m).

COLOUR New Forest ponies may be any colour except piebald, skewbald or blue-eyed cream. Bays and browns predominate. White markings on head and legs are permitted.

TYPE A New Forest pony should be of riding type, with substance. It should have a pony head, well set on, long sloping shoulders, strong quarters, plenty of bone, good depth of body, straight limbs and good hard round feet. The larger ponies, while narrow enough for children, are quite capable of carrying adults. The smaller ponies, though not up to so much weight, often show more quality.

ACTION This should be free, active and straight but not exaggerated.

TEMPERAMENT The New Forest pony has an ideal temperament and is very easy to train.

*Opposite* New Forest ponies are generally shown trimmed but unplaited.

# Showing the New Forest pony

In 1980 the Council of the New Forest Pony Breeding and Cattle Society, the regulatory body, issued the following letter to all judges:

> The Council of the above Society is very concerned at the loss of native pony type in the Breed, due to breeding away from the native habitat. Judges are, therefore, requested to give preference to ponies with depth and bone, even at the expense of quality. Action should be straight, with free movement, but not exaggerated pointed toes. Over refined heads and light bone are neither typical nor desirable. When judging brood mares, the condition of the foal should be taken into account.

The point was made that there are significant differences between the riding pony and the New Forest pony. Generally speaking the riding pony has a head length, shoulder length (from wither to point of shoulder) and back length (from wither to croup) which are roughly equal, the height exceeds the length of the body and the legs are longer than the depth of the body. The New Forest pony has a body length longer than the height of the pony, and the depth of the body equals the length of the legs.

# The judge's viewpoint

*The New Forest is a pony very different from all the other breeds because they have a specific height range, whereas the New Forest can vary from as small as you like right up to 14.2 hands. In fact in Germany they are allowed to be slightly taller because of the translation from metres to inches. They can also be all types, from the quite coarse and heavy to the less fortunate of the ponies running in the Forest. Although many of these have good conformation and would just benefit from better care and nutrition, some of them have conformation which leaves room for improvement, which is how the concern for maintenance of the native pony type came about following efforts to improve conformation. Other breeds have similarly made successful efforts to improve their stock by selective breeding, e.g. the Connemara and the Exmoor.*

*Efforts to increase the height of some New Forest breeding stock have resulted, in some cases, in rather flimsy stock with long cannon bones and weak hocks. In action they are just not right because this conformation causes them to trail their hocks behind them.*

*When it comes to recognising distinctive type, sometimes in big classes it can be confusing because the New Forest breed does have some big greys that can look a bit like the Connemara, and there can occasionally be throwbacks from some of the other breeds. Occasionally a Welsh Section B will be nice and big boned like they used to be and people will say what a good head that has got on a Forest pony. Then they realise that it is a much better Section B than many which have become very light boned, although very beautiful, and look more like show ponies than a Mountain and Moorland pony.*

*If one is watching for an inherent weakness in the breed it is the hind leg, which can be very weak, sickle trailing hocks and too much sideways action in the hock, and the short neck. Cow hocks can also be found and can be a consequence of physical weakness. The type considered the traditional native type has a short neck and a slightly big head, which together can result in a low head carriage which is not a good ride for a child. On the other hand, some of the old mares on the Forest have got a lovely length of rein. New Forest ponies are thus different from the other breeds which have a distinct set type. At different times stallions of other breeds have been put into the Forest to improve the breed, like the Anglo-Arab Field Marshal and the Welsh stallions Denny Danny and Goodenough. Nowadays this is not allowed.*

## Turnout and presentation

*Nowadays registered New Forest ponies cannot be plaited (although partbreds can). They can be trimmed under their chins and in their heels. Their manes can be pulled a bit but not very short. Tails can be pulled a little too but not like show hunters, and the tails can be cut off square. This does not apply to classes for ponies running in the Forest which must not be touched, but must just be clean and tidy.*

Great care has to be taken with tack for the New Forest pony, because the rules vary depending on the show. At the breed show it has to be white hemp halters for mares.

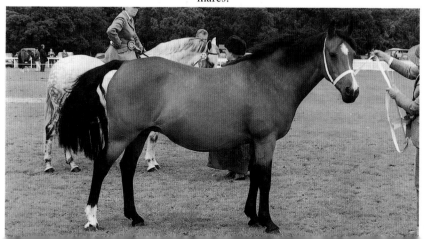

*Great care must be taken with tack, however. Different shows have different rules about this but it is always in the schedule which has to be read with close attention. At some it is acceptable to wear a normal bridle, e.g. a double or a snaffle, and at some they have to wear halters, or leather show halters without a bit attached, but at the breed show it has to be white hemp halters only. Partbreds can wear bridles, however. Stallions follow different rules and so do yearling colts. On most occasions coloured browbands can be worn with bridles but not, obviously, with white halters. When the rules state no decorations this does not refer to coloured browbands.*

## Clothing

*Wear a hat, if you can, and always look smart: riding clothes, jodhpurs, or some smart trousers, with a riding jacket, or, if you can't afford one, a neat anorak. Don't try and look fashionable or bright. Don't put on summer clothes. Try and look businesslike. Remember you have to run with the pony so wear suitable underwear and footwear!*

## Preparation

*It is very important to have the pony leading well. Going well at home is one thing, going well in the show ring is another matter. It is important not to get in front of the pony; you should be parallel with its shoulder. Even if it is idle don't try to pull but use your whip if necessary (maximum length allowed 30 inches), or click quietly so as not to upset the other ponies. A really good pony with presence and good presentation may not be as good as one further down the line, but*

It is very important to have the pony leading well.

*it will have caught the eye of the judge completely. A superb pony that has idled along, flicked at a fly and rested a leg can be overlooked.*

*They are usually bathed the night before the show. The professional producers keep them in for some time before the show, turning them out by day, and they are long reined and worked to get them muscled up and looking right with their weak points worked on. They are strapped and if necessary sweated on the fatty bits such as withers. They are also gromed to perfection. At the breed show no shoes are allowed at all in hand, but a ridden pony will wear shoes. Again schedules state the rules which can vary depending on the show. Some shows say front shoes only. Usually it is up to the owner.*

*Ringcraft*
*From the judge's point of view first appearances are very important, for example the outlook and balance and if the pony is going forward freely and easily. The judge's eye takes in the whole picture and forms an opinion of the class as a whole, which is then modified once they start to trot and the action confirms or changes this opinion, as does the pony looking very overbent. Later on individual faults and their importance will decide the difference between animals which might otherwise be of equal standard. It is in the beginning of the class that the presence of the animal will draw the attention of the judge.*

*Keep a close eye on the judge without being too obvious, and when she isn't watching try to jiggle the pony up quietly in the background, if necessary, so that when you lead it down in front of her it has its ears pricked and is taking an interest in life. Quite a lot of people go round the ring, like their ponies with their heads down, and not really doing anything for their ponies at all. You have to work terribly hard because the Forest pony is a very quiet pony on the whole and can get very bored if it is over-shown in hand. When it comes to trotting down you have to wake it up a bit before you start. Preferably start it just before the corner so that it is ready to come down straight.*

*Always keep it away, if you can, from the other ponies. Don't get on their tails. Some mean people (not many) will try and walk you off by getting close and then getting between you and the judge, obscuring the judge's view of you. Keep yourself isolated, keep an eye on the judge and try and make your pony look right when you are coming up.*

*If you've got a pony that you know moves wide behind when it is extending in front, trot fairly fast towards the judge and then slow right down and with luck its hocks will come together. Nowadays there is a tendency to look for the faults first before the general conformation, which is wrong. You've got to look to see if there is a really good animal before finding fault. If you've got a superb confor- mation animal which moves straight, even if it has one or two little faults or bumps, this shouldn't really matter. If the faults were congenital I wouldn't like it at all. Presence is very important and can make a big difference to final placing. When you are standing the pony up, though, it is a mistake to keep fidgeting around with the pony — a lot of judges don't like it. Don't make the mistake, as some people do, of leading the pony round and round near the judge's car before the competition. It usually biases the judge against you, however fair they are to your pony.*

# THE SHETLAND PONY

Classes for breeding stock are held at County Shows and the breed shows. There are many opportunities in mixed Mountain and Moorland classes at other shows.

## The judge's viewpoint

*As with every other horse and pony they must have good conformation and breed characteristics. Quality is what makes a Shetland special and immediately catches the eye. They must move well too. The action of Shetlands is somewhat different from other breeds because they have to pick their feet up and have a fairly high action. This is because they are used to living on rough ground. They also have slightly more upright pasterns for the same reason.*

*They should have a neat head and stallions must have slightly heavier heads than the females. You don't want dishy noses and tiny heads because they are miniature horses. They should have small to medium sized but thick-skinned pointed ears as a sign of hardiness. They should just stick out at the top of a closed fist. They should also have nice round feet, not donkey feet.*

*They must have plenty of bone. Showing has had a bad effect on a lot of breeds — the finer the bone a lot of these ponies have the better people like them. Children's riding ponies in particular are getting very fine boned, and it is getting pretty much the same with Shetland ponies. They seem to like them lighter and lighter and they shouldn't be. A pony must have plenty of substance, otherwise it would die if it was turned out on the moor. Our ponies always have plenty of bone*

# Official breed profile

HEIGHT   Registered stock must not exceed 40 inches (102 cm) at three years old or under, nor 42 inches (107 cm) at four years old and over. Ponies are measured from the withers to the ground, by measuring stick, and a level stance, preferably concrete, should be used.

COLOUR   Shetland ponies may be any colour known in horses, except spotted.

COAT   The coat changes according to the seasons of the year. A double coat in winter with guard hairs which shed the rain and keep the pony's skin completely dry in the worst of weather. By contrast, the summer coat is short and should carry a beautiful silky sheen. At all times the mane and tail hair should be long, straight and profuse and the feathering of the fetlocks straight and silky.

HEAD   The head should be small, carried well and in proportion. Ears should be small and erect, wide set, but pointing well forward. Forehead should be broad with bold, dark, intelligent eyes. Blue eyes are not acceptable. Muzzle must be broad with nostrils wide and open. Teeth and jaw must be correct.

BODY   The neck should be properly set on to the shoulder, which in turn should be sloping, not upright, and end in a well-defined wither. The body should be strong, with plenty of heart room, well-sprung ribs, the loin strong and muscular. The quarters should be broad and long with the tail set well up on them.

FORELEGS   Should be well-placed with sufficient good, flat bone. Strong forearm. Short, balanced cannon bone. Springy pasterns.

HIND LEGS   The thighs should be strong and muscular, with well-shaped hocks, neither hooky nor too straight. When viewed from behind, the hind legs should not be set too wide apart nor should the hocks be turned in.

FEET   Tough, round and well shaped – not short, narrow, contracted or thin.

ACTION   Straight, free action using every joint, tracking-up well.

GENERAL   A most salient and essential feature of the Shetland pony is its general air of vitality (presence), stamina and robustness.

A Shetland pony with plenty of substance.

*and if we see the bone slipping a bit we get concerned about it. Years ago ponies were kept more in their native areas but now with modern transport they travel all over, and different people are keeping them and in softer climates.*

*When they come in the ring I'd expect bone, knee action and a good bold eye, which the majority have, because it shows native intelligence. There are various other things you have to check too, like the teeth, which have to meet correctly, not be overshot. Quite a lot of ponies are wrong in the mouth. The Shetland Society are doing their best to stamp it out by inspecting the foals.*

*When you see a pony going away from you and coming towards you you only want to see two legs, not four. Some are wide in the front or close behind. A number of the small Shetlands travel wide behind. You don't find this so much with the standard ponies (38–40 inches).*

*It's just conformation, really. I look for good strong hind quarters. They want a good head carriage. So many people lead them in the ring letting them go as they like, with their noses down so that they are in a straight line from the top of the tail to the ears with no head carriage at all. They should be collected up with their heads up. You have to teach them to walk actively and trot. Rounded quarters is more a question of condition than strapping. A lot of people go wrong once they have been called in by talking to the other competitors instead of concentrating on the pony.*

*If you are going to do long distance showing you can't bring them in today, clean them up and then travel about two hundred miles to a show, because it just doesn't work on a regular basis. Ponies just fade away and are only half a pony the next day. To do this they have to have a certain amount of hard food twice a day as well as being cleaned once a day. Getting them fit is not so important as it is for a stallion.*

*Laminitis is a potential problem for some people but not living where we are [on Dartmoor] so how we produce them is different for us. We worked on them regularly from Christmas, targeting certain shows and not dragging them to every show. We had them in by day to work on them and out at night. It is harder for people on better land who are continually running into trouble with laminitis or the ponies getting itchy. The ponies are too fat, they can't feed them, and they are trying to keep the condition down, so they are fat, dull and lifeless. They should be on a rising plane of nutrition. They should get them in and work them or lead them out. They need to be sparky but absolutely under control.*

*Manes and tails should be as thick and long as possible. We train manes to hang over one side. We take off the hair under the jaw and fold the over to take the long hair off the edge of the ear and the hair that protrudes. We don't touch the long hairs around the nostrils and muzzle. We leave the legs alone completely and oil the hooves daily.*

*They are shown in leather, brass-mounted showing bridles with leather lead reins and vulcanite bar snaffles with small rings (1½ inches in diameter) in proportion to the size of the head.*

*When you first start handling a young Shetland a rope halter is the best thing, rather than a loose headcollar. They respond to them better. We practise leading in company at home so they learn to behave themselves before they get to the show and learn to walk up into their bridles so that you are not dragging them along. The work should be done at home including cleaning them regularly so that they never need bathing.*

*Handlers should be reasonably well dressed, not in jeans and T shirts, nor in flowing skirts and Ascot hats, because you are showing the pony, not yourself. Properly dressed you can go to a small show and a big show in the same clothes.*

*My advice is produce them properly, train them properly and show them properly, and don't forget your manners to the judge. Never arrive late for a class but arrive when the class is called. If you are showing you accept the judge's decision even if you don't agree with it. You should abide by the rules of the show. If you are prepared to go and show and win you should stay for the parade afterwards and parade in the way you are requested. Showing classes can be a bit monotonous for the public but they like to see the winners and the shows are put on for the public. The best way to learn showing is from the ringside, watching the successful competitors. A chequebook is not the solution to every problem.*

# CHAPTER TWELVE

# The Welsh Breeds

The Welsh breeds cover almost the entire range of weights and heights possible for riding and driving, so it is not surprising that they are divided by size, weight and type into four categories, Sections A, B, C, and D. The Welsh Pony and Cob Society differentiate them as follows:

Welsh Mountain Pony.

## The Welsh Mountain Pony (Section A)

*Height: Not exceeding 12 hh (122 cm)*

The Welsh Mountain Pony needs little introduction. Bred in the mountains and wild regions of Wales for many generations, their acknowledged beauty does not mean they are merely a 'pretty toy' — centuries of 'survival of the fittest' has ensured the sound constitution, iron hard limbs and great intelligence which, combined with the legendary Welsh temperament, makes the ideal child's pony of today. They can be seen ridden and driven all over the world — equally at home in the cold of Canada and Sweden or the heat of Africa and Australia.

The head of the Mountain Pony should be small, with neat pointed ears, big bold eyes and a wide forehead. The jaw should be clean cut, tapering to a small muzzle; the silhouette may be concave or 'dished' but never convex or too straight. The neck should be of a good length and well carried with shoulders sloping back to a clearly defined wither. The limbs must be set square with good flat bone and round dense hooves. The tail set high and gaily carried.

Action must be straight both in front and behind, quick and free with hocks well flexed.

## The Welsh Pony (Section B)

*Height: Not exceeding 13.2 hh (137 cm)*

The general description of the Welsh Mountain Pony can be applied to the Welsh Pony, with greater emphasis being placed on riding pony qualities whilst still retaining the true Welsh quality with substance.

For generations these ponies were the hill farmers' main means of transport, herding sheep and wild ponies over rough and mountainous country. They had to be hardy, balanced and fast to survive, which ensured that only the best were bred from. These qualities, combined with a natural jumping ability and the temperament of their Welsh Mountain Pony forebears make the Welsh Pony second to none in whatever field his young rider may choose. Today they hold their own among our top-class riding ponies both in performance competitions and in the show ring.

## The Welsh Pony of Cob Type (Section C)

*Height: Not exceeding 13.2 hh (137 cm)*

The Welsh Pony of Cob Type is the stronger counterpart of the Welsh Pony, but with Cob blood.

178

Their true worth as a dual purpose animal has been fully realised in recent years, and their numbers have increased accordingly.

Active, surefooted and hardy they are ideal for so many purposes both for adults and children.

Like all the Welsh breeds they are natural jumpers and they also excel in harness – there are in fact few things that they cannot be used for.

## The Welsh Cob (Section D)

*Height: Exceeding 13.2 hh (137 cm)*

Aptly described as 'the best ride and drive animal in the world', the Welsh Cob has been evolved throughout many centuries for his courage, tractability and powers of endurance.

The general character is the embodiment of strength, hardiness and agility. The head shows great quality with pony character. Bold prominent eyes, a broad forehead and neat, well set ears. The body must be deep, on strong limbs with good 'hard wearing' joints and an abundance of flat bone. Action must be straight, free and forceful, the knees should be bent and then the whole foreleg extended from the shoulders and as far forward as possible in all paces, with the hocks well flexed, producing powerful leverage.

The Welsh Cob is a good hunter and a most competent performer in all competitive sports, in recent years they have had great success in the international driving world. Their abilities in all spheres are now fully recognised throughout the world.

It should be added that these cobs can be as tall as 16 hands, although most are around 15 hh to 15.2 hh. The point has been made that the head should be small like a pony with a dished nose, never a Roman nose. It is interesting to discover that the breed, which was established by the fifteenth century, has many references in Welsh poetry, and in the sixteenth century the stallion was described, by the poet Tudur Aled in his poem, 'Abbot of Aberconwy', as follows:

The stallion should have the outlook and poise of a stag. The face should be dished; the forehead wide; the nostrils wide and open like the muzzle of a gun; the eyes like two ripe pears, bulging and dancing in his head; the ears should be small and fine, restless, and like two sage leaves; his coat like new silk. He can both trot and gallop, and when he trots on a stoned road, fire sparks from his shoes...his jump could be likened to a deer springing from an adder.

The breed was also known for swimming and jumping rivers.

179

# Showing the Welsh breeds

There are a number of rules governing various aspects of the showing of the Welsh breeds and these should be obtained from the Society. In the main they echo the general rules of the National Pony Society with regard to judges, exhibitors and the ages of foals and brood mares for showing purposes (see Chapter 11). One that relates specifically to Welsh breeds concerns the weight of shoes which is permitted, and has a bearing on the action.

# Weight of shoes

For ponies not exceeding 13.3 hands high, no shoe shall exceed 1 lb in weight in the case of stallions or 8 oz in the case of mares and youngstock.

For cobs exceeding 13.2 hands high and not exceeding 14.0 hands high, no shoe shall exceed 1½ lb in weight.

For cobs exceeding 14.0 hands high, no shoe shall exceed 2 lb in weight or in the case of yearling colts and fillies 1½ lb in weight.

Half an inch will be allowed in height for shoeing.

Sections A and B, if shod, should be shod with light shoes.

The Welsh Pony and Cob Society also gives the following guidance with regard to trimming:

# Trimming hints

*Section A*

Welsh Mountain Ponies should be shown in as natural a state as possible. However, very thick, long manes may be discreetly thinned, one long thin plait is usually put at the top of the mane behind the ear, the reason being to show off the line of the throat.

The long hairs under the jaw and those protruding from the ear may be trimmed off – leaving as natural a line as possible; the whiskers around the muzzle may be shortened.

The tail should look natural. A tail bandage will work wonders if the hairs at the top of the tail are very bushy.

*Section B*

It is recommended that Welsh Ponies are shown unplaited and, like a Mountain Pony, it should be realised that too much trimming and pulling of manes and tails detracts from their native pony character.

*Sections C and D*
  Welsh Cobs and Ponies of Cob Type, like the Welsh Mountain Pony,
  should be shown in as natural a state as possible.

From the above the inference can be drawn that the general procedure
for showing the Welsh breeds follows the lines of Mountain and
Moorland classes but with a relaxation of the rules regarding natural
condition. In effect the condition is anything but natural, with
exhibitors turning their ponies and cobs out to a very high standard
with all the attention to detail that one associates with conventional
show ring standards, apart from the plaiting. The exception to this
is the single plait at the top of the mane behind the ears in the case
of animals old enough to have a sufficiently long mane to benefit. In
this case the plait is secured at the bottom by stitching but not rolled
up. The mane is encouraged to lie over on the offside and damped
to sharpen the outline for the show ring. With regard to trimming,
the head is trimmed conventionally but not the heels. Tails are not
squared off but discreetly pulled so that they appear to end naturally
at a level that flatters rather than being left to drag along the
ground. The top of the tail is thinned and laid by the use of a tail
bandage so that the quarters are shown to their advantage, but the
tail is not pulled as such. The areas around the eyes and muzzle are
oiled in the conventional manner but preferably not artificially enhanced with make up! The hooves are oiled but not stained.

## Show ring procedure

This follows the pattern of Mountain and Moorland showing with
all competitors trotting in succession past the judge before their
individual show. A feature of the Welsh breeds is the trot and the
unique action which involves free movement of the shoulders as well
as hock engagement (see illustration p. 16). To show this well there
needs to be a good head of steam, so it is essential that the leader is
suitably dressed, fast enough and fit enough to keep up and carry on
round the ring. Men tend to wear caps and tweed rather than suits
and bowlers for showing the Welsh breeds. The extravagance of the
Welsh action makes it all the more important that the pony's head is
straight, otherwise any slight tendency to dish will be made worse.
For the same reason it is very important that the pony is well
balanced, which is helped additionally by a light but firm and even
contact on the rein (see illustration p. 66). Trailing hind legs and

Welsh Cob (Section D). Traditionally posed with front feet level and hind legs stretched out and parallel to each other; this is seen less commonly in England nowadays.

consequent hollow backs can be helped at home with work that builds up the back muscles, like active walking involving over-tracking of the hind feet.

### Standing up for the judge

Traditionally the Welsh breeds were posed in a more exaggerated manner than other British breeds, with the front feet level with each other and the hind legs stretched right out and parallel to each other. This is still seen today at the breed shows but to a lesser extent and more amongst the older generation. Elsewhere they are now shown in the more conventional British fashion, although some-times with one hind leg more stretched than usual.

## The producer/judge's viewpoint

### Preparation and training

*We start preparing our ponies in January when we get them in, rug them up and start feeding for the show ring. I like them to start the season fat. Yearlings, two and three year olds and mares live out all winter and are fed haylage which does not make them fat, but when they come in they are all rugged up including the foals. They are turned out daily and are fed hard food. Preparation is concerned with the general condition of the pony so the things you have to think about are teeth, feet, worms and lice. It is impossible to put condition on a pony if it has lice, which affect all horses at some time.*

*We don't do a lot of schooling. The foals are halter broken at weaning and taught to tie up and be touched and handled. They are then taught to lead with an assistant walking behind to keep them going until they can do it on their own. After that they practise as if they were in the show ring, even if they are just being led in and out of the field. They must not hang back but walk beside you.*

*Strapping is a good way to muscle up the pony if you have the time. Road work in hand is very good for muscling up provided it is active. Lungeing in circles is good for teaching them to go forward, interspersed with going in a straight line at the end of the lunge line.*

*Bathe the pony the day before the show. When you see pink skin through grey hair then you know it is really clean. With Section As I plait the tail in about three tight plaits right down to the bottom so that when they are combed out there is a crinkle to the hair. I don't do this to the manes because the effect would be wrong, but they do need to be laid with water or baby oil. The manes of youngstock might be plaited, though, to encourage them to lie over on the off side, but not just before a show.*

### Action and its artificial encouragement
*Foot care practices vary a great deal. Some people shoe their ponies with shoes weighing up to 1½ lb. This applies more to the cobs than the Section As. Some people shoe yearlings but in my opinion this causes a tendency to grow long boxy feet later on. Heavy shoes, if used, are worn until about four or five days before a show and then light shoes are put on. We don't agree with this practice, but we do trim the front feet to lighten the action and encourage it to flow. Another practice sometimes seen but not advocated is periodically attaching short chains to straps above the fetlocks so that they trail on the ground and encourage the pony to pick up its feet. If you choose your pony correctly with good action you will breed good action. Judges generally seem more concerned about front action with the hocks under them than dishing, and they also like to see the ponies well covered.*

*Turnout of pony*

Section As *are shown in special white webbing halters, which can be bought in Wales, from yearlings up to three year olds for mares. Colts are generally shown in white halters to start with and perhaps the second year but in a leather bridle with a brass browband and buckles and a bit (nylon/vulcanite snaffle so as not to damage the mouth) with a running chain through it as three year olds.*

*They should be shown in a natural state with a flowing mane and tail, so the tail should never be squared off but thinned a little, not pulled, at the sides of the dock to show off the quarters. The mane is tidied so that you can just see the line of the throat helped by the thin plait behind the ears. It is shaped to follow the line of the mane all the way to the withers but is not as short as conventional riding pony length. Whiskers are all trimmed off on the head but the heels are not touched.*

Section Bs *are never shown in white halters. Foals are shown in leather foal slips with leather lead reins, fillies in leather headcollars, mares in leather bridles with leather lead reins.*

*They also are shown with a flowing mane and tail officially although some people keep the manes shorter, but it does not look so good. They are turned out to a smarter standard but must not be plaited, although they were at one time but this is no longer allowed. Again they have the thin plait behind the ears. Their tails are pulled at the bottom to finish just below the hocks but are not cut off square, and again they are thinned at the dock but not pulled as such. The aim is to achieve a natural effect. The Welsh Pony carries its tail quite high and you aim to have the very bottom of the tail at the ideal length even though the widest part is higher.*

Section Cs and Ds *are shown in the same way as the Section As. Mares are always shown in white halters, colts with bridles and bits.*

Section D mare and foal in traditional white halters.

## Turnout of handler

*In the show ring a lot of people take a lot of trouble to make their pony look nice and then forget about themselves. To my mind a cane is part of the turnout and can be the steering wheel when it comes to turning the corners in the ring. Rather than hang on to the pony's head which will then turn towards you it is much better just to bring up the cane and the pony will automatically go round. Apart from that you may need it to deal with bad behaviour.*

*I like to see people come into the ring not dressed in jeans and a shirt but with a jacket on and trousers or perhaps cords, and a headscarf or a hat. Bowlers are never worn but caps are. Younger people seem not to wear hats very much but I think it is bad really, you don't have the same image. If it is a very hot day you can wear a shirt and a waistcoat, but for Section Bs you should always wear a jacket.*

## Ring procedure

*This is the same for all sections but details can vary according to the judge. You should not run into the ring but walk, and when called in by the judge you should walk to the line up. To do otherwise is bad manners, but sometimes it is a result of the cob being allowed to jog instead of learning to walk correctly. This can happen when the exhibitor is concentrating on producing an animal with presence, a bold eye and a fiery trot and gets carried away. This is less likely with true horsemen.*

*I was always taught to do two circuits of the ring and then watch the judge because, if there was a choice between two, if you were the one watching the judge the eye contact shows you are keen and might influence things.*

## The trot

*There is a difference between running a pony and showing a pony. A lot of people think that you have to run like hell to show a pony properly, but you haven't. If you have them balanced properly on all four feet then you just keep that pace going until you ask them to extend to the point where they are about to break into canter, so that they are really extending and really going forward. A lot of people run like hell and watch the front end but don't notice that at the back the pony may be going very wide. Showing is an art and if you know that the pony has this tendency then as you pass the judge you pull him back to bring the hocks back under him, rebalance, and then go on again. Never attempt to bring the pony round in front of the judge again once he has seen him because this is very bad manners.*

185

*With Section As the first thing I look for is conformation – depth and heart room, sloping shoulder, good head, bold eye, flaring nostrils and rounded quarters. In action I like to see a pony over-stride at the walk by about six to eight inches. At the trot, with the Welsh, I do not like to see daisy-cutting action. They have to go forwards, use the shoulder and cover the ground, not going up and down without travelling. I look for knee action that comes from the shoulder. Tied in, restricted action is not uncommon and when I look at a pony I look for room behind the elbow, between the elbow and the ribs, which usually means they can move.*

*You don't look for such high knee action with a Section B, more shoulder action. Even so a superb Section B would be an inferior show pony from the point of view of knee action, bearing in mind that the show pony is expected to have floating, daisy-cutting action. Conversely an attractive Section B without distinctive Welsh action may well be a very successful show pony.*

*The Section As, Cs and Ds should all look like different sized versions of the same thing, except that the C should look more ponyish. The Section Bs are the exception because of their added refinement.*

*Conformation is the first priority again, followed by action. Behaviour and temperament are very important too because they are children's ponies.*

### Standing up for the judge

*The pony should be stood up in exactly the same way as any other pony with all four legs visible from the side. They should be encouraged to reach out to show a length of rein. The only difference is that the head should be slightly higher to show off the crest and the arch of the neck rather than just poking the head out in front which does not show off the Welsh head to advantage. They are no longer shown with a leg in each corner and the hind legs stretched right out because this can make the back look weak. You must make an effort to stand the pony correctly, because a judge likes to see the handler working on the pony, not just standing there like a zombie. Never stand a pony facing downhill. Hocks can be weak – sickle and cow hocked and sometimes weak second thighs – so this affects how you stand the pony. Necks can be short and withers flat with the Cobs, but flattering these is more a question of preparation and turnout.*

*Opposite* A cane is part of the turnout and can be the steering wheel when it comes to turning the corners in the ring.

# CHAPTER THIRTEEN

# The Arabian Horse

Much prized for centuries for its qualities of classical beauty, courage and agility and for its unique light floating action, the influence of the Arabian on the evolution of the modern horse has been considerable. Not surprisingly centres of excellence of Arabian breeding are not restricted to Arab countries nor even to one continent, and valuable strains can be found all over the world. As one would expect the physical types vary tremendously and these are not identified by simple geographical location. Recognising them is a complex subject in its own right. From the point of view of the modern show ring, eligibility is a simple question of having your horse registered under the auspices of the World Arab Horse Organisation. In Britain this is administered by the Arab Horse Society, under whose authority the regional and national shows as well as the European qualifiers are run in conjunction with the European Arab Horse Show Commission. The rules for these shows are fairly extensive and very strictly administered by representatives of the disciplinary committee of the Arab Horse Society. You should obtain these rules and read them carefully, but some significant ones are as follows:

## Breed show rules

No mare or her foal may be shown unless the foal was born at least three weeks before the date of the judging.

Stallions and colts aged three years and over must be shown wearing suitable bridles with bits.

Sensible bridlework must be used on all exhibits.

Rigid metal nosebands or headpieces, or rigid inserts in flexible nosebands or headpieces, are banned.

Chains may not be used on foals under three months old.

Whips used in In-hand and Ridden classes must not exceed one metre in length, which includes the tassel.

*PLEASE NOTE*: Arab Horse Society does not condone the alteration of appearance of a horse or pony, i.e. the application of black hoof varnish or dye substances or colouring which alter or cover the basic colour of the hoof, skin, or coat.

The Arab Horse Society does not approve of the clipping of manes of Pure Bred Arab Horses.

## Trimming and clipping (ECAHO rule no. 31)

Pure Bred horses may not be shown with a clipped bridle path exceeding 1 inch in length unless imported on or after January 1st [same year]. Whilst a bridle path is growing out, the shorter mane may be plaited neatly, and the horse shown without penalty. Tactile hair (whiskers) should not be removed.

The Arab Horse Society offers the following guidelines for beginners showing in hand:

## Purebred Arabian horses

HORSE   To be shown with full mane and tail. No alteration of the basic colour of the skin, coat or hooves is permitted. This rule covers hoof paints and varnishes, coat dyes and cosmetic operations. Hoof oil, vaseline and whitening naturally white legs is permitted. Clipping of the eyelashes is not permitted. Foals, when shown, must be suitably haltered and led.

TACK   Neat leather halter and rein. Metal or wire-cored halters can be cruel and are not considered suitable. The bitting of colts and stallions is compulsory. Handlers are reminded that they are entirely responsible for the comfort and control of their exhibit.

HANDLER   Appearance must be neat and tidy. Tweed jackets and cord slacks or jodhpurs always look nice, and wear suitable shoes for running with your horse. Felt hats, bowlers or hunting caps look smart, and remember to wear gloves. Buttonholes should not be worn. Short whips, not exceeding one metre, or canes should be carried. These clothes are the normal showing wear at British shows. At International shows handlers in Arabian classes are expected to wear white clothing.

## Anglo-Arab and partbred Arabian horses

HORSE   To be shown with mane plaited, and the tail either pulled or plaited. The other rules applicable to purebred Arabians also apply to Anglos and partbreds.

TACK   Suitable leather halters or bridles. Most exhibits from yearlings onwards are shown bitted and horses from four years of age and upwards are usually shown in riding bridles, i.e. double bridle.

HANDLER   Dress as above, but whips are not really suitable for these classes, and a short stick or leather-covered cane look the part. A neat workmanlike appearance is what is wanted.

Success in the show ring is largely a question of correct conformation as it is defined for any horse, and the individual preference of the judge on the day with regard to specific features of type. Because it is such a complex subject the Arab Horse Society hesitates to issue an official breed profile. One of the most influential breeders and a pioneer of Arab breeding in Britain, Lady Anne Wentworth of the Crabbet Park Stud, recorded a summary of the features of the breed that she considered essential, in her book *The Swift Runner* (1957), but this is perhaps more relevant to her own stock and their descendants. It is a useful introduction, however, despite modern reservations about her views on vertebrae length, and is reproduced here.

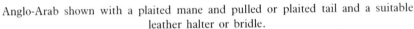

Anglo-Arab shown with a plaited mane and pulled or plaited tail and a suitable leather halter or bridle.

# Unofficial breed profile

HEAD   This is one of the most important points as it is the hallmark of the breed — small wedge shaped, broad at cheek bones and relatively short. Profile undulating with a concave dip just below eye level, tapering to a very fine muzzle without noticeable arching over the nose. Forehead very wide between the eyes and usually more prominent in mares than stallions, which sometimes have an almost flat forehead, but never narrow. A narrow bulging forehead is also wrong.

Jaws at joint of neck very wide apart, circular and deep with well-defined sharp edges, the hollow between them free of flesh and the throat well detached and loose, set into it in a pronounced very delicate arch.

Shafts of under jaw straight, without convexity, and tapering into a sharply defined firm chin. Mouth long and firm, with a pleasing expression.

EYES   Enormously large and dark, shaped like a blunted oval, set low in the head and almost at right angles to the profile. Very wide open and brilliant and sometimes showing white at the corners. A stallion's eyes should blaze and sparkle — a mare's eyes have a deer-like softness.

NOSTRILS   Exceptionally large, fine edged and flexible, exquisitely modelled and set nearly parallel with the profile when in repose, not semi-vertically at the end of the nose but capable of very great expansion when inflated.

EARS   Small, set wide apart but strongly pricked, quick and alert, sharply chiselled in most delicate curves with very fine edges. Thick clumsy ears and nostrils show degeneracy. Stallions have shorter ears than mares. Long ears in a stallion are a defect.

NECK   The longer the better. Decidedly arched, elastic and pliable with corresponding curves of crest and throat. The throat-latch beautifully modelled, never fleshy or thick. Stallions should have a strongly arched crest (never a gelding's neck) and no Arab should have an angular or stiff attachment of neck to head. Head and neck carried higher and more proudly than in most breeds. A mare's neck is lighter and often straighter, but should never lose the curve of throat.

SHOULDER AND WITHERS  Withers well marked and as high as possible, though seldom as high or lean as in Thoroughbreds, the vertebrae being shorter, and Arabs may be correspondingly wider and more muscled over the withers – this does not affect action which is dependent on the slope and length of shoulder blades allowing the humerus to swing the foreleg freely backwards and forward as on a pendulum.

A 'pudding shoulder', i.e. soft and shapeless with bulging breast, so often associated with bad Arabs, must be strictly barred. Shoulder should be long and well modelled. A straight shoulder with cow withers is a common and very bad fault.

CHEST AND RIBS  Wide and deep, lots of heart room and deep girth for stamina.

LOINS  Short and strong. As Arabians have only five lumbar vertebrae, any sagging of the spine in front of the hips is specially undesirable and stallions should never lose a slightly full curve of loins, even if saddle-backed or hollow with age – sagging loins are hereditary, in mares this is less important.

BACK  Short and level, the croup and quarters carrying on the horizontal line to root of tail and well muscled on each side of spine. Mares may have longer backs than stallions and many mares have deep backs.

BODY  Barrel much rounded with curved ribs – flanks must not be cut up or narrow.

QUARTERS  Long from hip to point of buttocks and very wide across hips and thighs. Gaskins and thighs strongly muscled with great length from stifle to hocks. Should not be higher than the withers in adult horses. Growing youngsters generally grow higher behind than in front.

HOCKS  Large and flat, with points well developed and a straight drop of hind leg. Weak, small, bent or cow hocks are most undesirable.

TAIL  Tail carriage is equal in importance to the shape of the head. Set level with back, strong at root and springing up in a perfect arch and carried high the moment the horse is in motion. Slight sideways carriage no defect; but it must never be exaggeratedly twisted and turned so as to show a long stretch of bare dock. Another approved carriage is cocked up closer to, but clear of, the body, like the crook handle of a walking stick.

FORELEGS  Large flat knees, short cannons. Tendons parallel with the cannon bone and exceptionally clean and prominent, the inner one like a violoncello string. If perfectly straight and defined with no inward slant, great measurement of 'bone' is immaterial so long as it is flat and not tied in below the knee or hock. Pasterns on the long side and sloping, but strong as steel.

FEET  Circular, hoofs dense, smooth and hard. Very contracted mule feet or splay feet very bad. Mares usually have larger feet than stallions.

Many good Arabs, like Thoroughbreds, turn out one or both hind feet slightly when standing. It is rather a characteristic of the breed and when hocks and action are straight, is quite immaterial, though a quite true stance is of course the ideal.

COAT, SKIN AND HAIR  Skin thin, fine and supple – satin coat with irridescent sheen – legs clean of hair – mane, tail and forelock fine and long and may have a wave, but not be coarse and curly.

COLOUR AND MARKINGS  Bright colours best. Chestnut, bay, brown and all stages of grey to white. Black, dun and roan are not Arab colours, though in the early stages of grey are often mistaken for them – foals never being white at birth are often a long time turning grey, from the birth colour of black and other dark browns. Dapple grey and white are the most celebrated colours. 'Roan' grey, dappled, iron and other greys are not permanent but transitional to ultimate white or flea-bitten grey. So called 'roan' seldom lasts beyond the fourth year and dapples begin to fade after twelve.

HEIGHT  Varies with feeding, care and climate. Owing to increasingly hard desert conditions modern imported horses rarely exceed 14.2 hh and are getting smaller. The Bahreyn breed, however, 200 years ago used to reach nearly 16 hands and some of Abbas Pasha's racehorses, notably Wazir's stock, measured 15.2 hh. In England and America height is notably increasing. There is no limit of height, but where type and quality are of equal merit, the biggest horse is likely to be the best as, height being measured at the withers, he is, except in rare cases, probably the horse with the best withers and shoulders.

# Showing the Arab

*Tack*

The increase in popularity of the Arab and the increasing influence of American show ring practices over the last few years have led to changes in the style of the bridles worn in the show ring. These have become much lighter, more ornamental and with a paradoxical tendency to be more severe in action. American bridles can be very severe in a number of ways. Consisting of a headpiece, cheekpieces and the front part of a noseband connected through small rings by a fine chain under the chin, they are frequently reinforced with metal running inside the leather. They are consequently narrow and hard so can cut and bruise in the wrong hands, particularly if the sanction of the chain is used, which is finer than an English curb chain. The Arab Horse Society is aware of this danger and the rules reflect their concern. Swift and public action is taken to ensure that reinforced bridles are not used in this country, or even bridles that might once have been reinforced.

Some examples of Arab bridles. *Below* Foal. *Above right* Mare. *Below right* Stallion.

There is considerable variation in Arab heads, so the choice of bridle is very important. Things have changed very much over the years from the days when Arabs wore lighter versions of the same kinds of bridles as other breeds. Many owners like colour on the bridle and there are strong views held on the most suitable colours to choose, like not putting red on chestnuts that seem to suit cool colours and brass better, whereas silver looks good on greys, and bays look good in anything, but this is purely a matter for the owner's taste. There is a belief that the correct choice of bridle can make the difference between winning and coming second, and there have been fashions with studs and silver buckles and rolled leather work. Not all bridles have chains. Mares and foals often have matching bridles. Generally speaking the better the head the finer the bridle. There are no customs regarding the type of Arab and the bridle chosen; it is purely a question of finding what suits the particular head best.

## Turnout

Manes and tails are fine and silky so are just washed and brushed out with a soft brush, taking care not to break the hair. Manes are not pulled but can be laid with a damp water brush. Tails are not cut off square but left to grow and the sides of the tail are encouraged to grow straight, so a tail guard is preferable to a tail bandage for travelling because it does not set the hair to follow the line of the dock, and creates a better effect when the horse is animated and carrying the tail flagged over the back. Facial hair is not trimmed but the appearance of the head is enhanced by the application of vaseline or baby oil, or a mixture of baby oil and liquid paraffin, around the eyes and muzzle.

## Handler

There are no hard and fast rules but most people adopt traditional English showing clothes: suits and bowlers, or slacks and tweed jackets and caps for the men; trousers, tweed jackets and hats for the ladies, or riding clothes. There also seems to be a higher percentage of ladies wearing mid-calf length skirts with shirts and waistcoats and long boots than for other breeds, which complements the romanticism of the breed.

# The judge's viewpoint

*Distinguishing features of the Arabian today*

HEAD *Widely spaced enormous eyes, wafer thin nostrils that are capable of great expansion, a peculiar jaw arrangement, small ears, dished profile (either dished or straight in the USA).*

THROAT *Peculiar curved entrance to the neck at the throat, like an upturned tea plate, called the 'mitbah', which is a prized feature of quality Arabians.*

BACK *Very short back, very long, broad and more level croup with a high set tail.*

ACTION *Light, dancing and airy.*

*A 15 hand Arab should have something between 7 and 7½ inches of bone, but in fact the density of the bone is such that the breed has a tremendous reputation for remaining sound even with 12 or 13 stone riders, so the actual diameter of the limb is of less importance, providing the tendons are well defined and the shape of the limbs is correct. The overall impression of balance is important, so that a lightweight horse can get away with less bone providing it is in proportion to the size of the body.*

## Training the Arabian

*Encountering the quality Arabian and learning that handling it correctly is a question of lightness and sensitivity, rather than brute force and strength, creates an enduring love of the breed. A relationship with an Arabian creates a bond that can deal with obstacles in an almost telepathic way, probably based on glances and posture and other non-verbal cues. Successful experts agree that force does not work with a Arab, and can have the reverse effect, but asking, playing and wanting an Arab to race, for example, brings out the best in them. They are different in character from other horses. Arabian horses love life and love learning something new. Teaching them something is about teaching them to want to do it rather than forcing or bribing them. They love achieving things, so are encouraged with lots of praise to enjoy learning.*

## Care and preparation

*It is a traditional belief that the Arabian is tough enough to cope with the poor grazing and cold nights of the desert and has legs like steel. It is also part of the mythology that their proud owners will take them*

197

*into their tents at night, ejecting their wives if necessary. While some owners may wish to strike a balance between these two points of view, it is quite normal in this country for in-foal mares and youngstock to live out all winter, whatever the conditions, providing they have access to water. Their coats grow accordingly but these can be shed in good time for the showing season. A feature of the breed is a lack of fleshiness around the head and cheekbones, and the limbs, called dryness, yet in the winter these areas become covered with fat and hair with no detrimental effect.*

*Production is very important. Unfortunately entries have to be in very early in the year and sometimes the horse is not right on the day for one reason or another. Horses have to be prepared gradually for the show and it is difficult to put a time scale on this. The amount of free grazing that they have has to be restricted in order to lose some of their grass belly. Weeks of work have to be spent grooming the coat until it is perfect, including strapping and perhaps sweating over the withers if they are prone to be fatty. A programme of work has to be followed in conjunction with this, depending on the age of the horse, to produce the correct outline. It will consist of lungeing, riding or even driving, or a combination of these activities. The horse has to be obedient and understand what standing up means and look alert.*

*Body fat is very important. The horse has to be well covered and fit looking but not fat. It must not be fat looking, pot bellied and over-topped. A lot of effort has to go into the feeding and the exercise, as well as the coat, general well being and training. Part of the preparation of the correct outline may involve strapping, and here the general principles of good conformation, which are common to all horses, will be your guide as to which muscles need particular development. Quarters can look weak in all breeds and can benefit from strapping, but this is really a strategy for the preparation of mature horses only. Yearlings should not be strapped and two year olds only rarely. In their case correct feeding and daily grooming are the most effective strategies, as their preparation should be as natural as possible. Coats can be helped if necessary with vitamin and mineral supplements. Nowadays with modern advances coarse mixes can take a lot of the guesswork out of the feeding, and with the range available a suitable balanced mix can be found for the individual needs of most horses, with added extras like vitamin supplements if necessary. On particularly good grazing, however, you hardly need to feed show stock at all. Character and temperament are the features that are the first to be affected by restrictions in the diet, and these are the components of the all-*

*important 'presence' which is so essential in attracting the eye of the judge when competing in top-class company. This is where experience tells in producing for the show ring.*

*One of the benefits of the American influence is that fat yearlings are not popular, which reduces the chance of problems in later life from this cause. This is of particular relevance to the production of Arabs which, if forced in any way, are rapidly prone to the condition of osteochondrosis (OCD) or knuckling over at the joints or alteration to the foot shape. If this semi-arthritic overgrowth of the joints should occur, which can only be properly diagnosed by scanning, with its intermittent lameness, you have to forget showing for a couple of years and put the horse on a maintenance diet, and usually they can be saved.*

*Many people believe that the Arabian, if it has a fault, has problems with the shape of the forelegs. It used to be hind legs and bent hocks but this is no longer the case, following careful breeding to correct this. Nowadays the degree of refinement has increased in the whole animal with a corresponding increase in fineness of the foreleg, and the slightest deviation, like an offset cannon or back at the knee, appears more marked. Another problem encountered is out-turning or in-turning toes.*

### The average day

*This is a misnomer because each horse is an individual and different personalities need different timetables. Generally speaking they are all fed in the morning, turned out on good grazing for a certain period of time, usually between three and four hours, and brought in before lunch. After a rest and a sleep they follow their personal work programme of lungeing, loose schooling, long reining, riding or driving, including in-hand training. Variety brings a sweetness to the horse's outlook that cannot be achieved by mechanical methods of production. Depending on the weather they are then washed off, dried, groomed, rugged up, bandaged and later on walked out in hand before bedding down and feeding.*

### Show ring procedure

*The way that the Arabian is shown in hand has changed considerably over the last ten years as a result of the influence of practices in America and more recently Europe, and extends even to the type of bridles worn, which are more detailed and finer in order to show off the beauty of the Arabian head. For the spectator the showing of*

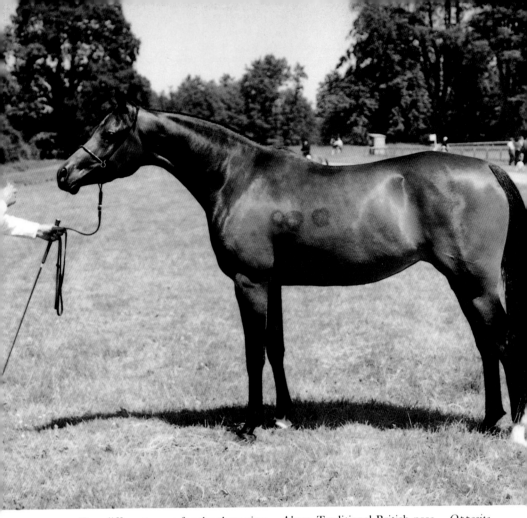

Two different poses for the show ring. *Above* Traditional British pose. *Opposite* American-influenced pose, found at national and international levels of competition, which gives the impression of a flatter top line. The distinctions between the two poses and the impressions they create have been the subject of some controversy.

*Arabians is particularly interesting, because it is possible to see elements of both the old and the new depending on the level of competition. Apart from specific techniques in the ring the fundamental procedures are of two kinds, either one or two judges comparing all the horses before them and conferring, or a panel of judges marking individual horses on a point system with no conferring. In this case ties are decided by the horse that is closest to the type required winning.*

*The point system can be very time consuming — one and a half to two hours per class is not unknown — and there is a danger that at the end of it they have forgotten what the standard was at the start of the*

competition. All the horses are seen together walking and trotting, all leave the arena and then return individually. First they are stood up for the judges, walked in a triangle, trotted in a larger triangle, stood up again and then put to one side while the marks are computerised. Very often there are five judges, so this is a weighty undertaking. There is a lot to be said for the discipline of the prescribed triangle, and the panel system encourages greater spectator awareness and appreciation because everybody can see what is going on, not just the people in the main grandstand, although there is not a significant difference in the results obtained with this system of judging. This, however, is the method employed for international competitions and also some regional breed shows, perhaps with fewer judges, and is on the increase.

*Standing the horse up for the judge*

Previously the custom was to show in the traditional English way with regard to the way the horse was presented to the judge. The horse was expected to be posed with all four legs visible from the side in a balanced way. The forelegs were supposed to be slightly in front of and behind the perpendicular and so were the hind legs, with the horse slightly stretched. The attention of the horse was held by rustling something in the pocket or feeding a mouthful of grass and this encouraged the horse to arch the neck forward towards the hand.

This changed gradually over the years so that the horse is set up with a slightly longer distance between the fore and the hind legs so that it is more stretched, but not exaggeratedly so in the way that Welsh cobs used to be shown. This has the effect of levelling the croup which is a requirement of the breed, as is showing as high a set of tail as possible which is also helped in this way. Nowadays the forelegs are placed more or less together and the whip is held up high and the horse is trained to reach upwards and outwards to touch the handler's end of the whip. This is meant to look like a stallion standing on top of a hill surveying his mares, looking animated and alert with his neck arched, a level top line, his tail up, nostrils flaring, and is supposed to show off the long curved neck set high on to the shoulders, the short back, the level quarters and the tail in the air which distinguish the breed from other horses.

While the Americans like to see a flat top line from the withers to the tail a certain amount of undulation is considered desirable in this country, and in fact is present in the American horses when they are not standing up in the show ring. This feature has been the subject of considerable controversy because an exaggeratedly flat top line would be detrimental to the performance of the horse.

In America, where showing is intended to be a spectator entertainment and huge sums of money are involved, this part of the process is quite flamboyant, with handlers using tassels on the end of the whip or waving the whip around to encourage the horse to reach out, and when these practices reached our shores they also caused much discussion. While the debate still continues, ambitious but conservative showmen have contributed to an acceptance of the modified technique in the interests of success at national and international level, where this is more the norm, by exercising British restraint.

With regard to the matter of the length of rein many people will agree that a medium length neck, well set on to the shoulders and curved with a very fine throat, and an arch to the throat (the mitbah), *is much more desirable than a horse that just happens to have a long neck. The way that the Arabian is shown nowadays is to emphasise the shape of the neck rather than the length of it.*

*At the average show the horses appear in the ring and parade around the judge in a clockwise direction with the handlers on the outside. As with other breeds the judge is trying to spot the first four prize winners at this stage and they will be called in in this order. The distinguishing features that catch the eye will be a nice outline, a beautiful make and shape and essentially Arabian type. On closer examination the horses will be stood up for him in a way that suits that particular animal best. Some horses look better with a hind leg further back and some look better more compact. The judge will take note of condition, conformation and breed type. The horse will be asked to walk away from him so he can see the hind action, towards him to see the front movement, and then it will trot towards him, past him and round the back line to show the profile movement. As it goes away round the back the horse is allowed to extend further to give as good an extended trot as possible. As they go down the back straight the leader will give more and more rein to encourage the horse to float away on its extended trot, without interference from the handler who has just got to keep up. At this time the head will be up in the air with the tail held very high, flagged over the back if possible and looking very animated. Showing practices tend towards the conservative at County Show level and become more flamboyant and modern at breed show European qualifier level and more still at international level.*

## Disguising conformation defects

*Most strategies to minimise faults, once again, are beacons to most judges to watch for them, so are self defeating. Crooked lines going towards judges suggest something wrong with the forelegs and their action. If a horse turns a toe out or in, trotting a bit faster may disguise it, which is reasonable showmanship in the hands of someone who knows what suits his horse best, but what is guaranteed to irritate a judge is when a horse trots well towards him and then when level with him gallops past him apparently out of control until it reaches the corner and then miraculously trots correctly around the corner and on round the ring. This will almost certainly result in the horse being called back to do it properly, with the judge's eagle eye fixed on its action behind, especially if it is likely to win the class. Hind action is very difficult to influence in hand when you are really only controlling the head. Wide action is worse the faster you go, especially on a loose rein. If the horse is close moving behind then a fast trot on a loose rein will improve things.*

*Tack*

*Most horses are shown in a slip, which resembles the front part of a drop noseband without the chinstrap, and then a chain is threaded through the two rings to give a plain and simple effect. The amount of decoration and the degree of fineness of the bridle varies from handler to handler, and the type of head of the horse. It is hard to flatter a head with a bridle but what you can do is not to accentuate the faults. The ideal is to have the finest and lightest possible, without cutting the horse, so that the beauty of the head speaks for itself. If the horse is long from its eye to its nostril this distance needs to be divided in some way, so a broader noseband would be called for, placed higher up the head so that the distance is divided into two halves and this gives the impression of a shorter head than it actually is. However much is spent on a bridle the effect can be totally lost if the noseband is fitted too low over the nostrils.*

*The overriding principle is to have your horse looking its best. Some horses need to carry more weight than others and you have to know your horse and plan ahead over a long period of time, i.e. two or three months. Artificial production is against the spirit of showing, which is to breed a better next generation of horses. Artificially produced results interfere with this, by disguising the faults of breeding stock so that these faults are perpetuated.*

# CHAPTER FOURTEEN

# Showing Classes Based on Coat Colour

There are a number of showing classes based on coat colours, namely for Palomino, Coloured (Skewbald and Piebald), Spotted and Appaloosa, all of which have in-hand as well as ridden classes at the major shows and all of which are regulated by societies which register stock. Invariably to show in these classes your horse has to be registered with the relevant society, which usually involves inspection, so it is not as simple as merely being what you think is the right colour.

Having said that, the Appaloosa is a breed and not a colour. In Britain registration is controlled by the British Appaloosa Society according to criteria in harmony with the American society and the breed is dealt with in the chapter for American breeds because of its American origins. Confusion arises from the increasing use of the term 'Appaloosa coat colour' to describe colouring once referred to as 'spotted', but Appaloosas proper are bred from Appaloosa stock and the only permitted outcrosses nowadays are with Arabs, Quarter Horses and Thoroughbreds.

Appaloosa or spotted colouring may come from other outcrosses, however, some of which may be eligible for the British Spotted Pony Society which runs competitions for its own members. It caters for British-bred ponies, which may also be registered as native ponies, where appropriate.

While a defining feature for entry, colour is not always a criterion of the judging process, which may come as a surprise.

## PALOMINO

The Palomino is not a breed but a colour. A number of breed societies permit the registration of stock of this colour, such as the Welsh Pony and Cob, the New Forest and the Connemara Pony Societies, so their members have the option of belonging to two societies and competing in both sets of competitions. The American breeds like the Saddlebred, Morgan and Quarter Horse also have Palominos, so the number of options open to their members for competing in horse shows is quite considerable, what with Western and English riding classes, their own breed society shows, American all-breed shows and Palomino classes. Not all of them may be eligible for the British Palomino Society, which inspects horses and ponies for registration. The criteria for approval are explained below by the judge. The society runs its own shows for members, as well as classes at County Shows. The rules to be observed for these classes relate to the organisation regulating the show on the day in question.

## The judge's viewpoint

*To show off the colour properly you need light and sun. Apart from looking nicer on a sunny day, sunlight can fade the colour, which should be borne in mind when turning Palominos out. Ideally a Palomino should be the colour of a 'newly minted gold coin' which is actually quite rare, but in any case nothing like a washed out chestnut. Coat colour can change with the seasons, being lighter in the winter, and with age when the coat gradually darkens. For this reason a yearling can successfully challenge a mature horse but become less successful over time. In practice success boils down to the preference of the judge on the day.*

*The coat should be a good even colour with no dappling, which is a fault, although this would not prevent a horse from being registered with the British Palomino Society. There is a kind of black marking called 'thumb marks' [not to be confused with the indentations of the 'prophet's thumb mark' on the neck] and this is a fault also, which could put a horse down the line. Dark colouring is not good. White markings are not permitted above trace height and must not grow from pink skin, which is a reason for failing the inspection of the society, which is compulsory for all horses over a year old. Blue or wall eyes are not permitted. Horses are allowed to have up to 15 per cent dark hair in their manes and tails, which should be light coloured. Yearlings are sometimes uneven coloured.*

*Turnout*
*Generally speaking the turnout should conform to the standards of conventional British in-hand showing. For the handler this means a*

The Palomino should be the coloure of 'a newly minted gold coin' with no dappling, dark colouring or pink skin.

*sensible shirt worn with a hacking jacket or waistcoat and not shirt sleeves; for the horse an accepted in-hand bridle, perhaps with a light chain behind the jaw. I personally don't approve of Arab bridles which some people use on the partbred Arabs that compete. Colts are expected to be bitted, but not fillies.*

*All Palominos must be shown with a full mane and tail and unplaited. If they wre plaited they would not be judged. Because of the variety of competitions that the horses compete in which may require them to be plaited, pulling and trimming are permitted within reason, and tails may be cut off square at the bottom.*

*Show ring procedure*
*The procedure in the ring follows the conventional pattern of showing at County Shows. When they enter the ring you pick them out roughly according to the best colours and then examine them more closely for conformation and action. They must be able to move! The balance between colour and conformation is difficult to define but the final line up should show the best coloured animals at the top of the line and the worst conformation at the bottom.*

# COLOURED

There are two organisations that register coloured horses and ponies, the Coloured Horse and Pony Society (UK) and the British Skewbald and Piebald Association. Both register animals according to colour and not type, size or genes, but there are differences in the registration criteria of the two societies.

The coat colours that permit horses and ponies to be eligible for membership of the British Skewbald and Piebald Association are 'Piebald, which is black and white only, and Skewbald, which is white with any other colour, i.e. bay, brown, chestnut, grey, dun or palomino. There may be some black marks in addition.' The BSPA specifies that:

If a horse or pony only have white markings on head, legs, belly and/ or mane or tail in isolation, it cannot be considered as Skewbald or Piebald.

Clyde markings do not constitute a Skewbald or Piebald in isolation from other markings.

White colour must be distributed in patches not spots, and have even and regular demarcation lines. If a horse/pony has only one patch or spot of white it cannot be described as Skewbald or Piebald.

The overall distribution and evenness of colour, patterns and markings will contribute to the percentage marks awarded to colour and markings. Ideally an overall symmetry and evenness of colour and markings should be present, with a depth and vibrance of colour and tone, for example, black, bay, brown, chestnut, dun, palomino, lemon and white.

Skewbald and Piebald horses are distinct from other 'coloured' or 'odd coloured' horses and are unique and not to be confused with 'splash marks, roans or Appaloosas'...

We require judges to give favourable recognition within each category to a well-marked animal with good depth and clarity of colour (as above). Ideally the markings should be clearly defined, regular and symmetric.

Where judges struggle to separate entries for their placings on conformation, type characteristics and/or performance and manners, we suggest this aspect of our criteria is *then used to assist them.*

No horse/pony should ever be placed only on colour and markings. Conformation and type characteristics and manners must *always* take precedence.

Only in Best Colour Markings classes is colour or markings ever given precedence over conformation and type characteristics, manners and/or performance requirements.

The Coloured Horse and Pony Society (CHAPS) oversees competitions at County Shows in addition to organising its own shows for members. To compete at a County Show membership is not compulsory but winners of qualifiers for the National Coloured Championship Show, both entrant and horse/pony, must become members within fourteen days of qualifying to compete at the final. The society has precise definitions of what constitutes 'coloured' to which all competitors must conform:

## Definition of coloured

The definition of a 'coloured' animal is black and white (Piebald), white and any other colour, e.g. bay, roan, grey, chestnut etc. (Skewbald) with a minimum patch of *naturally* occurring white of 6 inches in diameter. This white patch *must* be on the body (above the level of the stifle and elbow). Any white markings below this do not qualify. Manes and tails may also be white, or have white in them. Appaloosas with white belly markings do not qualify.

Skewbald mare in a class of coloured horses.

## Colour markings

There are two recognised Colour patterns: Tobiano and Overo.

*Overo (O-viaro)*  An Overo appears to be a coloured horse with white markings, the spots of white appear to be jagged and originate on the animal's side or belly, spreading toward the neck, tail, legs and back. The colour appears to frame the white spots, thus, an Overo often has a dark tail, mane, legs and backline. Bald or white faces often accompany the overo pattern. Some Overos show white legs with splashy white markings seemingly made up of round lacey white spots. The location of white almost never crosses the back or top line.

*Tobiano (Toe-bee-ah'no)*  A Tobiano appears to be white with large spots of colour, often overlapping on animals with a greater percentage of colour than white. Spots of colour typically originate from the head, chest, flank and buttock, often including the tail. Legs are generally white, giving the appearance of a white horse with large or flowing spots of colour. Generally the white crosses the centre of the back between the withers and the tail.

# Exhibiting and showing guide

## Exhibits

1. No Palomino, Roan, Dun, Spotted or Appaloosa are permitted in affiliated classes. However, 'roaning' within a solid patch is acceptable.
2. Clipping, trimmed manes, tails and feathers are acceptable and should not be penalized. However, horses/ponies especially native and vanner types may be shown as natural as possible.
3. Wall/Blue/Glass eyes are acceptable.
4. Ridden classes are open to any horse/pony 4 years old and over unless otherwise stated.
5. All animals when shown shall be SOUND.

The Society literature defines the categories under which animals may be shown and the specific expectations regarding tack and turnout which follow the usual conventions of show schedules and rules. The one exception is that of vanner, which is 'Usually considered the traditional type of Tradesman's horse of pre-motor days. Of mixed breeding, active and capable of a good trot. Frequently have an upright shoulder, and may exceed 16 hh. Can be shown traditionally with full manes, feather and tails or pulled tails and hogged.'
With regard to the in-hand classes:

*Youngstock*

Open to horses/ponies, fillies, colts and geldings not exceeding three years old. May be shown in halter, leather headcollar or snaffle bridle.

*Broodmares*

May be shown as above, or in pelham or double bridle.

*Foals*

Exceeding three weeks old must only be shown in a halter or leather headcollar.

*Stallions and colts*

Two years old and over. Must be adequately bitted in a snaffle type bridle. Must be well mannered and under control at all times.

With regard to general turnout there are guidelines:

Cosmetic hoof varnish is to be discouraged. Tack of all classes should be either a simple snaffle, double bridle or pelham.

*Attire – In hand*

Smart jacket and trousers (cords, jodhpurs, slacks)
Shirt and tie
Hat/cap
Gloves
Suitable footwear – jodhpur boots/walking shoes etc.

As with the other breeds, types and colours, both organisations hold classes for members at their shows. There are a limited but increasing number of opportunities to show at County level.

## The viewpoint of the Coloured Horse and Pony Society's judge

*There is only one native breed that permits the registration of coloured ponies and that is the Shetland Pony Society, so these would be shown unplaited in natural condition. Cobs are shown with pulled tails and hogged manes, but everybody else shows with a plaited mane and the option of either a pulled or plaited tail. This means that there is also the option of quarter marks if suitable. Any ornamentation attracts the eye so this should only be used with good features unless you are clever enough to disguise bad ones. The same applies to just how far down the dock you pull or plait the tail. With good quarters the tail could be plaited right down the dock; if not then it is best left unplaited or just plaited part of the way down.*

*As regards tack a standard British in-hand showing bridle is used, with a coloured or brass browband providing it flatters the head. If there is too much white on the head or if the head is particularly attractive a coloured browband is better. If the head is a bit plain then you would try to draw the judge's eye away from this feature. The handler would also wear conventional in-hand showing clothes.*

*With coloured horses conformation is the priority, and action. You look for quality more than any particular type because there can be so many common coloured horses. The goal for the breeder is to produce a quality horse because it can be used to improve the rest.*

# SPOTTED PONIES

Unlike the Palominos and the Coloured horses and ponies, the British Spotted Pony Society exists to register spotted ponies of known breeding. As the society points out in its literature:

> These ponies are truly British. Not Appaloosas. There have been spotted ponies in the British Isles for many centuries. It is not known whether they were feral or came in about the time of the First Crusade. They appear in many illustrated manuscripts, old paintings and drawings and were obviously widely used both in peace and in war. The most common size seems to have been a sturdy cob of about 14 hands.

Although the British Spotted Horse and Pony Society was formed in 1946 to register and help conserve them in this country, it split in 1976 and the British Spotted Pony Society now caters for the registration and encouragement of the breeding of ponies up to 14.2 hh. There is a temporary entry scheme for ponies of unknown or unregistered breeding which conform to the required breed characteristics which are as follows:

## General character

A quality pony with adequate bone and substance, hardy and active with real pony character of small, riding or cob type, up to and including 14.2 hh.

212

## Breed characteristics

All ponies MUST display some or all of the following:

White sclera round the eye.

Mottled skin. This part dark, part pink skin is usually most evident around the genitals, lips, muzzle, eyes and inside the ears.

Striped hooves.

*Colour*

*Leopard.* Spots of any colour on a white or light coloured background.

*Few spot leopard.* White base coat with only a few spots. Strong characteristics often accompanied by varnish marks (groupings of dark hairs within an area, usually nose, cheekbones, stifle, gaskin and knee).

*Snowflake.* White spots on a dark base coat. This colour can appear almost roan but must show strong characteristics, and often has varnish marks which distinguish it from an ordinary roan.

*Blanket.* An area of white over hips and hind quarters with or without spots. Any base colour. The blanket can extend over the entire back and shoulders.

Piebald and skewbald markings of any kind are not eligible. Solid colours are eligible for a separate Register but must be of proven spotted breeding, and preferably show some breed characteristics.

HEAD  Full of quality and true pony character. Big bold eyes set well apart. Ears should be well placed, small, neat and in proportion to the head. Prominant, open nostrils. Clean, well defined throat. A coarse head and Roman nose are to be discouraged.

NECK  Should have good length and be well carried. Moderately lean in mares but inclined to be more cresty in stallions. Slightly heavier neck is allowable in the cob type.

SHOULDERS  Good strong, sloping and well laid back. Withers should be well defined but not 'knifey'.

FORELEGS  Should be set square and true. Not tied in at the elbow. Long strong forearms with well developed knee. Short flat bone below knee. Pasterns of proportionate length and slope. Well shaped dense hooves. The cob type should have a greater abundance of bone without coarseness and a moderate quantity of fine feather when in the rough.

213

BODY  Muscular, strong, well coupled with plenty of heart room. Good deep girth and well sprung ribs.

HIND QUARTERS  Lengthy, strong, well muscled, not ragged or drooping, with well set on tail. Slightly finer in riding type.

HIND LEGS  Well let down hocks, large flat clean bone, prominent points. The hock not to be set behind a line from the point of quarter to fetlock joint. No sickle or cow hocks. Pasterns to be of proportionate length and slope. Hooves well shaped and dense.

ACTION  Low, straight, from the shoulder free flowing. Hocks well flexed with straight action coming well under the body. The cob type may show more knee action.

# Showing the spotted pony

The Society organises a national show where Mountain and Moorland judges officiate, the championships being decided by a points system awarded by all the judges of the day's classes.

## Presentation

The turnout and procedure of showing follow the customs of other pony breeds. Exhibitors can decide if they wish to plait or not according to the usual factors, including the thickness of the mane. Stallions tend not to be plaited but competitors in ridden classes usually are. Many of the bigger spotted ponies have sparse manes and tails whereas the smaller ponies of Welsh or Shetland descent have thicker ones which look better unplaited.

Trimming must be minimal, so the long hair under the chin and sticking out of the ears may be trimmed but no other cosmetic clipping or trimming is permitted. In times past Welsh breeders used to clip under the neck and the front of the face to accentuate the neck and the dish face but this is now banned.

*Opposite* A Spotted Pony stallion.

# CHAPTER FIFTEEN

# European Breeds

Since the Second World War, and especially during the last 25 years, there has been a significant influx to Britain of breeds from abroad. They have brought with them their own methods of showing, not only to show off their unique features but as a reflection of the methods employed in their countries of origin. This is partially a consequence of breeders wishing to breed stock that are eligible for membership of the parent breed society. The more firmly established breeds now have British-based breed societies to regulate standards which maintain close links with the parent society by using the same systems of assessment, including inviting judges from the country of origin to judge at the breed shows.

In practical terms every aspect of the showing process can vary from the British system, such as tack, turnout, handler's dress, numbers of judges and procedure in the ring. Each breed has its own tradition but in the main the European breeds rely on a system which has several judges marking each animal independently of each other as it demonstrates its gaits individually in a precisely defined manner. Each animal obtains a score against an ideal score for the breed, the highest cumulative score winning the competition.

The breeds covered in this chapter are those with shows and classes available, or planned, as in the case of the Caspian which, virtually extinct in its country of origin, has become a European breed. The Warmbloods, whose administration is based on the identification of the area in which they are foaled, share not only genetic roots in many cases, but also the same system of evaluation, and are represented here by the Trakehner.

## THE CASPIAN

It is, as yet, too early for the Caspian to have its own classes at mainstream horse shows but as their establishment is considered a

## Official breed profile

HEIGHT   Normally between 10.2 and 12.2 hands, averaging 11.3 hands.

COLOUR   Bay, grey, roan and chestnut, sometimes black or cream.

HEAD   Wide, vaulted forehead and deep cheekbones in a short, fine head that tapers to a small muzzle. Large, almond shaped and often prominent dark eyes. Nostrils large and set low.

EARS   Short, wide-apart, alert and finely drawn, often noticeably in-turned at the tips.

LIMBS   Slender, with strong dense flat bone and little or no feathering at the fetlocks.

HOOVES   Oval, neat and immensely strong. Often with small frog.

GENERAL APPEARANCE   A well-bred, elegant horse in miniature, with a fine silky coat, mane and tail. Tail carried gaily in action.

TEMPERAMENT   Highly intelligent, alert, kind and willing. Most Caspians are 'characters'.

ACTION AND PERFORMANCE   The Caspian has a natural floating action at all gaits; a long, low, swinging trot, smooth, rocking canter and rapid, flat gallop.

priority by the society, the information they will be based on is made available here.

## The history of the Caspian

The location of the Caspian pony is in one small area between the Elburz Mountains of Iran and the southern shores of the Caspian Sea. There is evidence that small, high quality ponies were sent as gifts to the ancient Kings of Persia. They were highly prized by King Darius the Great, who depicted horses of similar size and type both on his official Seal and on the huge stone staircase at his palace in Persepolis.

Now almost extinct in its native land, the Caspian survived either as a feral animal or as a working pony, escaping the coarse, Mongolian blood of other ponies in the area. Blood-typing has proved that there is a distinct link between the Caspian and the Arab horse.

In 1965, a stud was formed in Iran to re-establish the Caspian as a breed. Small numbers of foundation and first-generation stock were exported to the UK and subsequently to Australia and New Zealand.

Scientific research suggests that the Caspian is the oldest equine breed, and quite possibly the ancestor of the Arab horse that it predates by about 3000 years. Certainly the earliest domestication of the horse, as a species, was undertaken by the nomadic Aryan tribes of the Steppes bordering the Caspian Sea.

The Caspian possesses a number of quite unique conformation features, such as an extra molar in the upper jaw, a uniquely shaped scapula, and, most strikingly, a rounded or vaulted forehead. Although called a pony it is in fact a miniature horse with all that offers in comfort to the rider, and additionally has an extraordinary jumping ability.

## Showing the Caspian pony – breed society hints

Caspians should be shown untrimmed, in full mane and tail, which should be dense, fine and silky. Of course, if showing in ordinary pony [ridden] classes this entails plaiting so some tidying up is permissible; however, for pure Caspian classes the pony should be shown as close to natural as possible. Feathering should be minimal or non-

The Caspian, whose features include a vaulted forehead and straight knees as well as a kind temperament.

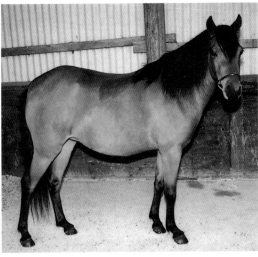

existent. Partbreds may be shown plaited or natural, but in practice most are plaited.

Having had a mountainous habitat over a long period of time, the Caspian has the skeletal structure normally associated with this terrain – sloping quarters, tendency to closeness behind, etc.; however, these tendencies should not be excessive. They will only expect to be shod if doing a lot of driving – their hard flat bone and hard feet being another product of their environment.

In many ways the method of showing the Caspian pony is similar to the Connemara, in that they are both native breeds and shown in natural condition, but because of their versatility concessions are made to the turnout requirements of other competitions. In-hand tack should aim to flatter the quality of the head and there are no formal rules about the style of bridles. Handlers dress in the usual manner for British showing.

# THE HAFLINGER

As the Haflinger Society of Great Britain explain in their literature:

Halflingers were first imported into Great Britain in the 1960s. They were the native ponies from the Alpine farms of Austria and have a long history on the continent. In the South Tyrol, where the breed originated, stallions have been registered for nearly one hundred years, and organised breeding by a government department has been in operation for more than fifty years. The breed was established by crossing the native Tyrolean pony with Arab blood brought back from the continental wars with the Turks – the result was a combination of native hardiness with spirit and elegance. They are now well established in many different countries in all five continents.

## The judge's viewpoint

*Inspectors are now going for selective breeding, which means increasingly a variety of type depending on the older or newer types sought. During the First World War in Austria animals were wanted for meat and for pulling so they bred from shorter stockier animals – about 12–13 hands – which was the type in the 1920s, 1930s and 1940s and which we see today, although the Haflinger used to be about 14–15 hands high. Now things are swinging the other way and breeding and selection are favouring the bigger animals again. There are height restrictions, although in the very near future I think that this is going*

## Official breed profile

These are the Inspection Standards as laid down by the World Haflinger Federation:

HEAD   Short, with slight dish, large dark and lively eyes, fine nostrils, small, pliable ears.

NECK   Strong, well-positioned and not too short, suitable for a riding pony.

BODY   Broad and deep chest, well-tensed back, broad loins with good joints, a muscular croup that is not too short, and a well-carried tail.
  Deep girth which should measure 67–75 inches, 170–190.5 cm.

LIMBS   Clean with hard, healthy hooves. Strong fore-arms and a good second thigh, short cannons.

BONE   Mare 6¾–7¾ inches, 17–19.6 cm.
     Stallion 7¼–9 inches, 18.4–22.8 cm.

HEIGHT AT 3 YEARS   Mares 134–147 cm (13.1–14.2 hh)
          Colts 140–149 cm (13.3–14.2½ hh)

COLOUR   Chestnut: Light, Middle, Liver, Red.

MANE AND TAIL   Flaxen. Red or grey is unacceptable.
White star, blaze or stripe is permissible. White on the body or limbs is not encouraged but will not bar registration.

*to change again. They are now being bred with longer necks, more sloping shoulders and more daylight under the belly. This is quite controversial. They are slow maturing so a filly can be quite gangly but will mature into a beautiful mare.*

*I am very hot on conformation and cannot bear to see beautiful animals bred from which close examination shows to move too close or with cow hocks. I like to see a judge pick up a horse's tail. I also like to see them give the handlers the opportunity to stand the horse up again if there is any difficulty choosing between two animals.*

*On the head you look for a neat small muzzle and lovely dished head with very wide eyes. On a stallion you automatically get a different head with a heavier jowl. I like to go for a good horse first*

The Haflinger mare and foal showing the lovely dished head, wide eyes and neat small muzzle.

*and type second, because at the end of the day the Haflinger has to have all the qualities of a good horse. I look for quality. I don't like an unmannerly horse that bites and kicks in the show ring because this is so rare in the breed. The head can be important in the Haflinger because you have to be able to look at it, and I look for a good kind eye as a mark of good temperament which is common in the breed, not a piggy eye. The legs have got to be correctly set and carried under the body because the body is heavy, so they must not be set like the legs on a table. You want the horse to move from the shoulder, otherwise being so wide chested you would end up with a duck waddle! Everything has to flow when the horse is moving and carrying himself correctly with the head at the right angle. They have to be fairly athletic.*

## Training

*I personally don't lunge but prefer to long rein, sending the horse forward, which I think can balance a horse just as well and is more natural. I think long reining is easier for a shorter necked animal as the Haflinger has to be to carry the depth of chest that it has. The neck*

The Haflinger stallion.

need not be ugly and you can still get a decent length of rein, however.

Nowadays we are looking for a multi-purpose animal. At one time the shoulder used to be fairly straight, and this was not considered a defect because the horse was pulling from the shoulder, but this can shorten the stride and is not so comfortable for a riding horse, although efficient in harness. The Haflinger gait is the trot. The walk is not a good walk out, although it can be improved with training, but naturally they are a docile, quiet breed and they don't walk out particularly well. They have to be encouraged to track up.

### Show ring presentation
The Haflinger is shown unplaited and the tail is not pulled. A certain amount of trimming is allowed, like behind the jaw, the whiskers round the muzzle and the edge of the ears, but it really isn't necessary. Not trimming would not stop you winning; bathing and grooming is really all you need.

### Tack
They are very strong but listen to the voice more quickly than anything and don't need weighing down with lots of equipment. For the show ring we found that the traditional Haflinger bridle did not flatter their heads, because the leatherwork was too thick and heavy. There are no hard and fast rules about this although colts need to have bits because

*they can be very strong. Haflingers need a fairly strong showing bridle, however, with thick sides to balance the strength of the head, so you may have to have one made.*

## Clothes
*There are no fixed rules and although ladies have been seen in Austrian clothes most people follow English conventions. [British men will probably be relieved they don't have to wear lederhosen!]*

## Faults and how to help them
*Faults that you have to watch out for are badly set front legs that are too wide apart and prevent the horse from carrying itself properly. The way to help this is not to let them carry too much fat, which improves their balance. They can also be cow hocked and move wide behind, but if you have to slow them down at the trot you might as well forget showing them because the trot is so important to the breed.*

## Show ring procedure
*At the breed show foreign judges are invited to judge and the procedure follows the European format. All the exhibitors are paraded in front of the judge in single file and then leave the ring. They are then brought back individually and stood up for the judge with all four feet square. The head has to be carried naturally and not artificially positioned. The handler is then expected to keep out of the judge's line of vision as he examines the horse from all angles. The horse is seen from the side that the mane hangs over and is also seen on the side without the mane. If the mane is split and hangs over both sides the handler is then expected to place the mane on one side so that the judge can see the line of the neck. Sometimes the handler is asked to turn the horse round and stand it up again for this purpose. The judge then stands outside a marked triangular track at one of the points and the horse is walked away from him to the second point, trotted in front of him to the third point and then trotted back towards him.*

*Other than at the breed show they are usually shown in mixed Mountain and Moorland classes following the usual Mountain and Moorland procedure, although these can be difficult classes to win, because of the popularity of the Welsh breeds which is a shame because the Haflinger is a fantastic horse but not well known enough. They are extremely kind and cooperative and keen to please. They are very versatile and can carry a disabled child one minute and a man the next, and are very economical to keep.*

# THE ICELANDIC

## Official breed profile

This is an extract from the FEIF (the International Federation of Icelandic Horse Associations) Breeding standard for Icelandic Horses:

The Icelandic Horse is bred for use, not for show. Highest priority is given to its rideability. It must be courageous and resourceful, cooperative and willing, with good forward action. Its typical robustness must always be preserved. It is easy to keep and should be of flawless disposition.

The Icelandic Horse is an extremely versatile riding horse for adults and is, under certain circumstances, also suitable as a children's horse. It can be used for long distance riding as well as five-gaited competition, as a family horse as well as in dressage.

The horse must possess at least four gaits. In addition to the normal gaits of walk, trot and canter/gallop, it must also have tølt (running walk, slow gait, single foot or rack). The fifth gait, 'flugskeid' or flying pace, is very highly valued but not always present.

The horse should be somewhat rectangular and well proportioned. The head must be clean cut and expressive, the neck long, supple and well set, so that the horse carries itself well balanced when ridden. The shoulder should be comparatively long and well angled, the back flexible and the croup sloping and well muscled. The limbs must be strong with well defined joints.

The horse must give an impression of courage and power, with a proud and attentive expression, especially when ridden.

The ideal size lies between 12.3 and 13.1 hands measured at the highest point of the withers, although horses may vary considerably in size and type. Commonly mares are between 12 and 13.2 hands, and stallions/geldings between 13 and 14.2 hands. All colours and markings are allowed.

When evaluating an Icelandic breeding horse, 40 per cent of the score derives from its conformation and 60 per cent from its rideability (action as well as disposition and other psychological traits of importance in a riding horse). An Icelandic Horse can therefore not be evaluated before it has been correctly trained. The Icelandic is a slow developing breed with a long working life (25–30 years is not unusual) so the horse should not begin training until it is five years of age.

As the Icelandic Horse Society of Great Britain explain in their literature:

The Icelandic horse is considered to be the only breed which has been bred pure, without any outside blood, for almost 1000 years. When the Vikings settled Iceland they took with them horses from Western Norway and the British Isles. These animals formed the basis of the breed and the horses of today are virtually the same as those original Viking horses. Importation after 1100 AD was forbidden in order to keep Iceland free of disease. Even today, no horse leaving the country, for instance, to compete in a European Championship, may ever return!

Because of this isolation in such a harsh environment, the breed is extremely robust, healthy and sure-footed, intelligent, good natured and able to take care of itself, and, unlike most other breeds, it has kept the gaits of tølt and pace, which were highly thought of in past ages. The horse has figured largely in the history of Iceland, and even earlier, one reads of famous horses in legends of the Gods and in the great Sagas, alongside the names of famous men. These same names are still given to horses of today. The country could hardly have been settled without the horse. He has carried everything needed for existence: hay, wood, building materials, wool, fish and supplies, and even coffins to the grave. He has followed the Icelandic people down through the centuries and shared in all the hardships endured by them, particularly after the volcanic eruptions, when the land was covered with ash, and nothing would grow. People and horses died in their thousands from starvation, and it took years of struggle to recover. With no roads or bridges the horse was the only means of transport over ice and snow, rocks and lava, sand deserts and raging rivers. Even today a high proportion of Icelanders own horses even in the towns. There are 45 Horse Clubs and everywhere one meets folk riding, often with one or two horses on the side. They will usually be seen gliding along in the tølt, that most famous gait of the Icelandic.

A breed society representative adds:

The horses which are judged at an Icelandic breeding show are those at the very top of a rigorous selection system which is unique to Europe, and probably much of the rest of the world.

In Iceland, selection starts at birth. The mares foal outside without assistance. If anything goes wrong, which is rare, both mother and foal may well die. The breeding stock and youngsters live out throughout the year. During the winter months they are fed on hay or silage, and have free access to barrels of salted herring, which they eat when they need the protein. Not only do the horses have to survive an inhospitable climate, they also have to cope with natural disasters. After the eruption in 1783 the horse population fell from 32,000 to 8,600, mainly due to the poisoning of the ground by the falling ash.

Iceland is unsuited to the rearing of beef cattle. The Icelandic horse was indispensable for transport, until recently in Iceland, but also very important for food. This means that the horses which survive nature's tough conditions then have to survive man's no less rigorous selection procedure. Horses with bad temperaments (biters and kickers), and which are no fun to ride (e.g. lazy or nappy individuals), end up in the pot.

## Showing the Icelandic horse

Although the Icelandic is bred for use and not show, breeding stock have to be evaluated and this is, after all, the real reason for in-hand showing competitions the world over. The difference is that the

The Icelandic horse has to be ridden to be evaluated but not 'beautified'. The unusual design of saddle is traditional but not compulsory. Note also the clips attaching the reins to the bit.

Icelandic is usually only evaluated once in this way, unless the owner thinks they can improve on their score which stays with the horse for its lifetime. As the breed society points out:

> the evaluation cannot take place until the horse has been trained to a level that can give a true idea of its ability – usually between 5 and 8 years of age.

This cuts out all the complications of immature stock not showing their potential or competing against more mature animals. These evaluations may take place at a breeding show and involve the services of three internationally accepted judges. Sometimes they confer and give one mark, sometimes they judge independently and the final mark given is the mean of their individual marks.

This is the only time that Icelandic horses are ever judged in hand at any time in their lives, and even then it is only part of an overall assessment of ability. As it is so important to the future use of the horse it is dealt with here in some depth.

## Breed society guidelines for presentation

Icelandic Horses should never have their manes or tails pulled or plaited. Most have very long, thick manes which help give them their special character; if they get over-long then they should be trimmed with scissors. In Iceland it is very rare to clip the horses because they are not worked from October to January, and if they get very sweaty after work, they will be put in a large enclosed barn to dry before being turned out. Of course in this country it is sometimes necessary, but a simple bib clip usually suffices.

Other society literature describes the standards of turnout and the evaluation criteria:

## Turnout

The horse should be clean and tidy, but with no artificial 'beautifying' treatment. The mane and tail may be trimmed if too long to be practical, and it is generally considered to be more beautiful when the mane is on both sides of the horse's neck.

An ordinary snaffle bridle, or Icelandic curb may be used. Any standard kind of saddle, with or without crupper, is permissible. Lightweight overreach boots may be used when showing fast tölt and pace.

227

Horses must be shod equally all round, with no thicker than 8 mm shoes.

The rider should look tidy, but may wear what he likes. Jacket and tie, with white jodhpurs and long boots are common, but it is quite all right to wear a sweatshirt and coloured jodhpurs. It is the *horse* that is being judged. Hard hats are optional, depending on the custom of the country in which the show takes place.

# Procedure

Horses are shown individually, and are presented to the judges four times:

1. Horses are measured with a tape, stick and calipers:

| *Tape* | *Average* |
|---|---|
| Height to the withers | 140–150 cm |
| Girth | approx. 160 cm |
| Knee circumference | 27–32 cm |
| Cannon bone circumference | 9–12 cm less than knee |

| *Stick* | |
|---|---|
| Height to withers | 128–140 cm |
| Height to the saddle dip | as above less 7–10 cm |
| Height to the croup | within 2 cm of wither height |
| Depth of chest (½ × stick height less 5 cm) | 60–62 cm |
| Length of body | approx. 3–10 cm longer than height |

| *Calipers* | |
|---|---|
| Width of chest | not less than 35 or more than 40 cm |
| Width of hips | 45–50 cm, no wider than 50 cm |
| Width of hip joints | no more than 5 cm less than above |
| Difference between hip and chest widths | 7–10 cm |

For height measurements only the tape measurement is 8–9 cm longer than the stick measurement, because the tape follows the contours of the body more closely.

All the above measurements are guidelines only to the ideal conformation as part of the overall assessment of the Icelandic horse.

The process of measuring provides an opportunity for the disposition and character to be assessed at close quarters. The girth measurement gives an indication of the chest and lung capacity but can be masked by the general condition of the horse.

2. Horses are judged for *conformation*. They stand still, and are then asked to walk (and occasionally trot) in hand so the judges can assess straightness of movement.

3. Horses are *ridden*, usually up and down a straight track. The rider chooses in which order he shows the gaits, and may continue until he feels the horse has shown all gaits to the best of his ability.

4. One or more of the *judges will ride* the horse to assess its temperament, willingness to go forward and its desire to cooperate with the rider's wishes.

## Judging the Icelandic horse

It is obvious from the above that there is no place here for ringcraft of any description and that a lot of effort has gone into precise definition of the features of the breed and their identification. On the few occasions when they are assessed time is not of the essence and optical illusions unimportant and exposed as such.

To summarise some of the many features looked for by the judges, horses are preferred that have powerful joints and slim, dry forearms with oval cannon bones. Heads may be concave but convex foreheads are not desired, although slighty convex noses are permitted. Jawbones should be well defined with room for a fist between them (8–10 cm) and strong enough to deal with rough fodder. Nostrils should be wide and thin-skinned. The body must be rectangular, so stick height must not be the same as body length. The height at the croup should not exceed the height at the withers; if it does the horse is described as overbuilt. Stallions are expected to be bigger and stronger than mares but not overbuilt.

As the British representative of FEIF explains:

*Horses are awarded marks out of ten for the following categories on a scale of 5–10, with 7.5 regarded as being the standard desired of an averagely good horse. In Iceland animals are only entered in the stud book if they have been judged and received a minimum mark, which is 7.5 for mares and 7.75 for stallions. Each category has a factor by which the mark is multiplied, depending on how important that particular category is perceived to be. The weighting of the categories is not the same in all the FEIF countries, as some countries perceive certain categories as being more important than others. The factors may also be changed from time to time, if it is felt that more emphasis should be put on improving a certain feature of the horse at a certain time.*

*The table [over] shows the different categories for which marks are awarded, and the factors by which the mark is multiplied under the FEIF international system, and in Iceland. This is just for interest.*

| Category | FEIF | Iceland |
|---|---|---|
| *Conformation (40%)* | | |
| Head | 4 | 4 |
| Neck/shoulders | 6 | 6 |
| Back/croup | 6 | 6 |
| Legs | 5 | 5 |
| Straightness | 6 | 6 |
| Hooves | 5 | 5 |
| Proportions | 8 | 8 |
| *Under saddle (60%)* | | |
| Walk | 6 | 0 |
| Trot | 6 | 8 |
| Tølt | 10 | 20 |
| Pace | 8 | 10 |
| Canter/gallop | 6 | 6 |
| Willingness | 10 | 12 |
| Disposition | 8 | 8 |
| General impression | 6 | 6 |

*A horse which has been judged ends up with a mark for conformation, one for its performance under saddle, and then an overall mark. It is this final mark which counts, although in some countries a stallion which receives less than 7 for any one category may not be used for breeding.*

# THE IRISH DRAUGHT HORSE

The Irish Draught horse was the multi-purpose farm horse of the traditional Irish farmer and was equally adept at ploughing a small acreage, turning hay, taking the milk to the creamery, taking the family to church and on social outings and, on its 'day off', taking the farmer hunting. In addition to all this the farm mare made a vital contribution to the economy of the small farm by producing a foal each year which was sold, often to foreign buyers. Crossed with a Thoroughbred stallion the Irish Draught horse gave the world the famous and highly prized 'Irish Hunter', renowned for its good sense, intelligence and phenomenal jumping ability. This same combination produced the international show jumper, and Irish-bred halfbreds have been at the forefront of modern international competitions since their inception, although more often under the flags of other countries. The same is true of the second cross, that is the halfbred crossed again with the Thoroughbred, which can always be found at the top levels of three-day eventing.

For this reason Irish Draughts were always bred to ride as well as drive and so, unusually for farm horses, were expected to have riding horse conformation. Often the only horse kept on a farm, they had to stay sound and be economical to keep, and as they were frequently cared for by children were expected to be, and are still, exceptionally good tempered and gentle.

In the past these horses were much in demand for the armies of Europe where they were eventually assimilated into the breeding programmes. Most notably halfbred Draughts formed part of the foundation stock of the Hanoverian and so influenced the modern warmbloods.

Their performance in the First World War led to the official recognition of the breed in 1917 and the publication of Volume I of the Irish Draught Horse Book in 1918, although they had first been registered by the Irish Department of Agriculture in 1907. All breeding stock have been inspected and subjected to stringent veterinary examination since those early days and where once they were tried and tested by the rigours of Irish rural life they now participate in formal performance testing to European breed society standards. Considered the mainstay of the Irish non-Thoroughbred performance horse industry they are bred all over the world including Britain, the USA, Australia and New Zealand.

## Showing the Irish Draught

As one would expect with such a pedigree the Irish Draught is shown in exactly the same way as the hunter at breed shows, although quarter marks are unnecessary. Potential breeding Irish Draughts should not have their legs trimmed for inspections, but do when competing in hunter and cob classes. There are a number of specialist classes nationally, as well as the breed shows.

## The judge's viewpoint

*As the horses enter the ring I like to watch each horse walk in turn over the same area of the track. At this point I note which horses are attractive and 'fill the eye'. I ask myself 'are they free movers', that is, loose and elastic and tracking up? Are they free, swinging and relaxed*

## Official breed profile

TYPE AND CHARACTER   The Irish Draught Horse is an active short-shinned powerful horse with substance and quality. Standing over a lot of ground he is proud of bearing, deep of girth, strong of back, loins and quarters. He has an exceptionally strong and sound constitution and is known for his intelligent and gentle nature and good sense. Height at 3 years old, stallions 16.0 hh and over, mares from 15.2 hh with 9 inches or more of clean flat bone.

HEAD   Good bold eyes set well apart, wide forehead and long, well-set ears. Head should be generous and pleasant, not coarse or hatchet headed. The jaw bones should have enough room to take the gullet and allow ease of breathing.

SHOULDERS, NECK AND FRONT   Shoulders should be clean-cut and not loaded. Withers well defined, not coarse. The neck set in high and carried proudly showing a good length of rein. The chest should not be too broad and beefy. The forearms large and generous, set near the ground. The cannon bone or shin short and straight with plenty of clean flat bone. Being back of the knee (calf-kneed) is forbidden in stallions and most undesirable in mares, i.e. should not slope forward from knee to fetlock. The bone never round or coarse, the legs should be clean and hard with a little silky hair at the back of the fetlock as a necessary protection. In winter the legs may become 'woolly' but never should the hair be stiff and coarse and at no time grown down the front of the hoof. The pasterns strong and in proportion, not short and upright nor long and weak. Hooves should be hard and sound, not large and flat like a carthorse, nor boxy or contracted and there should be plenty of room at the heel.

BACK, HIND QUARTERS, BODY AND HIND LEGS   The back strong and girth deep with strong loins and quarters, not forgetting the mares must have enough room to carry a foal. The croup to buttocks to be long and gently sloping, not short and rounded or flat topped. Hips not wide and plain, the upper thighs very powerful and at least as wide from the back view as the hips. The second thighs long and broad and powerful like forearm and well-developed. The hocks sound and generous and like the knees set into a good short shin. Hocks should not be too wide apart or close together. They must not be bent or weak in any way but should be in a line with the

---

buttocks to the heel. The cannon bone short and strong like the front leg or shin and not sloping forward or weak.

ACTION   Smooth and free but without exaggeration and not heavy and ponderous. Walk and trot straight and true with good flexion of the hocks and freedom of the shoulders.

COLOUR   Any strong whole colour including greys. Obvious Clydesdale markings not permitted, i.e. bay with white legs above the hocks and knees.

---

*as they walk round? After I have watched them, and made a mental note of each, I sometimes take the opportunity to see them trot on the circle, one at a time over my chosen ground. When judging Draughts I like to see slightly more knee action than with hunters, but the length of the stride must be even with no 'choppiness', and the movement made right through the shoulder, not from the elbow. Handlers should be encouraged to allow the horse to trot on and not restrict the stride otherwise the proper action cannot be seen, particularly the action of the hind leg.*

*The horses are then pulled in and lined up in their preliminary order. At this stage it helps to take a breath and concentrate particularly hard because this is when handlers are seeking to gain the advantage by using a little ringcraft. They try very hard to gain the judge's attention and eclipse the opposition. The horses are then drawn out individually and it is only then that the closest examination of conformation can take place.*

*An Irish Draught should stand squarely on well-kept, open feet that are in proportion to its size and bone, with flinty hard hooves. The pastern can be slightly shorter than in a Thoroughbred, and perhaps very slightly steeper, but the angle to the foot must be correct and certainly not upright. Cannon bones both fore and hind must be short with knees and hocks close to the ground. All joints should be of good size with no enlargements, giving a look of strength, as in a well-made piece of furniture. The amount of bone should be in proportion to the top of the animal. Forearms and gaskins must be strong and muscular with free elbows. Elbows and stifle should be equidistant from the ground. The angle of the hock and elbow should suggest spring and cadence in the stride.*

*An Irish Draught head should not be small and ponyish, nor as refined as a Thoroughbred, but must show quality with a kind and generous eye, and plenty of room between the jaw bones. The head should be set on to a neck that is well shaped and convex with a clearly defined neck and chest. One must not appear to merge with the other.*

*The withers should be well defined, giving the horse a narrow place for the saddle to fit. It is a great help to imagine a well-fitting saddle on the back of the horse. This gives a good indication of the angle of the shoulder, and of the length of the back. A deep shoulder will always put the saddle position well back and the girth groove will appear far behind the elbow. The area between the apparent back of the imaginary saddle and the line between the hips must be as short as possible. The depth of the horse should be the same from the girth to the flank, that is, the bottom of the rib cage should be as level as possible [so that the horse is not herring gutted], and there should be as little room as possible between the last rib and the hind leg.*

*Quarters should be well-rounded but not apple-shaped. They must be long from the point of the hip backwards, with the tail set not too*

The Irish Draught, in effect the heavyweight hunter, is shown as a hunter. Although not common, quarter marks are worn here and their effect can be judged.

*low, although a slight slope to the tail head is not too great a fault if the quarters are strong. When viewed from behind the hind quarters should be massive and muscular, as well as being wider at the second thigh than across the hips.*

*I stand back and take a look at the animal as a whole. It should be strong, deep and standing square. One way to see if a horse is balanced is to look first at the top half, and then just the limbs, and then compare the two to see if they match each other. You can do this with each end, fore and hind, separately too. If each part matches up you have a well-balanced and well-proportioned horse in front of you.*

*When each horse is walked in a straight line away from you, the fore and hind limbs and feet have to move straight and in line. Any deviation from what ought to be two parallel lines is undesirable and a weakness. At the trot some handlers tend to slow down as they go past the judge, when they should, if anything, go slightly faster to make the most of the stride, and take advantage of the main opportunity the judge has to see it.*

*One of the problems the Draught had in the past was a poor front leg and a tendency to be back at the knee. This has been helped considerably by the grading procedure for breeding stock and especially stallions, and I would look carefully for this. Draughts generally have very good, sound feet, which are broad, open and round, unlike many warmbloods.*

*A good Irish Draught mare is like a good heavyweight hunter mare, for which there are very few classes and few opportunities for the public to see them. Middle and lightweight hunter mares tend more towards the Thoroughbred type. The main difference between the Irish Draught and the show hunter is that the Irish Draught is slightly shorter in the leg, and in particular below the knee. Here they are shorter to the ground but they are not shorter in the forearm which should be more muscled. Irish Draughts generally carry more muscle than most hunters. In youngstock classes the Irish Draught may be less mature in its growth than one with more Thoroughbred blood, but this is quite acceptable, because the Irish Draught is not fully grown until six at the earliest, whereas the Thoroughbred, which races at two, is mature at four.*

*They are turned out like hunters. I think a well-fitting clean bridle is better than one with lots of brass buckles which can be a distraction. The goal is to be workmanlike, not flashy, and you try to take the eye away from the bad points and do nothing in the way of tack or turnout to distract the eye from the good ones. Heels should not need trimming because the Irish Draught does not grow feather, just a little hair around the ergot. Any tendency to hairiness can be groomed out. If I see a Draught with trimmed heels it makes me look much closer to see if coarseness has been disguised.*

# THE LUSITANO

It is quite recently, and then only in some areas, that differences are recognised between the Purebred Spanish Horse (Andalusian) and the Lusitano, the indigenous Portuguese horse, or to give it its other names, the Lusitano Andalusian, the Lusitanian, the Portuguese Iberian or the Iberian horse. It is not always possible to tell the two Iberian breeds apart. The main difference is the paperwork of the pedigrees, although near the border of the two countries there is some overlap with Portuguese horses with Spanish pedigrees and vice versa (see p. 242).

For those concerned with the issue of performance testing, an interesting explanation for the similarity of horses bred in two different countries, albeit with a shared frontier, is the continuing demands for horses with the abilities required for cattle ranching and, in both countries, the bull ring. Performance scores, and consequently breeding values, since Neolithic times right up to the present moment are the difference between the quick and the dead!

With both breeds, although stringent inspection standards regulate the registration of breeding stallions, there is an enduring 'macho' tradition of retaining rejected stallions uncastrated, for riding, and it is an expectation of the breed that the temperament is acceptable for this. To the uninitiated it is easy to see the appeal of these horses which seem to embody the most romantic and powerful qualities. To attend one of the breed shows is to encounter the drama and the passion of Hispanic culture evidenced by flaring nostrils and bold romantic eyes.

The Lusitano Breed Society in its literature argues that some breeders are moving away from the old-fashioned war horse image of the typical Lusitano and Andalusian, and therefore we are beginning to see Spanish horses with a more delicate head, and longer, more streamlined body conformation. The Lusitano, thanks to the necessity to breed a functional horse to work with cattle or in the bullring, which is still of prime importance in Portugal, has remained essentially as a handy combat horse, easy to manipulate, quick to turn and full of courage, once the chosen mount of kings and classical riding masters.

They maintain, in other words, that the Purebred Spanish Horse has evolved but the Lusitano remains true to the traditional profile of the breed thanks to modern needs sustaining the same qualities for which the breed was treasured in antiquity.

---

## Official breed profile

Lusitano horses are generally between 15.1 and 16.3 hh and may be any true colour, including dun and chestnut. Dappled grey is very popular. The characteristics which make this breed easily recognisable are as follows:

(a) A long noble head, with straight or slightly convex profile narrowing to a long finely curved nose.

(b) Large generous eyes, inclined to be almond shaped.

(c) A long powerful neck, deep at the base, and set at a rather wider angle to the shoulder than is normal in the Thoroughbred, for instance, giving the impression of being more upright.

(d) A high wither, powerful shoulder and deep rib-cage which is slightly flat at the sides.

(e) A short coupled body with broad, powerful loins.

(f) A gently sloping croup with the tail set low rather than high (unlike the Arab, where the tail springs free from the highest level of the quarters).

(g) The hind leg positioned well underneath the body axis, producing excellent hock action and powerful, forward impulsion, which also helps the horse to collect easily.

(h) Fine legs with excellent dense bone.

(i) A temperament of excellent courage, willingness and gentleness.

---

All these characteristics have withstood the passage of many centuries, and the established theory of many equestrian historians is that the Iberian horse is the oldest saddle horse of Europe. 'Together with the Thoroughbred and the Arab he is one of the trio of breeds acknowledged as hot blood. (The Thoroughbred gained its hot blood from its Oriental and Iberian genes.)'

# The society's viewpoint

*The criteria for showing and judging Lusitano horses in Britain should strictly follow those of the parent organisation in Portugal, where they hold single sex classes for yearlings, two year olds and three year olds. Good mares are essentially used for breeding, not for riding, so from then on they are shown with foal at foot, as a group of three mares with foal at foot, or as a member of a group of three siblings out of one mare by different stallions. The adult males have their own classes, four year olds shown ridden and then in hand, graded breeding stallions shown ridden and then in hand, and as part of a group of five horses all by the same stallion out of a minimum of three different mares. There is no requirement for stallions to be ridden in Britain, although this may change. In Portugal very few males are gelded and those that are may well have shown uncertain temperaments, which is never permitted in a stallion, and there are never any classes for geldings. Reject stallions are not always castrated but may be used for estate work herding cattle or the bull ring.*

*In Britain, unlike Portugal, there are in-hand classes for partbreds and they can be presented how the owner wishes: plaited, trimmed etc. As very few are bred from, the purpose is merely to find the horse with the best conformation. Luso-Arabs and Anglo-Lusos, who have to have full papers on both sides of the pedigree and are highly valued, tend to be shown as purebreds.*

# Presentation of purebred Lusitanos

*In Portugal farriers tend to keep the heels much longer. Yearlings of both sexes are hogged and their tails completely clipped in Portugal in the belief that it encourages better growth of the long silky manes and tails. Manes are hogged and the top two thirds of the dock clipped for protection against the vicious thistles and burrs peculiar to the Portuguese terrain. In Britain very few breeders do this but some do, although it does not influence the judging of the horses. Mares wear large bells on wide straps around their necks and ornamental versions of these when shown in Portugal. When shown in hand they wear head collars and when three mares are shown as a group there is only one handler who leads the mare on his right and the others are attached to each other by clipped on lead reins. The foals follow on loose.*

238

*In Britain, the society does not recommend the plaiting of young-stock which is considered not only incorrect but unnecessary because the judge can see the shape of the neck on the other side from the mane. Under saddle, English style, some owners may put in a simple running plait, and if ridden in the Portuguese style this may be reinforced by a wide silk ribbon [see Suffolk, p. 306 for rough guide], in both cases sewn at the end as with any other plait. Tails tend to be naturally wavy and just washing them and brushing them out shows this off best without using a tail bandage. Tails are not plaited except for the parade horse classes, which are ridden and follow the customs of the* feiras *(traditional horse shows), so the whole tail would be plaited right up.*

## Tack

*In Portugal tack is traditional and the idea of using specially designed equipment to enhance the look of the horse goes against the whole purpose of the show. Under saddle it is only rideability that is assessed.*

*There are no hard and fast rules about tack in Britain as the emphasis is on encouraging owners to show their animals.*

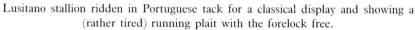

Lusitano stallion ridden in Portuguese tack for a classical display and showing a (rather tired) running plait with the forelock free.

*Clothing*

*Owners can wear traditional Portuguese dress providing it is correct and consistent, including the horse's tack, but the whole outfit can cost over £1000. There is a distinction between owners' clothes and grooms' clothes in Portugal. Grooms from some studs wear white cotton trousers and shirts with the stud brand embroidered on the left breast; others, depending on the region, wear a cheaper simpler version of the owners' traditional clothes or their own traditional outfit, which includes knee breeches, cummerbunds and long tasselled knitted woollen hats hanging over the shoulder. Owners never wear grooms' clothes. Traditional country clothes consist of a wide brimmed low crowned hat, a white shirt with an unpointed collar with a gold or silver collar clip, a short waistcoat with lapels, a waist-length jacket and high-waisted and straight-legged trousers (with no turn-ups or decoration at the ankle like Spanish trousers) which are worn with braces and a cummerbund. In place of traditional country clothes Portuguese owners may wear English riding dress of black hunt cap, white shirt and stock, black jacket, white breeches and long black boots with spurs.*

*Ladies may wear a full length divided skirt, with or without trousers underneath depending on style, or side saddle dress with a full skirt, or men's style trousers. Their shirts may have frills and the hats may have a curl in the brim and a slight taper to the crown.*

*Colours are plain and sober, grey or brown with black trimming and gold or silver clips, but no stripes or patterns. Boots are traditional Portuguese with a wider bottom to the stacked heel on which the spur rests, and are worn inside the trousers.*

*There is a strong word of caution here from the Society on the subject of mixing British and Portuguese traditions with regard to tack and turnout, all the more so if owners here wear Portuguese worker's clothes, which can appear to mock traditions and is very unpopular with the judges, although they would not penalise a good horse for this. They really prefer to see British owners wearing proper British dress. Whatever you choose it has to be smart.*

# Show ring procedure

*Portuguese judges from the official panel are always invited to judge at the Annual Breed Show. Because the Lusitano is a riding breed there is an emphasis on the requirement to show ability, both mental and physical, under saddle, so they are all top level riders and many, even most, are vets too.*

*It is usual, although not compulsory, for three judges to officiate in every class. First of all the horses are walked together around the ring and then those that have not been eliminated are brought back individually when they are shown on an equilateral triangle, each side 40 metres long. The judge(s) stands at the apex of the triangle and the horse is walked away from them along the first side. It is then trotted along the second side so that the action is seen in profile and then trotted towards them on the third side. Stallions are also judged in a ridden phase, and at each stage eliminations occur so that only the final prize winners come back for the stripped phase, when they are compared and examined from all angles for congenital defects (but not acquired defects).*

### *Role of the handler*

*The handler must not get between the horse and the judge either in movement or standing still. Their job is to show off the horse's natural paces to the best advantage and to present the best natural posture when standing. The lead rein should be slack and not used to force the horse into an unnatural posture or pace. The horse should be trained to walk and trot comfortably in hand, showing its best natural paces and outline. The handler is allowed to give spoken instruction to the horse to get it to stand up smartly, trot out well, and so on, and an assistant is allowed to follow behind with a dressage-type whip and calmly encourage the horse to go forward at its best, if the handler wishes it. The horse is given every fair opportunity to show itself at its best but any sort of 'ringcraft' will result in elimination.*

## The action

The action should be high and rounded. Dishing is not considered a fault but in recent years the trend has been to look for straightness in the movement. Despite the closeness of the two breeds, Lusitano enthusiasts consider the Portuguese horse to have the straighter action, which is more apparent at the trot. The Iberian breeds tend not to cover as much ground as, say, the Thoroughbred because they are much shorter striding. The Lusitano, like the Spanish Horse, is capable of distinctive exaggerated action at the walk.

# THE PUREBRED SPANISH HORSE

Historically there is proof that horses of the Iberian Peninsula were used by the ancient warriors, certainly as long ago as the Neolithic Age, to protect them against invaders, and were so successful that the Romans set up remount depots in Spain and Portugal around the time of the Carthaginian Wars to make them available to their own cavalry. Even today with the establishment of two distinct breed societies, the major difference is the country of origin of the horses and hence the location of the main stud books, and the name of the breed. The horse in Spain was always known as the Andalusian and in Portugal the Lusitano. Very recently the Spanish Ministry of Defence, which is still responsible for the administration of the breed in Spain, insisted that the two breeds be administered separately and the name of the society dealing with Spanish horses indicates the difference. For this reason the British Andalusian Society has changed its name to the British Society of the Purebred Spanish Horse.

## Breed profile

A detailed formal breed profile was not available from the British Society of the Purebred Spanish Horse at the time of writing, but it is maintained that there are significant physical differences from the Lusitano, so it is recommended that the breed profile be obtained when available. For history and discussion see pp. 236–7.

## The producer's viewpoint

*Show ring turnout*
*There are no hard and fast rules but it is better for the horse and leader to be turned out in either all English traditional manner or all Spanish style. Showing generally is a much more relaxed affair, although within a system of rules, than the traditional English method.*

*Spanish style: the handler*
*Spanish costume consists of trousers, usually grey or striped, with turn ups; leather boots with a small stacked heel; white blouse/shirt with*

*no collar; a grey, black or white short jacket, preferably to match the trousers, although you can wear a white jacket with grey trousers; a Spanish hat, either grey or black to match the outfit; and a cummerbund to match or tone with the overall colour scheme. Gloves are not worn.*

## The horse

*Both stallions and mares wear Spanish bridles without bits, consisting of a reinforced leather-covered noseband (sheepskin covered for stallions), and a chain to which the lead rein is attached. Young horses wear nosebands with solid protrusions on the inside [which I hesitate to call spikes], which exert a controlling influence on youthful exuberance! Training the ridden horse involves the transition from the reinforced noseband (imported from Spain) with reins attached, to the reins on the bit, and a necessary phase is the use of double reins combining the two. For haute école some trainers use the rein on the noseband in the same way that English trainers use the curb of the double bridle to increase flexion.*

*Stallions also wear coloured browbands with small rosettes on the sides in the traditional Spanish combinations of colours of red and gold or white and green.*

*Foals are hogged and their tails are clipped until they are yearlings.*

*Mares are always hogged and their tails are clipped roughly half to three quarters of the way down the dock, to suit the quarters, and the rest of the tail is left to grow to hock length. Often the forelock is left to grow as protection against flies.*

*Stallions' manes and tails are left unpulled and untrimmed from the age of a year onwards.*

*Whiskers are trimmed but there is no grease put around the eyes and muzzle.*

## Show ring procedure

*Everybody walks around together in single file, in an anti-clockwise direction, which puts the leader on the inside of the ring between the judge and the horse. They are then called in and lined up. This is followed by the individual show of walking and trotting which is under the specific direction of the judge.*

*When the horse is stood up for the judge all four feet have to be square, unlike the stretched pose of English showing. Head carriage has to be natural rather than stretced too, so there isn't a need for titbits.*

243

*Below* Purebred Spanish mare produced in the Spanish way, the tail clipped three-quarters of the way down the dock and the mane hogged. This owner has left the forelock unclipped and the heels are not trimmed. *Above* Purebred Spanish mare with her foal, also hogged and tail clipped, showing the brand of registered stock.

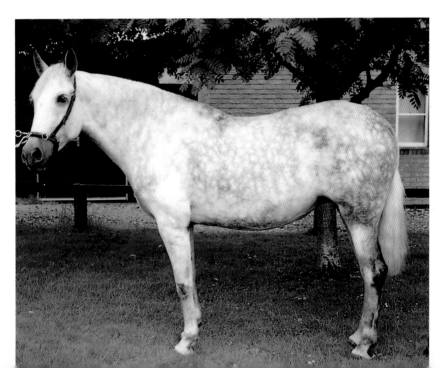

*Hock engagement is not a problem for the Spanish horse. It is one of the reasons why this is the horse of the haute école, but care must be taken to trot on well because they tend to be short striding, although naturally supple. You are advised to ensure that your horse shows free forward movement, particularly at the trot. It is not uncommon to see leaders running in front of their horses at this time, although perhaps not strictly necessary.*

*Dishing is typical of the breed but the horse has to go forward at the same time. Another characteristic is the exaggerated 'paddling' action of the forelegs at the walk particularly, otherwise known as the 'Spanish Walk', which would be called pawing or striking if restricted to one movement of one leg in an English horse. Far from being a circus trick this is a natural movement.*

## THE TRAKEHNER

Trakehner horses, in addition to being the progeny, as one would expect, of two registered, purebred Trakehner horses approved for breeding, may also be bred from one purebred, registered (and approved for breeding) Trakehner, and one purebred, registered Arab, Anglo-Arab or Thoroughbred approved for breeding within the Trakehner breed by the Trakehner Verband or its associated bodies.

The history of the breed is outlined in the literature:

> The Trakehner breed was founded as a light cavalry horse by Frederick the Great of Prussia at his State Stud at Trakehnen, East Prussia, in the early eighteenth century, using native East Prussian horses, Thoroughbred and Arabian blood. The stud book has been closed since 1732, making the Trakehner the oldest established riding horse breed in the world and the oldest German warmblood.
>
> In 1945 the Red Army occupied East Prussia and some 700 of the breeding horses from Trakehnen escaped to West Germany in an historic trek. The breed has since been rebuilt and today about 2000 active breeders carry on the breeding of Trakehners in West Germany, with 4500 registered mares and 300 approved stallions. Trakehner stallions are used by every German warmblood breeding district to improve and perfect the various breeds, and they are also in demand in other countries. The German breed society has affiliates all over the world, with sizeable Trakehner populations in the USA, Canada, Denmark, Holland, Switzerland, Britain, and New Zealand.

Performance testing and selection for breeding has been a breed policy since the early days and the standard is deliberately maintained at a high level. Today, Trakehners can be found at the top in all equestrian disciplines and are frequent Olympic competitors. Equally their all-round abilities and unrivalled temperament makes them ideal for the owner who rides only for pleasure.

---

### Official breed profile

*Definition of a Trakehner horse*
HEIGHT   15.2 hh upwards.

COLOUR   Any solid colour.

*Conformation*
HEAD   Refined with large eyes and small muzzle.

NECK   Elegant and tapering.

SHOULDERS   Well sloped.

BODY   Medium length – well ribbed up and strong.

HIND QUARTERS   Well developed, strong thighs and hocks.

LIMBS   Hard with strong cannons and excellent sound feet.

ACTION   Straight and true with great freedom giving the impression of floating.

TEMPERAMENT   Spirited but kind.

SPECIAL CHARACTERISTICS   Tremendous stamina.

---

The regulatory body for the breed is the Trakehner Verband of Germany which licenses the Trakehner Breeders Fraternity in Britain to register, grade, performance test and brand purebred Trakehner horses for the British section of the stud book. An annual breed show is held which is the main venue for the in-hand showing of Trakehners in the UK. This is where they are judged as a breed, as under saddle they are expected to compete in the classes for competition horses in various disciplines. They are also found competing in hunter and hack classes throughout the country.

At breed society events the emphasis throughout is on athletic movement, particularly in the trot, rather than static beauty, and, of course, details of conformation. This means that the handlers have to be athletic as well to show the horse to advantage. In-hand showing is not an end in itself but a means of assessing potential breeding stock. Good colts are prepared with the goal of successful grading as stallions, so are shown less as youngsters. The larger studs show foals which are then sold. The Trakehner is not at its best as a yearling so these classes are not large, but the classes for brood mares are keenly contested.

On the occasions when the Trakehner is judged as a breed certain specific conformation details are looked for, described by a Fraternity spokesman as follows:

Trakehner mare showing the features of the breed. When plaited in the warmblood manner the plaits are highlighted with contrasting white tape.

*The ideal Trakehner should be of the noblest appearance; eyes set a handspan apart, ears set forward with tapering curves, a broad forehead and a 'champagne glass' muzzle (muzzle should fit into same!). The angle between the head and neck should be wide with the neck set high on the sloping shoulder. The body and limbs should exemplify compactness and strength with strong forearms and second thighs. Overall the horse should be chiselled in outline showing the raised blood vessels of the noblest of warmbloods.*

The annual breed show is held at the same time as the grading (and auction) in the second week in September, so the regulations concerning presentation and turnout for the grading apply also to the in-hand showing of Trakehners. When plaiting, the warmblood custom of highlighting the plaits with white tape may be followed.

### Preparation

Mares and stallions should be trained to walk and trot in hand. It is advantageous to lunge/long rein them regularly before the inspection. Mares should be in good condition, turned out well and have plaited manes. In addition stallions for grading should practise loose jumping.

### Handlers

All handlers should be dressed in white tops with black or white trousers. The handler should be someone who is able to move well enough himself to be able to show the horse's maximum ability. The horse is judged on the quality of the trot because the Trakehner has the most exceptional movement, and so demonstrating it is a demanding and skilful job and much underrated by newcomers to the breed. Professional handlers are available for the grading.

### Horses

Horses must be shown in an in-hand bridle or snaffle bridle.

### Grading procedure

This is for potential breeding stock and those eligible, the property of members of the Fraternity, should have a Certificate of Freedom from Hereditary Disease plus an explanatory letter from a vet concerning any acquired blemishes if relevant. They are inspected individually in hand and then loose after another veterinary inspection on the grading day. Stallions are also jumped loose to assess their outline and all the successful horses are not branded on the left side of the neck. There are random drug tests.

The individual inspection involves the assessment of walk, trot and canter, and includes trotting around a triangle of two sides of 20 metres and one side of 30 metres viewed from the apex by the judges. [In-hand showing procedure does not rigidly follow the grading format of judging 'on the triangle', but the principles of assessment are the same.]

*Judging the Trakehner is according to the following criteria*:
1. Breed type.
2. Conformation.
3. Swing and elasticity of stride.
4. Movement/paces.
5. General impression.

Trakehner mares must achieve a minimum of 5 marks out of 10 in each section to be considered graded, i.e. 25 out of 50. Those achieving a minimum of 7.8 in each section earn the title of Premium mare and one is chosen to be Champion Trakehner mare.

Stallions have to achieve a minimum of 35 out of 50 marks to be graded. Thoroughbred, Anglo-Arab and Arab mares must achieve an average of 7.8 out of 10, i.e. 39 out of 50.

## The producer's viewpoint

*An advantage of the grading procedure is that potential faults can be eliminated. One such potential fault that the Trakehner has is a tendency to thickness through the jaw. Some dressage movements require the jaw-to-neck angle to be closed, which is difficult in this case. Some of the old blood lines had a tendency to pigeon toes too, but this was eliminated by the grading. When the Trakehner is shown in open competitions some features can be misunderstood, such as the shape of the Trakehner foot which is not round and flat like the Thoroughbred foot but more narrow and upright. This is often viewed with doubt and suspicion in the mistaken belief that it might lead to navicular disease. A survey carried out in Germany actually showed that the Trakehner had the least incidence of navicular disease of continental horses. Some British farriers try to trim them to the Thoroughbred shape, which does not work; they should shoe the foot that they see. The feet are, in fact, very strong and do not spread. From a commercial point of view I try to avoid breeding horses with a tendency to white membranes around the eye because this can give a false impression of bad temperament.*

# CHAPTER SIXTEEN

# American Breeds

Looking at the art of showing from a British perspective, some of the practices involved in showing horses in America come as a shock. The place of the horse in the American culture has evolved uniquely and reflects the beliefs of the wider society. Innovation is embraced, not feared, and success is pursued with as much dedication and efficiency in this sphere as in others. Nowadays the show ring is seen as an important aspect of the leisure industry with rich rewards. Producing horses for competitions is a high profile and highly paid career with a number of precisely defined rungs in the career development ladder. Grooms groom, trainers train and winning is hugely important, and has become so because of the spectacle that it is believed that the show ring should be, for all, not just the knowledgeable few. Consequently no stone is left unturned in the art of the optical illusion. No factor is neglected in showing the unique features of each breed to maximum effect.

Show ring procedure is strikingly different from the moment the horses enter the arena, which may be one at a time. Breeds that have unusual gaits or a particularly dramatic profile endeavour to demonstrate them immediately by entering the ring in a characteristic manner, in sharp contrast to the sedate walk of the British and European methods.

After entering the ring and demonstrating their action individually they may then be judged in comparison with each other by standing head to tail for the judge's examination. In-hand showing classes are called halter classes and have their own conventions regarding the handler's role.

It is in the area of the underlying principles of horse rearing and showing, however, that the greatest differences lie. Production is everything. The basic philosophy in neatly summarised in the remarks of an American-trained European producer and judge of American Quarter Horses:

*It is not always the best horses that win but the judge can only judge what they are allowed to see. If the better horse stands with a leg turned out or won't stand still, the judge has to judge what they see. When I walk into the arena with my horse I haven't left anything to chance; if I have, I have made a mistake. You don't win because you are lucky, you win because you work at it.*

'Working at it' in this context included the routine weaning of foals at three months, regular lungeing of foals specifically for 'weanling' classes, and ad lib hard feed for youngstock. These practices may come as a surprise to British producers.

# THE AMERICAN QUARTER HORSE

The Quarter Horse, so-called because of its ability to run a quarter mile faster than any other breed, is the most popular of the American breeds. As the American Quarter Horse Association (AQHA) points out in its literature:

> The American Quarter Horse originated in colonial America in the early 1600s and was used primarily for sprint racing because of his quick acceleration and muscular build. Its foundation bloodlines were a mix of Arab, Barb and Turk horses bred to English mares which produced a compact, heavily muscled horse that could run short distances faster than any other horse. But as the new country grew so did the American Quarter Horse and it adapted into more of a work horse that could be used for almost any kind of task. Along with the first pioneers the American Quarter Horse forged its way westward pulling wagons, herding cattle and exploring the wide open plains.
>
> Today the American Quarter Horse is known as 'The World's Most Versatile Horse' and its popularity has grown as fast as the breed which now numbers in excess of 3 million AQHA registered horses worldwide. It is still used on ranches and racetracks, as well as having become popular in the show ring and as a pleasure riding horse. There are more than one million American Quarter Horse owners in all 50 states and 64 countries worldwide.

## Official breed profile

HEAD  The head of an American Quarter Horse reflects alert intelligence. This is due to his short, broad head topped by little 'fox ears' and by his wide-set kind eyes and large nostrils, short muzzle and firm mouth. Well developed jaws give the impression of great strength.

251

NECK   The head of the American Quarter Horse joins the neck at a near 45-degree angle, with a distinct space between jawbone and neck muscles, to allow him to work with his head down and not restrict his breathing. The medium length, slightly arched, full neck blends into sloping shoulders.

SHOULDERS   The American Quarter Horse's unusually good saddle back is created by his medium-high but sharp withers, extending well-back and combining with his deep sloping shoulders, so that the saddle is held in proper position for balanced action.

CHEST AND FORELEGS   The Quarter Horse is deep and broad chested, as indicated by his great heart girth and wide-set forelegs which blend into his shoulders. The smooth joints and very short cannons are set on clean fetlocks and the medium length pasterns are supported by sound feet. The powerfully muscled forearm tapers to the knee, whether viewed from the front or back.

BACK   The short saddle back of the Quarter Horse is characterised by being close coupled and especially full and powerful across the kidneys. The barrel is formed by deep, well-sprung ribs back to the hip joints and the underline comes back straight to the flank.

REAR QUARTERS   The rear quarters are broad, deep and heavy, viewed from either side or rear, and are muscled so they are full through the thigh, stifle, gaskin and down to the hock. The hind leg is muscled inside and out, the whole indicating the great driving power the Quarter Horse possesses. When viewed from the rear there is great width extending evenly from the top of the thigh to the bottom of the stifle and gaskin. The hocks are wide, deep, straight and clean.

BONES, LEGS AND HOOVES   The flat, clean, flinty bones are free from fleshiness and puffs but still show much substance. The foot should be well-rounded and roomy, with an especially deep open heel.

STANCE   The Quarter Horse normally stands perfectly at ease with his legs well under him; this explains his ability to move quickly in any direction.

ACTION   The American Quarter Horse is uniquely collected in his action and turns or stops with noticeable ease and balance, with his hocks always well under him.

In Britain, shows and classes for purebred Quarter Horses are run under the rules of the American Quarter Horse Association and judged by an American judge, whereas classes for partbreds are run under the rules of the British Quarter Horse Association and are more normally judged by a British judge.

## Presentation

Purebreds can be shown with the mane and tail free or alternatively with the mane banded. This means that the mane is divided up as if for conventional plaiting in the British style but with each individual bunch of mane secured with an elastic band wound round the hair, close to the crest, several times so that it is secure. This is exactly the same way that the mane is trained, at home, to hang over to one side. The mane is pulled so that it ends at a flattering length, although for horses taking part in reining classes (a type of ridden class) the mane is often left to grow to its natural length. In America there is a great specialisation in the show ring, so a halter horse, even aged four and over, may never be shown under saddle, but in Britain horses are more likely to be entered in a variety of classes.

Purebreds would only be plaited conventionally for English ridden classes, but partbreds may be shown in a conventional English way or in the same way as purebreds, as described below.

## Tack

When shown in hand in halter classes, purebreds are never shown in a bit but in a special leather in-hand halter – hence the name for the classes. A feature of these halters which is used for controlling high spirits is a length of chain which passes either over the nose or behind the jaw like a curb chain and to which the lead rein is attached. These American halters are not compulsory in Britain, and a clean, well-fitting headcollar will do instead. In this case the chain section of a stallion-type lead rein would be attached to the ring to which the throat lash is sewn, pass through the D at the side of the noseband and pass either under or over the nose to the corresponding D on the handler's side, through it and into the hand of the handler.

## Clothing

The general rule is that if you show in the Western style then the

253

American Quarter Horse showing the detail of the method of attaching the lead rein to the headcollar for showing in the American manner in Britain.

handler wears Western clothing too, which the American rules define as Western hat and boots. However, women often wear make up and jewelry and the latest fashion of Western riding clothing.

## Show ring procedure

How you show your horse in the ring varies slightly according to the judge. Normally competitors enter the ring one at a time, show a few strides of walk and trot, and then walk around the ring counter clockwise (handler on the inside) until all the competitors have entered. The rest of the judging then takes place with the horse halted.

The main thing is that you leave room for the judge to walk round your horse and you don't obscure his view, so you move from one side to another as he looks at your horse from all angles. American judges expect you to maintain eye contact with them all the time apart from when you are setting up your horse. They also expect to be able to examine your horse's teeth so your horse has to be trained for this.

Be ready for your class in good time, and later on if you are eligible for a championship stay near the ring, because the judging is very much faster than British judging and you don't want to be caught out.

American Quarter Horse shown in Western tack with the handler dressed accordingly. In the show ring the horse would be posed with the feet four square.

## Standing up for the judge

As implied in the breed profile, the American Quarter Horse is stood up with all four feet square. They are not stretched in any way and the weight should be evenly distributed on all four feet. The horse is expected to stand immobile throughout the judging and any fidgeting or moving around may be penalised.

## The American judge's viewpoint

*The first thing you must do is to determine whether your horse is a good show horse or not. If you can't make your own judgement, ask an expert — it need not be an AQHA judge, any expert horseman will do.*

*To me, the first thing to look at is balance and proportionality. Good horses are well balanced, with no excesses of deficiencies. To be balanced, the shoulder, the back, and the hind quarter should be about equal lengths. The distance from the withers to the chest [brisket] and chest to the ground should be about equal. The body of the horse should fit into an imaginary rectangle. For example, if the horse is extremely short in the hip [across the croup] or shallow in the shoulder it is not balanced.*

*The top line should show a distinct wither and a powerful loin. For the loin to be as powerful as possible, the back must be shortened, and this happens when the shoulder is long and sloping and there is good length of hip [length from the flank to the point of buttock].*

*The length of the horse's neck should be proportional to the length of the shoulder or hip. Longer, leaner necks are preferred over shorter, thicker necks. The neck should come out of the top of the shoulder and should be free of excessive 'meatiness' in the throat area, over the top and at the base of the neck.*

*The next thing to look at is skeletal structure. If a horse is not straight in its legs and feet I will not place it — if I have the choice! Skeletal structure is particularly important in the halter horse, as the halter horse should emulate the extremely good individual of the breed. Genetic law states that things regress to an average, so you cannot breed good horses from mediocre horses. How can a horse be a good athlete without good skeletal structure? That is what it is all about.*

*You should look for a long sloping shoulder — the shoulder can never be too long or too sloping. From the side, the foreleg should be straight, not back at the knee. If it is a little forward at the knee, this is acceptable, as long as it is not excessive. The knee should be in the lower half of the leg, in other words the cannon bone should be short. The pastern needs slope. The knees should be big and flat, and in that joint and the ankle joint you should be able to see bone, muscle, tendon, skin and nothing else. From the front, the leg should be straight through the knee — the forearm should come into the joint directly above where the cannon bone comes out, so neither part of the leg is offset. Toes should point straight ahead. In the hind leg, you must stay away from extremes: avoid the sickle leg (too much angle) and the post legged horse (too little angle). It is not the case that Quarter Horses should be straighter in the hind leg than other breeds. There is a correct angle. Looking at the horse from behind, the legs should come out from the centre of the hock. Like the other joints, you should only be able to see bone, muscle, tendon and skin in the hocks — no puffiness.*

*If I see crooked front legs or weak pasterns or crooked hocks I am going to discriminate against that horse.*

*An important feature of the Quarter Horse is the amount and distribution of muscling: how much is there, where is it, and what type. The halter horse needs more muscle than average, as it is meant to be the excellent horse, and you cannot breed the muscle in if it isn't there. Stallions should be particularly heavily muscled. But we are not looking for a really short muscle pattern, which inhibits stride length. The muscle pattern should be long. Look for muscle particularly at the stifle, the gaskin and the forearm — forearm muscling is the best predictor of total body muscling. If you can't tell the difference between fat and heavy muscling, look at the horse from the rear. A heavy muscled horse will be wider through the stifle than through the hip, but a fat horse will be the other way.*

*You must have the right breed and sex characteristics. The head must be appropriate to the sex. Mares should not have big coarse heads. It is proven that female animals with large coarse heads do not have a high level of productivity. Stallions should look masculine, and geldings somewhere in between. A Quarter Horse should look like a Quarter Horse.*

*By definition, the halter horse is the phenotypic extreme of the breed. Any extreme features must contribute to athletic ability, but in a halter horse quality is a factor. You cannot ignore presence and prettiness in a show horse. The head, brightness of eye, width across the face, cleanness of the neck, condition of coat and skin, even colour and markings all go towards prettiness and quality. With quality, the further you are from a horse, the more you can see it. But watch out for the 'counterfeit' horse: the pretty horse which grabs your attention, but the closer you get to it the worse it gets in its conformation. Quality needs to be considered* after *the other features I've described.*

*Ideally, you want a horse which has both structural soundness and prettiness. But when you see a really pretty horse make sure it can stand close inspection and you aren't being taken in by its prettiness.*

*When you have looked at your horse with all this in mind or had your expert look at it, ask yourself if the horse is good enough to win the class. Don't be blind about it. Get someone to hold the horse as it should be set up in the show ring and look at it. If it's not good enough to win, that shouldn't stop you entering the class, but don't be disappointed with the result.*

## Preparation
*Horses should be kept in the peak of health whether they are being*

*shown or not, so there should be nothing different about the way you feed the horse or about its foot care or parasite control. But it will take two to three months to prepare the horse to look its best, particularly with regard to coat quality. It is an insult to the judge in this day and age to bring a horse straight out of the pasture and take it to a show, because among other things it will not have the right coat.*

*The horse should preferably be stabled, and if it is not old enough to be ridden it should be turned out at night rather than by day, so that the coat doesn't get bleached in the sun. There are various ways of improving coat quality (rugging, lights etc.), so do whatever you know works.*

*A halter horse should not be obese, but it should not be so thin that the ribs and hip bones stand out. Medium flesh is best, but if a horse is in good flesh that is all right as long as it is fit.*

### Show ring procedure

*If you cannot make your horse stand up correctly without having to place its feet with your hands then not enough time has been spent on training it. The horse must stand still. It does not have to stand like a rock for thirty minutes, but must stand the whole time the judge is looking at him. The handler should get the horse to stand correctly when the judge is looking at one or two horses down the line. The horse must stand square — front legs and hind legs lined up. From the front, the forelegs must be placed where the shoulder dictates, and the same at the back. From the side, the legs must be perpendicular with the ground, not with forelegs back or hind legs forward or stretched back. There is just one place where the hind legs should be for the horse to look right.*

*The horse should be set up so as to look the best he possibly can. Teach him where to stand and how to stand still, then ask him to hold his head up. This can be taught, and then you just need to cue him, for example if you click your tongue and rattle the lead chain. Just as the judge comes to look at him, get the horse's ears up. There are two reasons for a horse putting its ears forward: curiosity (interest) or fright. Do something unusual — make an unusual noise, or make the horse anticipate something, by showing it food, for example. You hear of abusive methods of doing this, for instance burning a horse with a cigarette lighter at home and then flicking the lighter when you're in the arena. This is unnecessary and inhumane.*

*Normal show ring procedure is that the judge stands near the entrance. The exhibitors walk into the arena one at a time, walking towards the judge and then trotting away on the left hand rein, so the handler is between the judge and the horse. But you must be prepared to walk or trot wherever or whenever the command is given, so the horse must be trained to do that. For most of the class, however, the horses stand still head to tail. When trotting for the judge, the horse should go forward at a big, bold, brisk trot – you cannot evaluate a horse's movement if it's jogging.*

## Training

*Don't expect to do well at halter if your horse is not fit and ready and properly trained. The best exercise for a young horse is free exercise: put it out in a safe paddock and let it run and play. Some people lunge weanlings and yearlings or work them in a round pen. Working a horse under 24 months on the lunge or in any sort of circle is a short cut to disaster. It's all right as a way of teaching commands, to walk on and halt, but to work it enough to create physical fitness it can ruin the joints. It should be exercised in as straight a line as possible. If the horse has no access to pasture, or if it doesn't exercise itself at pasture, then pony it [lead it beside a ridden horse]. You must not overstress the skeleton. If you go at fast speeds, it should only be for a few seconds at a time, and then the horse must be given free exercise to allow the skeleton to settle. The ideal programme for a young horse is to exercise it straight and fast for a short time (by ponying or leading behind a suitable vehicle), and then let it have free exercise. It has been proven that if a horse stands in its stable all day and is only given ten minutes' exercise on the lunge or in a round pen, its skeleton will demineralise.*

*But with regard to exercise, remember that if God didn't put muscle on that horse, you are not going to put it on him. All you can do is tone it up.*

*I cannot stress enough that a halter horse must be trained. You cannot get him out of the pasture, bathe him and take him to a show. He must be trained for his job just like any horse in a ridden class. He must be a gentleman on the end of the lead rein, and this takes time, effort and discipline. If you can show your horse, the judge can see it.*

## Turnout

*It is normal in the USA for the horse's whiskers to be trimmed, for the inside of the ears to be clipped out, and a long bridle path clipped.*

259

*If you are going to show in front of an American judge and clip it out like this, you must understand what you have done to the horse, and be prepared to compensate. For example, you must protect the horse's ears against insects if you have clipped the ear out entirely rather than just tidied up the long hairs. I would be worried that if you didn't trim the horse up in the normal way, some US judges may assume – even subconsciously – that this is not such a good horse and overlook it. The clipping of legs is less important – it is fashionable to clip out white markings, but as long as the long hairs at the fetlock and the back of the leg are trimmed, shaving the leg is not necessary. It is immaterial to me whether feet are blackened or oiled or even left as they are.*

*Similarly, it is common practice in the USA for the horse to wear a neck sweat. If a horse has a naturally long, clean neck, sweating the neck will not be necessary. If the neck is sweated, care must be taken to avoid blistering the skin.*

*I don't care what kind of halter [leather show headcollar] the horse is wearing – I probably won't even see it – but It should be a neat, clean leather halter and you must make sure that it fits the horse snugly. Whether it has silver on it is a personal choice.*

*A lot is written about the fashions of the handler's clothes, but all that is necessary is that the handler should understand that they are in a 'show', so they should have clean and neat clothing: a white shirt and jeans, or more expensive suits and jackets if that is what you want. The rules require you to wear Western hat and 'cowboy' boots, but the boots can be a range of types; English jodhpur or paddock boots should be acceptable if they look like the popular 'roper' boots. You must keep in mind that you are giving signals to the judge – I know what I'm doing, so pay attention to me. Dress appropriately for the situation.*

## Abuses

*We hear a lot about drug abuses. Apart from the fact that it is against the rules, it is poor horsemanship, cruel and inhumane treatment to give a healthy horse steroids. I would never administer steroids to a healthy horse for any reason. And if you can't handle a horse without giving it tranquillisers, you shouldn't be showing it. You must have professional ethics. And you should never be led into going along with something which you know is wrong.*

# THE APPALOOSA

The inclusion of the Appaloosa in the section on American breeds is based on the modern association of the breed with American history, but in fact the ancient roots of these horses are middle European. As with other modern European breeds, migration of spotted horses has been recorded across Northern Europe from Africa and Persia to Spain, from whence the breed travelled around Europe with the Romans and much later to America with the conquistadores.

The Nez Percé Indians, responsible for the highly efficient selective breeding of Appaloosas, only acquired their horses around the beginning of the eighteenth century. Since their defeat in 1877 and the subsequent enforced dilution of their Appaloosa stock in a determined attempt by the authorities to restrict their mobility, modern efforts have been made to restore the purity and quality of the breed. Outcrosses permitted in the Appaloosa Horse Club of America are with Thoroughbred, American Quarter Horse and Arab horses. The establishment of the British Appaloosa Society in the 1970s and the acknowledged respect for the standards of the British Society now account for a two-way international traffic of good examples of the breed.

## Coat colour patterns

There are a number of identifiable patterns which to the uninitiated define the breed. In fact, whilst most Appaloosas possess them in one form or another, there are a number of purebred Appaloosas that do not. Therefore the type of marking is not a crucial feature of the judging process, but it may well be a decider between two animals of equally good conformation in a purebred class.

### Leopard
Black or chestnut spots on a white or light-coloured base coat. Spots any shape or size from 1 to 5 inches across, distributed at random over the body but usually more concentrated over the hind quarters. If there are not many spots it is called a few-spot leopard.

### Snowflake
The reverse colouring of the leopard with the base coat dark and the spots resembling the light dusting of snowflakes. This is quite rare

and not to be confused with the markings of some greys which do not have the other Appaloosa characteristics.

## Frosted

Like the snowflake, but the spots are very small like a light dusting of frost, and there are not so many of them, or else they are distributed like a blanket over the hip, rump and loin.

## Marble

Usually red or blue roan base colour, frequently with clusters of darker hairs called 'varnish marks' on the face, elbows, girth, stifle and hip areas. They may have a few spots irregularly distributed. Young horses may start out marbled and then 'colour out' to few-spot leopard.

## Blanket

Two sorts: completely white rump with solid coloured body, or white rump irregularly patterned with spots. The blanket can just cover the rump or extend forward as far as the withers. It can sometimes look like lace on a darker base colour.

# Showing the Appaloosa

All horses in affiliated classes must have been accepted for registration by the British Appaloosa Society. There are no hard and fast rules regarding turnout. It is accepted that different types have different needs in order to be shown to advantage. The thickness of the mane can vary enormously, as can the height and weight of the horse, so some will suit being plaited, others may look better hogged and others may look best with a natural mane. Similarly there is the option of showing in English or Western turnout. The rule of thumb is that if the horse wears Western tack then the handler must also wear Western showing clothes.

With regard to stallions, the British Appaloosa Society requires stallions to be shown bitted, but the halter classes run under the rules of the Appaloosa Horse Club of America require them to be shown in halter only, and if they were uncontrollable they would be penalised. In the future it is possible that some international championships may be run in Britain according to these rules, so it is most important to check the rules of the specific competition.

262

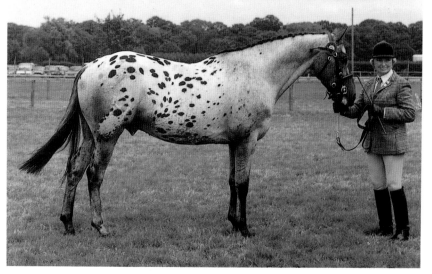

Appaloosa shown in the British manner.

In addition to the Main (Regular) Register there is also a Non-Characteristic Register for horses that do not fulfil the criteria required for full registration, that is, if the horse does not display a characteristic coat pattern or mottled skin (around the eyes, nose and/or dock), and one other visual characteristic, such as white sclera around the eye or striped feet (on dark legs). In recognition of the value to the gene pool of these horses, showing classes have now been introduced, but at regional shows these may well be combined with the classes for the horses registered on the Partbred Register. The following guidelines may apply less to the partbred, depending on the other parent, although the general aim of this register is still to provide good riding horses, albeit with a wider range of height and type than in the Appaloosa registers.

## Appaloosa type and conformation

The British Appaloosa Society Judging Guide offers the following description:

In general appearance the Appaloosa horse is symmetrical and smooth. Weight ranges from 950 to 1175 lb, and height from 14.0 hh upwards, with NO maximum height.

*Appaloosas come in a very wide range of types. These are ALL equally acceptable.* They also have a very wide range of colour and markings ranging from:

Solid colour with mottled skin and one other characteristic, either white sclera (like the human eye) or striped feet (on dark legs), through snowflake, marble, roan, frosted hip, blanket with or without spots, near leopard, leopard, few-spot leopard (white with some roaning, maybe one or two spots).

Appaloosas often have a very fine, thin mane and tail. If the tail is heavy it should be trimmed.

The head is straight and lean, usually showing parti-coloured skin about the nostrils and lips. The forehead is wide. The sclera of the eye is white (like the human eye). The ears are pointed and of medium size. The neck shows quality, having a clean cut throatlatch and large windpipe. It blends into a deep chest with long sloping shoulders. Excessive width or narrowness in the chest is counted against. The withers are prominent and well defined. Low, poorly defined withers are counted against.

The forearm is well muscled, long, wide and tapered down to a broad knee. The cannons are short, wide and flat, ending in wide, smooth and strongly supported fetlocks. The pastern is long and sloping. Short, straight pasterns are counted against. The hoof is rounded, deep, open and wide at the heel.

Viewed from the front, a perpendicular line from the point of the shoulder should fall upon the centre of the knee, cannon, pastern and foot. From the side, a perpendicular line dropped from the centre of the elbow joint should fall upon the centre of the knee, pastern joints and back of foot.

The back should appear short and straight and the loin short and wide. The underline should be long and the flank well let down. The hips are smoothly covered, being long, sloping and muscular. The thighs are long, muscular and deep, giving the quarters a smooth, well rounded appearance. The gaskins are long, wide and muscular extending to clean, clearly defined, wide, straight hocks. The back feet are a trifle narrower than the front: the hoof is dense, having a large elastic frog, strong bars, concave sole and wide high heel.

Viewed from behind, a perpendicular line from the point of the buttock should fall upon the centre of the hock, cannon, pastern and foot. From the side, a perpendicular line from the hip joint should fall upon the centre of the foot and divide the gaskin in the middle, and a perpendicular line from the point of the buttock should run parallel with the line of the cannon.

In conclusion the Appaloosa should be deep but not wide, have well defined prominent withers, and have length and slope to the pastern, shoulder and hip. He should have balance and a 'saddle' back. He must be sound, have good conformation, and have action that is long, brisk, elastic and straight.

## Appaloosa temperament

The Appaloosa temperament is a very important feature of the breed. They should be basically sensible and good natured. Allowance can be made for youngstock and stallions, but obviously bad temperament is a serious fault.

## In-hand classes

Horses shall enter the ring and be lined up at the discretion of the judge. Entries are to be judged individually, standing, and at a walk and trot on the line. Horses should stand squarely on all four feet, and should not be stretched. Horses are to be judged on conformation, soundness and action and should be suitable for use as a good riding horse.

A blemish is a disfiguring defect which does not interfere with the usefulness of the animal and should not be considered in judging. Common blemishes are scars.

As regards dress and tack for in-hand classes, English tack or American show halters are equally acceptable. Stallions and colts over two years are required to be led bitted unless the Show Rules state otherwise. Side reins and rollers are NOT permitted.

Some competitors may choose to wear western style clothing, this is acceptable.

# THE MORGAN HORSE

As the British Morgan Horse Society explains in its literature:

Versatility has been the hallmark of the Morgan since those early days 200 years ago when Justin Morgan, the music teacher, made the long hard journey from Massachusetts to Vermont with his proud little stallion destined to outrace, outpull and outshine all other horses with a grace and style all his own. The thrifty New Englanders soon recognised the value of the offspring of the equine Justin Morgan (named after his owner), and the Morgan breed became established.

# Official breed profile

1. The head should be expressive with broad forehead, large, prominent eyes, with straight or slightly dished short face, firm, fine lips, large nostrils, and well-rounded jowl. The ears should be short and shapely, set rather wide apart and carried alertly. Mares may have a slightly longer ear.

2. The throatlatch is slightly deeper than other breeds and should be refined sufficiently to allow proper flexion at the poll, and normal respiration.

3. The neck should come out on top of an extremely well-angulated shoulder with depth from top of withers to point of shoulder. The Morgan is renowned for its generous crest in both sexes. It should vary in degree according to age, and whether the individual is male or female. It should be slightly arched and should blend with the withers and back. The top line should be considerably longer than the bottom line. The stallion should have more crest than the mare or gelding. An animal gelded late in life may resemble the stallion more closely.

4. The wither should be well laid back and part of the continuous line from poll to the rear of the shoulder blade and extended into the back in proportion to the angulation of the shoulder.

5. The body should be compact, with a short back, close coupling, broad loins, deep flank, well sprung ribs, croup long and well muscled with tail attached high, carried gracefully and straight.

6. The stifle should be placed well forward and low in the flank area.

7. The legs should be straight and sound with short cannons, flat bone, and an appearance of over-all substance with refinement. The forearm should be relatively long in proportion to the cannon. The pasterns should have sufficient length and angulation to provide a light springy step.

8. The feet should be in proportion to the size of the horse, round, open at heel, with concave sole and hoof of dense structure.

9. Viewed from the front, the chest should be well developed. The front legs should be perpendicular to the ground and closely attached to the body.

10. Viewed from the side, the top line represents a gentle curve from the poll to the back, giving the impression of the neck sitting on top of the withers rather than in front of them continuing to a

short, straight back, a relatively level croup rounding into a well-muscled thigh. The tail should be attached high and carried well arched. At maturity the croup should NOT be higher than the withers. The under-line should be long with good depth through the heart, girth, and flanks. The extreme angulation of the shoulder results in the arm being a little more vertical than other breeds, placing the front legs slightly farther forward on the body. The front legs should be straight and perpendicular to the ground. The rear cannons should be perpendicular to the ground when points of hocks and buttocks are in the same vertical lines.

11. Viewed from the rear, the croup should be well rounded, thighs and gaskins well muscled. Legs should be straight. The gaskin should be relatively long in relation to the cannon.

12. The height ranges from 14.1 to 15.2 hh with some individuals under or over.

13. Horses must be serviceably sound – i.e. must not show evidence of lameness, broken wind or impairment of vision.

14. Stallions two years old and over must have all the fully developed physical characteristics of a stallion. Mature stallions must be masculine in appearance. Mares must be feminine in appearance.

*Other distinctive attributes* of the Morgan Horse are his presence and personality. These include:
Animation
Stamina
Vigor
Alertness
Adaptability
Attitude
Tractability

The British Morgan Horse Society's Morgan Horse Judging Standards give the following suggestions:

## Correct way of going for in-hand classes

*It is imperative that height of action, while higher than most other British breeds, should not take precedence over correct way of going. Emphasis shall be on type and conformation with consideration given to the horse's ability to move correctly when in hand.*

1. The walk should be rapid, flat-footed, a four-beat cadence, and

elastic with the accent of flexion in the pastern.

2. The trot should be a two-beat diagonal gait, animated, elastic, square and collected. The rear action should balance with the front.

3. Emphasis should be on the horse's ability to perform as described in (1) and (2) above, regardless of the type of shoeing or the type of training the horse has received.

4. All horses should exhibit good manners in the ring. The way of going and presence are equally as distinctive as the type itself.

5. Stress should be on a quiet, orderly presentation of the horse. He should move straight and true on the line, without a tendency to break gait or resist the handler. A gay vivacious way of going is expected of all Morgans, a greater degree being seen in the Park horses.

## Suggested procedures for judging in-hand classes

1. Enter the ring and line up at the discretion of the judge.

2. Horses to be judged individually standing, then at a walk and trot on the line along the rail.

3. Horses must stand squarely on all four feet with the front legs perpendicular to the ground, rear legs placed back in the traditional Morgan Park or 'stretch' position. Judge may ask exhibitor to move hind legs up for inspection.

4. Suggested procedures for elimination in large classes:

(a) At the discretion of the judge, the horses, after being worked on the rail, may be placed in two groups: one group to remain under consideration and another group to be excused. However, before being excused, the second group is again reviewed to ensure that a qualifying horse is not overlooked. Then the second group may be excused.

(b) The judge may take the numbers of superior animals as they are being worked on the rail. When all horses have been worked, superior horses are separated and others are reevaluated and excused.

5. The final placings of the horses may be made evident to the spectators by placing them head to tail in their proper order.

6. The winners are announced and given rosettes in ascending order. The winners of the first and second prize remain in the ring, and do a victory pass. The winner is the last horse to leave the ring.

The above guidelines for judges refer to the characteristics of all Morgans as distinct from Park horses. The Park Horse Division is a type of class for ridden and driven Morgans. There are no fewer than ten classes of competition, each with their own demands and conventions regarding gaits, way of going, turnout and equipment, that the Morgan can enjoy, many of which are open to the other breeds. The point is made that:

268

there must be one recognised standard for judging the Morgan horse. There is sufficient variation within the breed to make possible the selection of horses better suited than others for a particular purpose. To be shown in the ring a horse should be a show horse, regardless of what class or section he is shown in. We put him in competition before the public because we think he is a superior individual worthy to represent the breed.

## Official show rules

These extracts are not comprehensive and there are two documents that should be obtained from the Society: the British Morgan Horse Society (BMHS) Show Rules and the BMHS Morgan Horse Judging Standards.

Only horses with up-to-date BMHS registrations may enter Morgan classes.

All classes must be BMHS accredited.

All competitors must present themselves on time in the ring, properly dressed and turned out and with their horses in the right tack. Dress should be as follows:

*In-hand classes*: Neat trousers (not jeans) and shirt with tie, waistcoat and preferably a buttonhole. Gents usually wear a trilby. In more formal shows jackets may be worn.

*The steward will refuse entry to those not properly dressed.*

*Tack*: In-hand horses should be shown in a curb bit only, not a double bridle. This is not permissible for a riding class where the full bridle should be worn, though a pelham is also permissible, but not recommended (see Judging Standards). Yearlings should be shown in a show halter or snaffle.

For in-hand classes weanlings are shown in leather show halter sets, and are bare-footed. Yearlings may be shown in halter set or appropriate bridle and are bare-footed. The use of an appropriate bridle with snaffle, curb or stallion bit is recommended for all others. In certain areas it may be customary to show western-type horses in a halter.

No person under the age of 16 may show a stallion of three years or over in any class, and no stallions are allowed in any youth class.

## Presentation

The Morgan Horse and the two breeds described below, the Tennessee Walking Horse and the American Saddlebred, are all presented in the show ring in the same way, particularly for in-hand showing, because they have a number of features in common – high head carriage, poll flexion, flat top line and energetic and flamboyant knee and hock action.

Manes and tails are left to grow naturally and are washed and combed for the show. The tail would be plaited below the dock when damp so that it has a wavy appearance when it is brushed out before going into the ring. Ideally it should be long enough to trail on the ground, although the demands of other activities might rule this out and you would not be penalised.

The mane is hogged from behind the ears for about six to eight inches, in order to emphasise the flexion at the poll, and the hair next to this section has one long plait with ribbon plaited into it which is not rolled up in the British manner. This plait matches the forelock, which is plaited in an identical manner except that the finished plait is wound around the bridle beside the browband so that it does not obscure the horse's vision, because the hair can be as long as eighteen inches in all. This applies to both inhand and ridden classes.

Plaiting the ribbons into the forelock and the first lock of the mane is quite a skilled technique so requires practice. Three ribbons are needed for each plait and they have to be all the same length and knotted together at one end, with about an inch of ends sticking up and each with a V cut out of the middle so that the ends collectively

Morgan posed 'parked out' in the American manner and demonstrating the high head carriage, poll flexion and flat top line that is required. Note the American bridle with matching browband and noseband, the single curb bit and the forelock behind the browband.

consist of six points. The colours should match the colours of the browband, noseband, girth (ridden classes) and handler's buttonhole, which are all one colour, and the saddlesuit and boots (another colour), and the shirt (a third toning colour). The knot is placed close to the horse's head or crest and the three portions of the hair to be plaited are taken up each with a ribbon. The hair and ribbons are plaited all the way down to the ends of the hair, and then the ribbon is knotted to secure the plait and about an inch of ribbon hangs down below this, ending again in six points that have been cut into the ribbons.

The rest of the mane is trained to lie over on the offside. Whiskers are trimmed, ears are trimmed inside because ideally they should look pointed. Hooves are blacked and white feet are normally whitened but blackened for American showing.

## Tack

All three breeds wear an ordinary good quality riding bridle with matching leather browbands and nosebands that are quite deep and have single coloured panels set in them. Strictly speaking the correct bit to use is a single curb, a modified version of which is used by the Tennessee Walking Horse.

## Clothes

There are a number of conventions to observe in American showing as such, although most societies make concessions to British customs, particularly when animals are shown in the British manner. In hand, the horse can be presented in the all-English style, particularly for partbreds at mixed shows, but more usually purebreds at the breed shows observe the American customs of derby hat, waistcoat, long sleeved shirt and buttonhole (colour coordinated with the tack and plaits) and Kentucky breeches or smart trousers.

# THE GAITED AMERICAN BREEDS

The other breeds described in this chapter may demonstrate, in addition to the expected three gaits of walk, trot and, under saddle, canter, an additional two gaits reminiscent of the gait of ancient breeds of riding horses, such as the Hobby that was popular in medieval times before the widespread use of stirrups, and similar to the tølt and flying pace of the Icelandic horse.

These additional gaits are generally shown under saddle. It is believed that the ability to perform them is congenital, and so related to hip conformation, which therefore links in with the meticulous measurement process of the Icelandic horse assessment procedure. In-hand classes judge, in the main, conformation and straightness of action.

For the Tennessee Walking Horse, in addition to the 'flat-foot walk' described below, there is also the running walk which is typified by the overtracking by the hind feet of the front feet by up to 12–16 inches in some cases.

For the American Saddlebred these are referred to as the 'easy' gaits of 'slow gait' and 'rack'. Slow gait, originally known as the stepping pace, is an airy precise gait involving a long moment of hesitation between footfalls. Rack is a much faster version of this in which speeds of up to 35 mph can be attained.

In both gaits, which require a steady back and are very comfortable to sit on, the footfalls should be quite distinct and only one foot should strike the ground at a time.

For show ring presentation, see pp. 269–71.

## Tennessee Walking Horse

While the American Quarter Horse is described as 'The World's Most Versatile Horse' and the Morgan as 'The Versatile Family Horse – The Horse for all Reasons', the Tennessee Walking Horse is the 'Gentleman of the Equines – The Ride of Your Life', and 'the world's greatest show, pleasure, and trail horse'.

In 1885, a cross between a stallion called Allandorf, from the Hambletonian family of trotters, and Maggie Marshall, a Morgan mare, resulted in a black colt with a white blaze, off-hind coronet and near hind sock, Black Allan, foal of 1886. He was later to be chosen by the Tennessee Walking Horse Breeders' Association as the foundation sire of the Tennessee Walking Horse and designated as Allan F-1. It was a cross between Allan and the Tennessee Pacer that produced today's Tennessee Walking Horse.

---

## Breed profile

According to promotional literature:

> This horse is named for its graceful walk which provides a very smooth comfortable ride. Its three gaits are the flat-foot walk, the running walk, and the canter. The flat-foot walk is a smooth, four-beat gait that is easy on the rider, covering five to seven miles per hour with no posting or jolting. The running walk is a more accelerated version of the flat-foot walk, covering eight to ten miles per hour. The canter is a collected version of the gallop, called the 'rocking chair' gait.
>
> First bred 150 years ago in the central basin of Tennessee from Thoroughbred, Standardbred, Morgan, and American Saddle Horses, the Tennessee Walking Horse is a tough breed with great stamina. Many walking horses have been known to work long after the age of 20. And the distinctive walk that is the mark of a true Tennessee Walking Horse is a natural trait that can be seen in young horses soon after birth ... Being used as a utility animal for all types of farm work, as well as family transportation and recreation, the old Plantation type horse was not trained for showing in those days. This natural gait was most often inherited from his breeding.
>
> There are many practical uses for this versatile breed including working livestock and other general ranch work. The breed is also well suited for driving, jumping, and western style gaming events. Most families, however, use their walking horses just for recreational trail riding.

---

The show running walk, referred to above, is a 'spectacular gait with extremely high knee action and a gliding rear stride which oversteps the front hoofprint by up to 16 inches. The canter has a high rolling action and is very slow and animated.'

## The American Saddlebred

According to promotional literature:

> The American Saddlebred is shown in America under three basic categories – five gaited, three gaited and fine harness. Their role as America's premier show horse is a culmination of over 200 years of specialised breeding. The pioneers and plantation owners of old Kentucky mixed the blood of fine examples of the Narragansett Pacer, the English Ambler and Arabian to produce a mount of exquisite

presence, indomitable stamina and impressive turn of speed. This breed of horse was used for tours of inspection of the vast cotton plantations, drew the family carriage to church on Sundays and competed in races on holiday weekends. The hours spent 'turning the rows' of cotton necessitated a supremely comfortable mount, and this led to the enhancement of the breed's natural easy gaits. As the combustion engine outmoded the horse the breed was diverted for leisure use only where its spectacular hock and knee action and flashy gaits made it a natural for drawing the crowds to the show ring.

At all times he must carry himself very tall, his neck leaves his shoulders at a much sharper angle than other breeds and he has natural full flexion at the poll. This leads him easily into his stylish carriage, exciting walk, ground covering trot and rolling canter.

Outside of the show ring the American Saddlebred has established itself as a fine competition and pleasure horse. He can be found in the USA punching cows alongside the Quarter Horse, show-jumping in his nation's team and executing a top-class dressage test. The competition driving fraternity have discovered that his courage and speedy trot are ideal for their discipline, and many have excelled in endurance.

## Judging the American Saddlebred, and show ring procedure for the gaited breeds – the English judge's viewpoint

*The gait is something they are born to do, they inherit the ability and it is a single foot motion, one foot hitting the ground at a time. They can do this day after day after day, and this is why the famous 'minute men' of the Civil War chose to ride them because they could get to battle quicker than anybody else mounted on any other breed, up to 40 mph.*

*When it comes to showing them, for glamour and presence, you want the knees and the hocks coming up. Although you don't slow the horse down, at the same time you can't expect it to do that at 40 mph in the ring and it is not supposed to anyway. To make it a glamorous show horse that attracts non-horsy crowds in America they have brought all this elevation into it, which is not to be confused with the gaits.*

*The breed falls into two basic categories, the five gaited naturally and the three gaited naturally. They are like people with certain talents for certain things. A horse that is born to want to gait will give it to you; a horse that is naturally three-gaited can be trained to do it, as you can train them to do a good working trot, but it won't offer it naturally, so these tend to do three gaited showing. This comes down through the blood lines. For example, the stock of Supreme Sovereign, considered to be one of the finest sires ever, don't naturally rack, but the stock of Wing Commander always does.*

*The rules of showing in Britain allow for everybody to participate, so if they want to do it the English way and compete in what is called Hunt Seat classes they ride as they would a hunter/hack type horse, if they want to do it the American way they enter Saddle Seat classes and produce the horse the American way. The same applies for in hand. The purebred that is going to do it the American way has to be turned out with the coloured browband and noseband. These are colour coordinated with the handler's clothes (button hole, and cummerbund for men) and the ribbons in the mane.*

*We want to see upheadedness, knee action, hock action, flat top line and a naturally very flexed poll which should come naturally to a Saddlebred. In fact the difficulty you have with Saddlebreds when you want to do dressage with them is that their carriage is naturally too far advanced for the preliminary stages.*

*In America if you have a three gaited horse you enter the ring at the trot, if a five gaited horse you have the choice of trot, slow gait or rack. Most choose to enter at the rack because it is so spectacular and it gees the crowds up as well. In England we do it the English way and walk sedately in and start from there, although this may change in the future.*

*Some competitors, who carry a schooling whip, have an assistant (in matching outfit) with a schooling whip following behind the horse,*

American Saddlebred shown in the American manner. Note the clothing of the handlers – derby hat, waistcoat, longsleeved shirt and buttonhole (toning). The horse is being asked to 'park out' for the judge's inspection.

Partbred Palomino Saddlebred posed (*above*) the British way and (*below*) the American way. Note the mane and tail length and the change of tack.

*and to our eyes it looks as if it is part of the continuing education of the horse. It is purely to make sure they present themselves 'up, up, up'! Everything must be up all the time for American showing. It helps the handler at the front end to help keep the horse up because it is being driven from behind, otherwise you tend to get in to a drag situation, and everything starts to come down. Having an assistant is not seen as a sign of failure as it might in England because you are looking for a completely different type of obedience and energy, which is much harder for the horse to keep up without the impetus of the rider on the back. A lot will do it without the handler at the back but it has become accepted practice. Very often you'll notice that the handler at the back doesn't do anything, he's just there.*

## Feet

*If you are importing an American breed don't mess about [switching from the American system of foot care to the British]. You'll find that the foot looks long but actually it isn't. If you measure it it is probably no more than four or maybe four and a quarter inches, which the average hunter foot is, but because they pad them to protect them from the concussion of their very rapid foot movement you tend to get more heel. A leather/manmade pad is placed between the shoe and the foot so the horse tends to grow more heel, which gives the impression that the foot is longer, but it isn't, it is just at a slightly different angle from the one we are used to seeing. It is still at the correct angle to the pastern that it should be, and the frog will always be in contact with the pad which will be in contact with the ground.*

## Standing up for the judge

*In order to enhance the flat top line Saddlebreds, Tennessee Walking Horses and Morgans are posed 'parked out', which means with the hind legs stretched right out behind them and level with each other. To train them to do this you usually start them young, although you can train older ones, and you tell them that when you push their head up slightly then they bring their front legs out. Most of them, because of their conformation, will just do that naturally. Actually they will either pull their front legs out or push their back legs back. Every horse does it slightly differently. There is no particular technique, you just shake the head up a little bit and if they don't do it you tap them, just with your toe, on the fetlock and say 'park out' or alternatively 'stand up'. It takes about three or four times to show them until they've got it. They like doing it. It doesn't put them under any stress at all, Hackneys do it and so do Welsh Cobs.*

## Tack

*Saddlebreds require very fine leather so a hunter bridle wouldn't do, just a fine showing bridle. You might have to have a bit made specially, though, because a lot of Saddlebreds have low roofs to their mouths and they require thinner bits. These are easily imported from America. The Society is growing and hasn't imposed any particular rules for the choice of bit. You often find that they are ridden in an ordinary English curb and bridoon. In hand there is no set rule. Strictly speaking it should be just a curb bit for the Morgan and the Saddlebred, and a Tennessee Walking Horse curb for the Tennessee Walking Horse, but in practice Saddlebreds can show in what they like. As time goes on this may change.*

## Common faults

*You can get horses that are more low headed than you would like, and in England particularly, you can get horses with rather heavy plain heads. That won't necessarily go against them but if there was a horse of equal ability that had a fine head it would win.*

### Clothes
*In hand any smartness is permissible. You won't be marked down because you aren't wearing Kentucky jodhpurs, a waistcoat and a derby hat, but colour coordination of tack and handler's clothes is desirable. Saddlesuits can be worn for in-hand showing providing the trousers aren't too long.*

# CHAPTER SEVENTEEN

# The Heavy Horses

As with all forms of showing the object of the presentation and turnout of the heavy horses is to accentuate the features specific to the breed. Uniting them all is the need to demonstrate the attributes of the breed which enable it to carry out the job for which it is bred – in this case strength and the physical and mental ability to work for long periods of time under difficult physical conditions.

Various customs dictate the way that heavy horses are led in the ring and these can vary from one part of the country to the other. The Suffolk and the Percheron are always led clockwise around the ring with the handler on the outside of the horse to give the judge an uninterrupted view of the horse. In the south and the West Country this applies also to the Shire, but in the rest of the country the Shire is led anti-clockwise so that the handler is on the inside of the ring. The Clydesdale is always led anti-clockwise round the ring. The horse should not be allowed to carry its head lower than the level roughly of the shafts, as apart from detracting from the general appearance of the horse it loosens the plait or worse, pulls the mane out.

## Turnout and presentation

It goes without saying that the horse should be as clean and shiny as possible and the mane and tail squeaky clean and tangle free. All the usual skills of feeding and grooming as for other spheres of showing are employed, including strapping, to produce the horse with as correct an overall outline as possible. In the past a feature of the preparation, called 'larding' in some parts of Britain, involved fluffing up the hair on the body, assisted by resin or soap, to ensure a stronger appearance, but this is no longer standard practice. It is actually against the rules of the Shire Horse Society which warns that 'The use of soap and resin or any other substance on coats is prohibited. Damping of coats with clean water only will be allowed.

Shire foal with its coat treated with soap/resin/water (called larding) to enhance the impression of strength. This practice is commonplace in Scotland with Clydesdale foals. The tail is decorated but not the mane.

This ruling does not of course apply to foals.'

Older horses are generally shown shod, not only to protect the feet but also so they can participate in shoeing competitions which are commonly a feature of horse shows with heavy horse classes. Foot care is tremendously important for a heavy horse that has to cope with the regular additional strain of heavy loads and is only of use while it remains sound.

Cosmetic trimming of whiskers around the head is unnecessary because heavy horses are not expected to have the light, fine heads of riding horses, but strategic plucking of feather to allow the judge to see correct limb conformation where this might otherwise be obscured does occur.

### Tack

Foals, youngsters and mares are shown in white halters unless very strong, and male horses in bridles with bits. Stallion harness is

Shire stallion.

permitted. There tends to be more brass around heavy horse bridles generally but not a great tradition of varying the weight of the bridle to flatter the head, because fine heads are not desirable, unlike riding horses that were traditionally thought to tire more quickly if they had coarse, common heads. If a horse has a particularly long head then the showman might consider fitting a more flattering bridle, or using a fine noseband (or leaving it off altogether) for a particularly small head, but this is not given the priority it is in other breeds.

### The handler

Conventional British showing clothes are worn: tweeds and trousers, strong boots, caps or hats (men wear bowlers for high profile shows), collars and ties, etc. A significant difference is that the length of whips or canes is not restricted and schooling whips or similar are often carried, the exception being the Clydesdale which is not usually shown with a whip. For the breeds that use them the more professional producers can be seen to use them as an aid to turning the horse by holding them up in front of the nose to guide the horse round, a procedure that is undertaken with great care so that the horse is held up together and the feet moved slowly and precisely, and hopefully

*Above* Trotting in hand.   *Below* Turning with care aided by the whip.

with the hocks together. It is an interesting observation that the so-called gentle giants when produced in show condition are very bright and lively as well as extremely powerful, so calm and control are very much the order of the day.

## Plaiting or braiding

Individual owners choose a personal combination of toning coloured wool, ribbon or braid strands to plait, or as it is sometimes called, to braid in with the manes and tails, sometimes in conjunction with raffia strands. A useful tip is to use polo bandages that have been split lengthwise. They are made of stretchy fabric that allows more leeway with the level of the horse's head carriage. Apart from personal choice, colours are chosen to enhance the coat colours of the horse. The main feature of the mane plaiting is that a single plait runs the length of the mane, as high as possible to enhance the power of the neck. For the Suffolk, all the mane is plaited in and for the other breeds – Shire, Clydesdale and Percheron – the strands of mane are plaited in with the left hand, secured by plaiting in the strand in the right hand, and then separated out with the right hand to allow the mane to hang down freely below the plait. They all have ornaments attached at intervals that stand up above the mane and which also highlight the curve and hence the strength of the neck. Foals do not have their manes braided.

Fashions vary in the way the tails are plaited but the overall principle is of a tail tidied out of harm's way and prevented from getting caught up in the harness while working, while at the same time plaited and ornamented to enhance the width and apparent power of the quarters.

The horse should be tied up short with its head fairly high before you start plaiting, and it really is a time when an assistant is helpful to keep the horse steady because once you start you have to keep going in order to get the plait nice and firm. For obvious reasons a secure box is needed to stand on, which places you at the height where there is the least possible strain lifting your arms.

## Tails

Tails are plaited in all breeds at all ages, including foals, to follow the line of the dock. Traditionally and generally more popularly the hair is allowed to grow and plaited in down the centre of the dock in the conventional way, taking a piece of hair from the middle and from each side to encase the dock. Once the end of the dock is reached all the hair is then plaited in right down to the ends, which are secured with string, folded back up the outside of the dock and again secured with string, which is concealed with oversewing of braid threaded into a large upholstery needle. The tail is then decorated with ribbon or braid bows or knots at intervals down the tail.

283

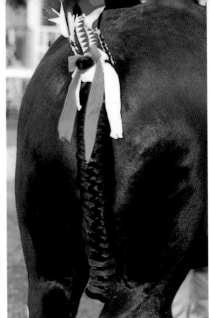

*Left* Traditional tail plait for the full tail (not Suffolks).

*Right* Alternative method.

The object of the dock plaiting is to make your horse look square. The higher the tail the better the horse will look. Higher-set tails are valued and give a square line, which is why the ornaments are added. The finished tail should look as if it is sitting in to the quarters rather than hanging down, and like this it makes the horse look wide in the quarters which is desirable. Fine-boned horses are undesirable.

## Ringcraft

The showing of heavy horses follows the customs of British showing generally with horses being led round the ring in single file at the walk in the custom of their breed for that part of the country. They are called in in approximate order of merit and then led out individually and stood up for the judge. The handler stands the horse so that it appears to cover as much ground as possible, usually with the hind feet parallel to each other, and with the head and neck stretched out slightly. This is done to show off the shoulder, rather than the length of rein that riding horses need for the greater comfort of their riders. They are then walked away from the judge, turned and walked back, trotted away, turned again and trotted back so that straightness and correctness of action can be assessed. They are then halted and backed about four steps. Turning is undertaken with great care so that ideally the horse pivots on the hind legs. Working horse action is not assessed in exactly the same way as riding horses because different demands are made of them. All the heavy horses are turned away from the handler, like riding horses, with the notable exception of the Clydesdale that is turned around the handler.

# THE SHIRE
## Official standard of points for Shires

A scale of points for the breed has been carefully drawn up and this has been amended when necessary, to meet modern requirements. For instance, years ago, a great characteristic of the Shire was the wealth of hair, or feather, on the legs. Today the demand is for a cleaner-legged horse, with straight, fine, silky hair.

The standard of points laid down by the Council of the Shire Horse Society is as follows:

*Stallions*

COLOUR  Black, brown, bay or grey. No good stallion should be splashed with large patches over the body. He must not be roan or chestnut.

HEIGHT  From 16.2 hands high. Standard 17 hands and upwards. Average about 17.2 hands.

HEAD  Long and lean, neither too large nor too small, with long neck in proportion to the body. Large jaw bone should be avoided.

EYES  Large, well set and docile in expression. Wall eyes not acceptable.

NOSE  Slightly Roman nostrils thin and wide; lips together.

EARS  Long, lean, sharp and sensitive.

THROAT  Clean cut and lean.

SHOULDER  Deep and oblique, wide enough to support the collar.

NECK  Long, slightly arched, well set on to give the horse a commanding appearance.

GIRTH   The girth varies from 6 ft to 8 ft in stallions of from 16.2 to 18 hands.

BACK   Short, strong and muscular. Should not be dipped or roached.

LOINS   Standing well up, denoting good constitution (must not be flat).

FORE-END   Wide across the chest, with legs well under the body and well enveloped in muscle, or action is impeded.

HIND QUARTERS   Long and sweeping, wide and full of muscle, well let down towards the thighs.

RIBS   Round, deep and well sprung, not flat.

FORELEGS   Should be as straight as possible down to pastern.

HIND LEGS   Hocks should be not too far back and in line with the hind quarters with ample width broadside and narrow in front. 'Puffy' and 'sickle' hocks should be avoided. The leg sinews should be clean cut and hard like fine cords to touch, and clear of short cannon bone.

BONE MEASUREMENT   Of flat bone 11 inches is ample, although occasionally 12½ inches is recorded — flat bone is heavier and stronger than spongy bone. Hocks must be broad, deep and flat, and set at the correct angle for leverage.

FEET   Deep, solid and wide, with thick open walls. Coronets should be hard and sinewy with substance.

HAIR   Not too much, fine, straight and silky.

A good Shire stallion should stand from 16.2 upwards, and weigh from 18 cwt to 22 cwt when matured, without being overdone in condition. He should possess a masculine head, and a good crest with sloping, not upright, shoulders running well into the back, which should be short and well coupled with the loins. The tail should be well set up, and not what is known as 'goose-rumped'. Both head and tail should be carried erect. The ribs should be well sprung, not flat sided, with good middle, which denotes good constitution. A stallion should have good feet and joints; the feet should be wide and big around the top of the coronets with sufficient length in the pasterns. When in motion, he should go with force using both knees and hocks, which latter should be kept close together. He should go straight and true before and behind.

A good Shire stallion should have strong character.

*Modification or variation of stallion standard of points for mares*
COLOUR   Black, brown, bay, grey, roan.

HEIGHT   16 hands upwards.

HEAD   Long and lean, neither too large nor too small, long neck in proportion to the body, but of feminine appearance.

EYES   Large, well set and docile in expression. Wall eyes are acceptable except for animals in Grade A and B register.

NECK   Long and slightly arched, and not of masculine appearance.

GIRTH   5 ft to 7 ft (matured) according to size and age of animal.

BACK   Strong and in some instances longer than a male.

LEGS   Short, with short cannons.

BONE MEASUREMENT   9 to 11 inches of flat bone, with clean cut sinews.

A mare should be on the quality side, long and deep with free action, of a feminine and matronly appearance, standing from 16 hands and upwards on short legs; she should have plenty of room to carry her foal.

*Modification or variation of stallion standard of points for geldings*
COLOUR   As for mares.

HEIGHT   16.2 hands and upwards.

GIRTH   From 6 ft to 7 ft 6 ins.

BONE MEASUREMENT   10 to 11 inches under knee, slightly more under hock and broadside on, of flat hard quality.

A gelding should be upstanding, thick, well-balanced, very active and a gay mover; he should be full of courage, and he should look like, and be able to do, a full day's work. Geldings weigh from 17 to 22 cwt.

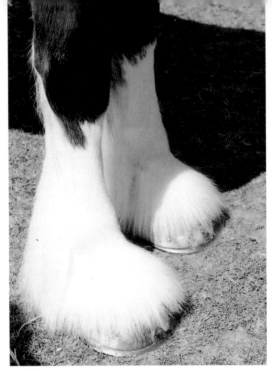

Bevelling is a feature of the shoes that aims to enhance the size of the feet by following the angle of the wall of the hoof. Note also the strategic plucking of feather down the sides of the legs to display the bone which would otherwise be obscured. It is left untouched down the back of the legs and around the coronet.

## Turnout

### Shoeing

The Shire Horse Society offers precise guidance on the correct shoeing for Shire horses, in view of the importance of the feet to working horses. In addition to ensuring frog pressure the shoe should provide good cover, especially at the heels for support, the clips should be broad and not terminated in a sharp point, and the base and height of the clip should be relative to the width of the shoe. Clenches should be of even height, a third of the way up the wall. Bevelling should follow the contour of the wall, because excessive bevelling can lead to injury, e.g. treads or brushing, and resulting ringbone. The Society warns of the dangers of overlong feet or unbalanced shoes (e.g. single calkin), which they say can lead to tearing of the lamina of the wall of the hoof from the sensitive laminae covering the pedal bone, excessive wear on joints and bones resulting in ringbone or sidebone, and excessive strain and wear on the flexor tendons. Spavins may form as the result of hind shoes fitted with a single calkin. Judges are instructed that:

288

If a judge is of the opinion that a horse's feet and the shoes are not in accordance with the published guidelines, *then the horse should be placed down the line.* Equally if a judge is of the opinion that the shoes fitted to a horse affect its movement, then this fact will be taken into consideration when placing horses in their respective classes. Horses shown without bevelled shoes should not be penalised.

*The mane*

The mane is left long and either raffia, sometimes called bass, coloured lengths of braid, thick strands of wool, or ribbon are plaited into it at the level of the crest for the entire length of the mane, starting from behind the poll. The strands are knotted together at one end, with the ends protruding a couple of inches out of the knot and each with V's cut into them if appropriate (not for raffia or wool). Your assistant holds the knot in place just behind the poll until you have plaited two or three lengths of mane in and it is quite secure.

This is done in such a way that pieces of hair taken from the top of the mane are picked up along the crest (not all of the mane) and plaited for a couple of turns of the braid and then allowed to hang down freely with the rest of the mane. The plaiting continues down to the withers if the horse is shown in hand, but if one of the classes involves the wearing of harness then it stops just in front of the collar to avoid chafing. The object while plaiting is to conceal the hair in the plait under the raffia/braid. The mane is not pulled because the longer the hair the easier it is to plait tightly. The lower end of the plait is secured with strong mane thread or string and then decorated with more ribbons, which are knotted together around the string to conceal it and the ends left hanging down a couple of inches. The ends of the ribbon or braid should have V's cut in them, not only to stop them fraying but to look attractive.

Either during the plaiting process or, more easily for the novice, afterwards, at roughly three-inch intervals, wire reinforced ribbon/braid ornaments called flights, flags, standards or flyers are inserted, and wrapped around the plait to emerge vertically above the crest. You try to get as many as possible in to enhance the impression of strength.

The forelock is left unplaited. Another ribbon is tied round the neck following the line of the shoulders in such a way that it takes in the chest rather than just the neck. The lower you can get it the greater the impression of breadth and hence power. The competitor's

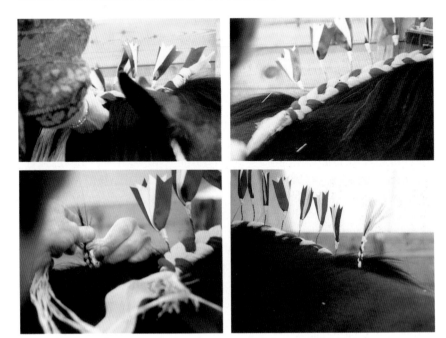

Stages in plaiting the mane with bass and braid.
A Plaiting the mane so it is concealed by the braid and attaching the wired flights at intervals.  B Securing the end of the plait.  C Plaiting bass and hair together to form a point of attachment for the neck ribbon as close to the withers as possible.
D The mane from the near side with the plait visible.

number is threaded through this and worn under the neck. Purists attach the neck ribbon to the mane with plaited rafia and ribbon (see illustrations). This enables the slope of the shoulder to be shown to advantage.

## The tail

At the top of the tail an arc of reinforced plaited braid called a jug handle is secured behind the central plait and then two flights, one on each side of the jug handle, are secured so that all three stand above the top of the central plait. Braid is wound around the end of the folded up tail to conceal the end of the tail attractively. Bows or knots of matching ribbon or braid are tied around the plait down the centre of the tail at intervals to decorate the plait.

It was traditional to clip around the dock below the level where the end of the tail might have been docked in the past. In the unplaited tail the effect is of unrestricted growth to this level. This

Stages in tail plaiting when the dock is clipped.
A Similar attachment points are plaited in on either side of the top of the tail so the decoration remains high on the tail, which flatters most.   B The top of the tail is plaited and the plait rolled into a bun which is secured and decorated with braid. Flights are attached to their points.   C The finished effect.

practice is only acceptable where the owner can undertake full responsibility for protecting the horse from flies and inclement weather, for the same reasons that horses are no longer docked. As with any other decision regarding show ring turnout you have to evaluate your horse carefully to decide which effect is most likely to flatter it and in this case to give the impression of power. Judges are formally instructed not to penalise horses with full tails. If the dock has been clipped, the hair at the top is plaited in the conventional way and the end of the plait folded back on itself and secured to make a bun, which is then decorated with ribbon or braid. The tail is decorated at the top in the same way as the full tail, to accentuate the height of the tail with the symmetrical flights and the jug handle.

Foals have their tails plaited and ornamented where possible but not, obviously, their manes. They also wear a matching ribbon, and hence their number, round their necks.

The overall picture. Note the addition of a jug handle to the top of the tail.

# Judging the Shire

Action must be straight and dishing is undesirable. If the horse does not trot in a straight line for whatever reason, including bad (or good) showmanship, it is marked down.

As a respected producer told me, judges look for height and depth in a Shire. The increased height in the Shire nowadays, when many are about 18 hands as opposed to the average height of about 16.2 in years gone by, is considered to be a result of crossing with Clydesdales when the numbers of Shires dropped. At the same time there have been a number of improvements over the years in general conformation regarding legs, feet, joints and the quality of the hair. Unfortunately, many Shires are back at the knee which is still considered a fault, as is tied in below the knee. Good shoeing is very important for the long-term soundness of a working horse and the foot should be well balanced without too much toe. The shoulder should slope back to the withers for the collar to be carried well, and a straight shoulder is just as bad for a working horse as a riding horse, only for reasons of soundness rather than the comfort of a rider.

Although a Shire should have lots of feather, to present one for the show the feather is pulled out at the front and sides of the leg to display the knee and the flatness of the bone if you are lucky enough to have one with these qualities. Flat bone was one of the good qualities that the Clydesdale influence brought to the modern Shire, as well as silky feather, but the price paid was the depth of the body, for Clydesdales have longer legs, a lighter body and rather more white about them.

When leading a Shire you have to keep them straight with their heads at a comfortable height – shaft height. This may mean keeping the arm nearest the horse stiff. As with other breeds the hind feet should follow in the tracks of the front feet. Great care is taken when turning Shires so that the hocks remain close – a feature of the breed.

# THE CLYDESDALE

## Official breed profile

The Clydesdale Horse Society issues the following description:

The Clydesdale horse is the pride of Scotland and is a native breed which was founded in Lanarkshire – Clydesdale being the old name for the district. The history of the breed dates from the middle of the eighteenth century, when the native horses of Lanarkshire were graded up in an effort to produce greater weight and substance by the use of imported Flemish stallions. This became necessary on account of the greatly improved roads brought about by the development of the coalfields, thus replacing the old pack-carrying horses and ponies...

The outstanding characteristics of this renowned horse are a combination of weight, size and activity, and what is looked for first and last by a Clydesdale man is the exceptional wearing qualities of feet and limbs. The former must be round and open with hoof heads [heels] wide and springy, for any suspicion of contraction might lead to sidebones or ringbones. To some extent the further requirements of this breed vary somewhat from the orthodox and should be noted.

The horse must have action, but not exaggerated, the inside of every shoe being made visible to anyone walking behind. The forelegs must be well under the shoulders, not carried bull-dog fashion – the legs, in fact, must hang straight from shoulder to fetlock joint, with no openness at the knee, yet with no inclination to knock. The hind legs must be similar, with the points of the hocks turned inwards rather than outwards, and the pasterns must be long.

The head must have an open forehead, broad across the eyes, the front of the face must be flat, neither dished nor roman, wide muzzle, large nostrils and a bright, clear, intelligent eye. A well-arched and long neck must spring out of an oblique shoulder with high withers, while the back should be short, with well-sprung ribs, and as befits a draught horse, the thighs must be packed with muscle and sinew. The colour is bay, brown or black, with much white on the face and legs, often running into the body. It should be noted that chestnuts are rarely seen.

It is claimed of the Clydesdales that they are possessed of quality and weight without displaying grossness and bulk, and this is largely true. They are certainly active movers for their size and weight, and in consequence, are very popular in many cities and on numerous farms, especially in the north of England...

The close action of the Clydesdale that judges and breeders look for is associated with a good grip of the ground. They say that a horse needs a fairly big head and wide-placed ears to give it room for brains, and that the Clydesdale has brains and is perhaps one of the most docile of breeds. As a producer told me:

*The ideal Clydesdale is approximately 17 hands high, some a little more, some a little less, weighing about 15−16 cwt. A good Clydesdale must have clean 'ankles' and a wealth of straight hair both round its hoof heads and the back of its legs. This is a unique feature of the Clydesdale. Feather must be straight and silky.*

*Producing the Clydesdale for the show ring is an expert job and needs time, patience and expertise to keep their feet right. The Clydesdale has to be kept shod to keep their feet round and solid and to prevent them from breaking.*

*The feather needs to be oiled regularly to promote growth and to keep it straight. Show horses have to be fed daily with bulky feeding, not solid feeding. This keeps them healthy, and most exhibitors give the horse two months without hard feed to rest the system before starting to feed again, which gives them a 'fresh spark' and a 'rich look'.*

294

## Presentation

Clydesdales are led anti-clockwise round the ring and handlers tend not to carry whips. There is not the same need for them because they turn their horses around them rather than using a whip to help them turn the horse away from them.

There are traditional ways of turning out Clydesdales, some of which are unique to the breed, but these are seen infrequently and more usually in Scotland. Others may once have been common to other breeds too but are less frequently practised by them now, such as the 'larding' of foals. Very often manes and tails are plaited in the same way as Shires and this is quite correct.

## Manes

In Scotland especially, at high profile shows, the mane is left unplaited for in-hand showing, but when the horse is to be shown in harness as well, plaiting makes for a smarter appearance, and in this case the plait would end in front of the collar.

In addition to the standard Shire method of mane plaiting there is a traditional method, called the foursome plait, which employs four strands of braid or ribbon, two of each colour. You plait in the strands of braid with the strands of hair 'top to top and bottom to bottom', so that you plait in two strands of hair consecutively with the braid of one colour and then the next two strands with the other colour, by crossing the braid behind the plait. This way, you end up with alternate colours for each 'rung' of the plait. The standards (flags) should strictly speaking be plaited in, although they are often put in afterwards. There is a much bigger traditional showing standard for the Clydesdale, made of raffia and ribbon, and these do go in afterwards on the same principle as the flags.

## Tails

Tails can be the same as for the Shire with the plough bob for the full tail previously described. The only difference is that some believe that Clydesdales should not have jug handles. If the horse has had the lower part of the dock clipped, which some say was a traditional way of ensuring the cleanliness and health of the horse working on peat bogs and sweating copiously, the top section is sometimes cut off square so that at first glance the tail looks as if it is docked. For the Clydesdale, it is then partially plaited, at the top of the dock only, into a small bun which is bound with ribbon, and segs (flags) are plaited in, using hair that has been left out specially for the purpose, at the top of the tail on either side, to increase the impression of height. In this way some hair may be left to hang down, ending squarely part of the way down the dock.

Another variation of the plaiting of a tail with a clipped-out lower dock is to plait in all the hair on the dock apart from the pieces for plaiting in the segs. The bun is bound with ribbon in the same way.

### Shoes

Because close action behind is desirable in a Clydesdale the hind shoes often have strong calkins on the outside of the heels to enhance this impression, but this has to be done with care because extensive use causes uneven wear on the joints and eventual unsoundness.

### Tack

Clydesdale showing bridles are simpler and less ornamented than Shire bridles, although both are correct. They do not have brass on them apart from the buckles.

A Clydesdale with the tail cut off square at the level it would have been docked at in past times. The top only is plaited to make a decorated bun.

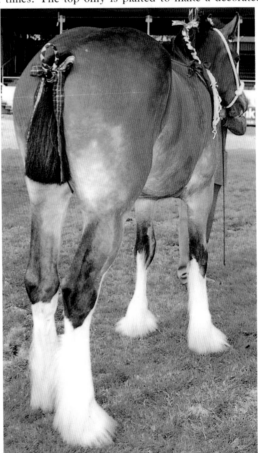

# THE PERCHERON

As the British Percheron Horse Society points out:

The Percheron horse originated in the area known as La Perche in
the north west of France. In 732 AD Arabian horses abandoned by
the Moors after their defeat in the Battle of Tours were crossed with
the massive Flemish stock and from this cross came the Percheron
type which has endured for twelve centuries.

During the Crusades a further infusion of Arab blood was made.
Arab sires procured in the Holy Land were bred to the Percheron
and in the early 1880s the French Government's stud at La Pin
introduced further Arab blood into the Percheron breed by covering
selected mares with two outstanding Arab sires, and now all contemporary Percherons share this common heritage descending from the
foundation stock which originated in La Perche.

The introduction of the Percheron into England came about at the
conclusion of the First World War. Many farmers serving with the
British Forces in France became familiar with the Percheron and
impressed with its docility, activity and power and ability to work
both in mud and on hard surfaces. At the conclusion of activities the
Percheron was imported to England as a general work horse, and
large numbers were to be seen working throughout the arable counties
of East Anglia and the Fens in particular, and they quickly spread to
other parts of the country.

The formation of the British Percheron Horse Society took place in
1918, and during 1918–1922, 36 stallions and 321 mares were imported
from France. The aim of the Society was to encourage the breeding
of a clean legged draught horse with short legs, short back, ample
bone, powerful, active and quick in work with a good temper and
easy to handle. The docility of the breed was very important as
experienced horsemen were declining on the farms.

## The producer/judge's viewpoint

*Percherons should not be washed above the knee and hock. A certain
amount of tidying of whiskers, chins and ears is done, because the
Percheron has an attractive head where the Arab influence shows,
although this is not done in France. The heels are meant to be clean
and tidy. The custom of plaiting the mane and tail closely follows the
methods used with the Shire (and Clydesdale): a single plait with the
mane hanging down below it, flags, free forelock, plaited tail doubled*

# Official breed profile

*Characteristics of the Percheron horse*

GENERAL    The British Percheron horse is essentially a heavy draught horse possessing great muscular development combined with style and activity. It should possess ample bone of good quality, and give a general impression of balance and power.

COLOUR    Grey or black, with a minimum of white. No other colour in stallions is eligible for entry in the Stud Book. Skin and coat should be of fine quality.

SIZE    Stallions should not be less than 16 hands 3 inches in height and mares not less than 16 hands 1 inch, but width and depth must not be sacrificed to height at maturity.

AVERAGE WEIGHT    Stallions    914 kilos – 1016 kilos
Mares    812 kilos – 914 kilos

HEAD    Wide across the eyes, which should be full and docile, ears medium in size and erect; deep cheek, curved on lower side, not long from eye to nose; intelligent expression.

BODY    Strong neck, not short, full arched crest in case of stallions; wide chest, deep well-laid shoulders, back strong and short; ribs wide and deep, deep at flank, hind quarters of exceptional width and long from hips to tail, avoiding any suggestions of a goose rump.

LIMBS    Strong arms and full second thighs, big knees and broad hocks, heavy flat bone, short cannons, pasterns of medium length, feet of reasonable size, of good quality hard blue horn. Limbs as clean and free from hair as possible.

ACTION    Typical of the breed; straight, bold, with a long free stride rather than short snappy action. Hocks well flexed and kept close.

*back on itself with a bun and decorated with ribbons. The dock is not clipped, however. Percherons, too, wear a ribbon round the neck to which the number is attached.*

*The style of turnout is a matter of individual choice. The plaiting of the mane emphasises the crest and the plaited dock helps to create the impression of a high-set tail and rounded croup, and improves the look*

Percheron mares whose heads have been tidied to show off their quality, a consequence of the Arab influence in their breeding.

*of the quarters. The single plait of the mane can be decorated with wool, ribbon, flights [flags] and plumes, but not pom-poms which are exclusive to Suffolks. They are shown in a show bridle with a bit, with or without a browband or noseband according to which flatters the horse best, although mares and youngstock are shown in white hemp halters. Stallions wear harness, because control is everything, which consists of a roller, a side check-rein on the offside (to stop them eating/biting) and a bearing rein which goes through a loop on the roller. There is also a crupper. The roller pad, the browband (if worn) and the flights are all the same colour.*

*The Percheron is shown with the handler on the nearside of the horse, which is led clockwise around the ring. During the individual show the horse is turned away from the handler. It used to be common for them to be asked to back during the individual show so that they could demonstrate, by backing evenly, the absence of stringhalt and a clean movement of the hocks, as well as receptiveness to discipline. This is not done so much nowadays although it always used to be expected of cart horses. When it is asked for the horse walks out and*

Percheron stallion in full harness.

*back, trots up and down and then halts. It is then asked to back up a few strides, rather like parking.*

*When they are stood up for the judge they stand four square and stretched slightly.*

# THE SUFFOLK

As the Suffolk Horse Society points out in its literature:

The Suffolk horse is the oldest breed of heavy horse in Great Britain to exist in its present state. The breed dates at least into the sixteenth century, but all animals alive today trace their male lines back to one stallion, a horse called Crisp's Horse of Ufford, who was foaled in 1768...

The Suffolk horse is always chesnut. A few white hairs well mixed with the chesnut on the body, and a star, stripe or blaze is allowed. Seven shades of chesnut are recognised: Bright, red, golden, yellow, light, dark, and dull dark. The legs are rather short, and the impression that the breed gives is that the body is too big for the legs. This shape gives the Suffolk its nick-name, the Suffolk Punch, and its great strength. The height of the mare is about 16.1 to 16.2 hands, and that of the stallion 17 to 17.1 hands. The legs are clean with no feather, thus making the working Suffolk an easy animal to care for in the stable. Temperament, so important in a working animal, is exceptionally good, and a long working life and economy of feeding are well-known features. Common practice on East Anglian farms was to feed the Suffolks loose in yards. Pulling matches were popular in Suffolk in the eighteenth century, and their recent revival has shown the Suffolk to be the equal of any in strength.

## Official scale of points for Suffolk horses

COLOUR  Chesnut [note the spelling – unique to Suffolks]       5
A star, little white on face, or few silver hairs is no basic detriment.

*Head + Neck + Shoulders + Carcase*                           25
HEAD  Big with broad forehead.

NECK  Deep in collar, tapering gracefully towards the setting of the head.

SHOULDERS  Long and muscular, well thrown back at the withers.

CARCASE  Deep, round ribbed from shoulder to flank, with graceful outline in back, loin and hind quarters; wide in front and behind, the tail well up with good second thighs.

FEET, JOINTS AND LEGS  The legs should be straight with fair sloping pasterns, big knees and long clean hocks on short cannon bones free from coarse hair. Elbows turned in regarded as a serious defect. Feet having plenty of size, with circular form protecting the frog.                                                          50

*Walk + Trot*                                                 20
WALK  Smart and true.

TROT  Well balanced all round with good action.

                                                             100

## Turnout

*The mane*

Unlike the other heavy horses, the Suffolk's entire mane is plaited in and concealed by the raffia or braid. The effect is similar to the riding horse turnout in that the neck is exposed, the big difference being that there is one continuous running plait edged by the raffia etc. Flyers again are employed and can be of three kinds: flights, bows (ribbon/braid) or pom-poms (wool).

There is no set length for the mane so practicality rules – a very long mane would get caught up in the collar. The more traditional raffia is more accommodating of long manes, which make the running

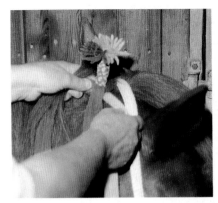

Stages in plaiting the Suffolk mane.
A Plaiting in the braid with the top knot standing up.   B The running plait with the braid concealing the hair.

plait bulkier. Ornaments, like ribbons, are added after the plait is completed just before you go into the ring (to protect them), and especially those on the tail to avoid them being rubbed out, during travelling for example, but all the plaiting and sewing can be done at home.

When plaiting in the braid the aim is to have the topknot standing up just behind the ears. Every time you take a piece of mane with the left hand and plait it in with the braid you have the braid on top so that the hair is concealed. The finished effect is of a coloured plait along the offside of the top of the crest. Once you have reached the place on the neck where the plait must finish – the withers if in hand, in front of the collar if harnessed – you stop picking up the mane and just continue plaiting the hair and braid together until all the hair is plaited in. Then you secure the plait by stitching it with very strong mane thread/fine string and finish it off with the braid threaded into it and knotted around it and with the ends hanging down for three or four inches.

The forelock is not plaited but is secured behind the browband by a ribbon or braid bow tied at the front of the browband.

When shown in hand the number is worn under the neck attached to another length of braid/wool/ribbon around the neck whose ends are knotted together and usually tied to the end of the plait.

### The tail
Unlike the other heavy horses a length of braid/ribbon/wool identical to the one in the mane is plaited in down the centre of the dock, and

Suffolk foal wearing a neck ribbon and tail decoration only, in the same colours as the mare.

once again you need to have the knot at the end held at the top of the tail by your assistant until the plait is well established and secure. The actual plaiting is very similar to the way riding horses' tails are plaited. Hair is taken from each side of the dock and, initially, from the hair down the middle of the dock. However, once the plait is well established the hair is picked up from the sides only and continued down to the end of the dock. From here on the entire tail is plaited in a continuous plait to the end of the tail, secured by stitching, and then folded back on itself to lie flat on the outside of the dock to make a bun. This is secured independently before it is attached to the braiding on the outside of the tail, about three-quarters of the way down the dock. It is then decorated with double coloured braid, to match the mane, which is tied around the bun. Three shorter lengths of braid are threaded through the tail at intervals and tied on the outside of the dock by way of decoration.

### Trimming
Whiskers and chins are not trimmed at all but hooves are oiled. The Suffolk is a clean legged, i.e. non-hairy, horse making it less prone than other breeds to the problems associated with working in mud, and in particular the clay soil of East Anglia. Such feather as they have is not meant to be trimmed or tidied in any way.

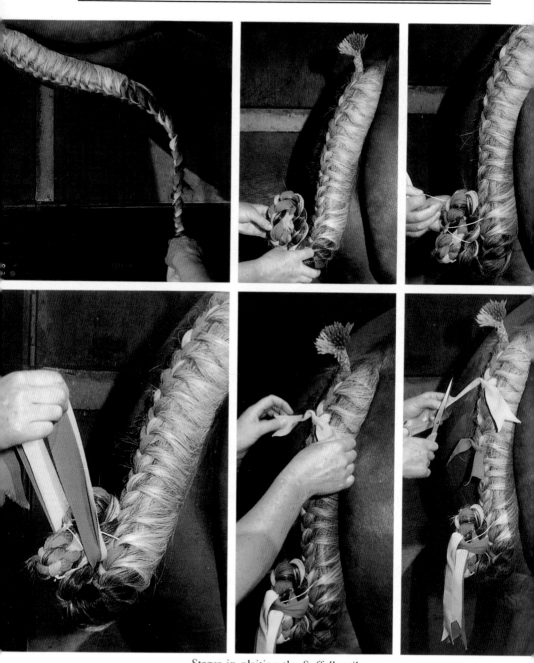

Stages in plaiting the Suffolk tail.
A The tail is plaited conventionally but with three lengths of braid down the centre to the end of the tail and secured.   B The tail is rolled up to make a bun on the outside of the dock.   C The bun is secured.   D and decorated.   E Ribbons are put in at intervals down the tail.   F and trimmed.

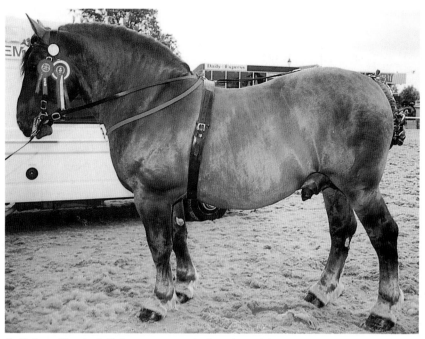

Suffolk stallion in full show turnout. A clean-legged breed, no trimming of the legs is necessary.

# JUDGING HEAVY HORSES: THE JUDGE'S VIEWPOINT

*In-hand showing is a waste of time and should be forbidden – function is the only test of a horse!*

*One of the blessings of judging a mixed class of heavy horses is that you can only judge what is in front of you, you can't judge what isn't there! With the breed standards fresh in your mind you still, unfortunately, see the way they are shown. If the horse is towing the handler all over the place and not doing what you ask them to do, turning the wrong way, not trotting where they are told and so on, it influences their ranking in order of merit, because you can't compare like with like. Mixed classes are difficult to judge and disheartening to compete in because judges have a natural preference for their own breed. Large classes are difficult to judge, too. If you are given twenty mares to judge in forty minutes there is not much time to consider the essentials of feet, limbs, eyes and heights. When I am judging brood mares they have to look as if they are capable of breeding, including width across*

305

The end result.

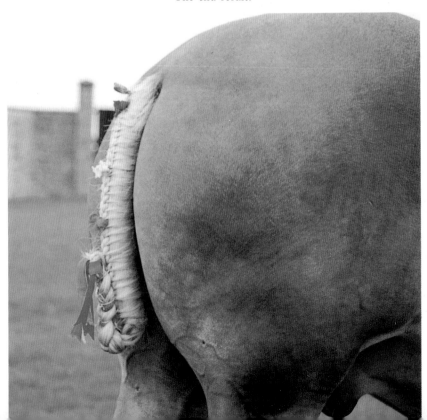

*the pelvis, and have the ability to be a mother, which is expressed in their behaviour, as well as pure show points. This doesn't vary much between breeds.*

*With regard to conformation, the most fundamental feature is the feet. No foot – no horse. This is followed by the limbs, just like any other horse. Heavy horses have to have a deep chest for work, a good shoulder for the collar, and strong quarters to push them along, which are helped by the weight of the horse. The heavier they are the more pulling power when they lean forward. A Shire can weigh between 17 and 23 cwt.*

*The feet should have good hard horn, which has to be blue in the case of the Percheron. For all of them there should be no cracks, or rings which might suggest nutritional or management problems. Side-bones don't bother me because heavy horses have not done any work for years. In a middle-aged horse the lateral cartilages may have ossified a bit, but providing they are still moving well they will have some merit over a spindly object with no bone.*

*They should be properly shod and the shoes must not be excessively large. For showing they can be quite exaggerated but they are only show shoes. Nobody would consider working in them. A feature of show shoes, particularly for the Shire and the Clydesdale, is bevelling, which continues the angle of the wall of the hoof to make the foot appear enormous. Suffolks and Percherons do this to a lesser extent because they have a neater foot. In North America they use what they call a Scotch shoe, which is about a foot square and the sides of the hoof are built up with car body filler to correct and exaggerate the action of the foot. They believe they have to do this to win, but special show shoes don't impress me.*

*Another feature of showing in North America is that the horses are very tall. Percherons in France fall into two height ranges: up to 16.2 hh and 16.2 hh and above. In North America they are between 17.2 and 18 hands, so that they are tall and fast for four, six and eight horse turnouts, but they would not be capable of pulling a ten-ton tree trunk.*

*When they are standing up for me to look at them they should be standing square and trying to cover the ground. If they are doing anything else I look to see if they have a bad stifle or hocks which they are trying to conceal which is betrayed by the stance. With regard to the limbs, I look for clean tendons with no signs of sprains and strains. I don't like to see long cannon bones and a tiny body at the top. We do see some spindly specimens in the Shire competitions in*

307

*inexperienced hands. I think this is the consequence of so many being bred and sold. There are a certain number of horses back at the knee in all breeds and no breed is worse than any other. Providing they move well it will not do much harm. The hind legs have to be good in a working horse, as well as any other, and I look for clean hocks. Osteochondrosis is quite widespread as a consequence of growing horses too fast. If the hocks are not moving properly I feel them. As with riding horses they must be in proportion and every joint must do its job. There should be well-rounded muscles at the thigh and the gaskin and the overall impression should be one of strength.*

*I look for flowing action where the horse covers the ground, rather than high flexion which is so uneconomic of energy and has the horse bashing its feet into the ground. The whole horse must move, not just part of the limbs. A bit of dishing is all right but not close action. I personally like to see the hocks separated but the Clydesdale people believe that close hocks give better pulling power. In the old days, of course, the working horses were never trotted. They wanted their goods carried and the horse to last for years. Over the years the purpose of working horses has evolved and so has their conformation. I think that their characteristics have to be preserved in a form that could work, even if they do not work very much nowadays.*

*Good shoulders for a collar should not be upright nor very sloping, but somewhere in the middle so that the collar sits comfortably and the draught line is in the right place, because the traces have to go back from the hames to the vehicle.*

*The head must be compatible with the body and preferably not a coffin head, or long with the chin on the ground. The teeth are important too and have to deal with a lifetime's food, so parrot mouth is unacceptable. I look for a bold eye, particularly with the Percheron which has Arab blood and a slight dish to the head. The neck should sit on the shoulders well. The rein runs through a ring on the collar to the bit and I try to imagine how it will look, and if the horse is 'bittable' as a consequence.*

*Character is extremely important. Stupidity and uncontrollability get marked down because they are not conducive to work. Handlers need to know what they are doing, not hanging on to the head and preventing the horse from trotting out. They should be level with the horse's shoulder and moving with it. A small handler makes a horse look bigger. They should be well turned out themselves and, ideally, carry a stick because it gives you so much more control. Sticks do not have to be long, although some are, and they help with turning the horse. I prefer to see the horse turned away from the handler because I can see the horse better but the Clydesdales turn around the handler. Either way great care has to be taken because you do not want to be trodden on!*

*There are various customs with the turnout of the horses. In Scotland Clydesdales are shown in bridles with white metal – in England buckles are brass. In-hand bridles are open, unlike driving bridles that have blinkers. Stallions are shown in stallion harness for the extra control. Feathers must not be whitened artificially so chalk is not allowed. Wood flour is used instead, which is very fine sawdust. Some people clip the docks of Shires and Clydesdales which I cannot say enough against, for the same reasons that docking has been against the law since 1946. There is nothing that this achieves that cannot be achieved by plaiting the tail up.*

*As I judge a class I think to myself which ones would I like to take home and for which purpose – breeding or eating! There isn't enough for the working horse to do nowadays. Some are now working in forestry, some opening pubs and others doing weddings. Many of those that do work might be successful in the show ring, but the main value of the show ring these days is public relations for the breeds. My advice is to get them fit, put them in a vehicle and see what they can do.*

# Bibliography

Akrill, Caroline. *Showing the Ridden Pony* (J.A. Allen 1981)

Baker, Sue. *Survival of the Fittest* (Exmoor Books 1993)

Bennett, Deb. *Principles of Conformation Analysis*, Vol. 1 (Fleet Street Publishing Corporation 1988)

Bloom, Lynda. *Fitting and Showing the Halter Horse* (Prentice Hall Press, New York 1987)

Cymbaluk, Nadia F., Christison, G.I. and Leach, D.H. 'Longitudinal growth analysis of horses following limited and *ad libitum* feeding', *Equine Veterinary Journal* (1990)

Fell, Alex. *The Irish Draught Horse* (J.A. Allen 1991)

Griffith, Moses. 'The Welsh Cob (1955)', *The Welsh Pony and Cob Society Journal* (1993)

Hartley Edwards, Elwyn. 'Breed Profile 63: The Caspian', *Horse and Hound*

Hume, Susan. *Native Ponies of the British Isles* (Saiga 1980)

Hyland, Ann. *The Appaloosa* (J.A. Allen 1990)

Jonsson, Marit. *Judging Icelandic Breeding Horses* (Dansk Islandshesteforening 1988 (for FEIF))

Schweisgut, Otto. *Haflinger Horses* (BLV Verlagsgesellschaft, Munich 1988)

Spooner, Glenda. *The Handbook of Showing* (J.A. Allen 1990)

Thorne, John and Susan. *Winning with Hunter Ponies* (J.A. Allen 1989)

Wentworth, Lady Anne. *The Swift Runner* (Allen & Unwin 1957)

# Index